model MARKETS of the world

everything
you need to know about
the top modeling markets

Marcia Rothschild Moellers

Published by Peter Glenn Publications / www.pgdirect.com

Model Markets of the World
© 2005 Marcia Rothschild Moellers
ISBN: 0-87314-325-6
$24.95 US

All Rights Reserved: No part of this publication may be reproduced, or transmitted in any form, by any means, electronic, mechanical, photocopying, recording or otherwise, without permission in writing from the copyright owner or his representatives. Contact publisher for details.

Cover Design:	Daniela Procupez / www.danielaprocupez.com
Typesetting:	Nurhan Thompson / www.redperfect.com
Printed by:	Times Offset Printing
Published by:	Peter Glenn Publications / www.pgdirect.com
	824 East Atlantic Avenue, Suite 7
	Delray Beach, Florida 33483 USA
	T: 1.888.332.6700
	T: 1.561.999.8930
	F: 1.561.999.8931

Bulk Discounts available upon request

MARCIA ROTHSCHILD MOELLERS
TABLE OF CONTENTS

NORTH AMERICA
- Atlanta 8
- Boston 11
- Chicago 14
- Dallas. 17
- Greensboro/Charlotte. 20
- Houston 23
- Los Angeles 26
- Miami. 30
- Milwaukee 33
- Minneapolis 36
- New York City. 39
- Philadelphia 43
- Phoenix 46
- Pittsburgh 49
- Portland 52
- San Diego 55
- San Francisco 58
- Seattle 61
- Tampa 64

- Montreal 67
- Toronto. 70
- Vancouver 73

AFRICA
- Capetown. 78
- Johannesburg 82

ASIA
- Bangkok 87
- Dubai. 91
- Hong Kong. 95
- Istanbul 99
- Kuala Lampur 102
- Osaka 105
- Seoul 109
- Shanghai 113
- Singapore. 116
- Taipei 119
- Tel Aviv 123
- Tokyo 126

EUROPE
- Amsterdam 131
- Athens 134
- Barcelona. 137
- Berlin 140
- Brussels 144
- Copenhagen. 147
- Dusseldorf 150
- Geneva 154
- Hamburg 157
- Lisbon. 160
- London 163
- Madrid 166
- Milan 169
- Munich 173
- Oslo. 177
- Paris. 180
- Stockholm. 184
- Vienna 187
- Zurich. 190

OCEANIA
- Auckland 194
- Melbourne 197
- Sydney. 201

SOUTH AMERICA
- Rio de Janiero. 206
- Santiago. 209
- Sao Paulo. 212

GLOSSARY
- Terms & Phrases 215

MODEL MARKETS OF THE WORLD
DEDICATION

This book is Dedicated To:

Santi: An honest, sincere, and passionate individual who reignited my desire and belief that this industry can be the best it can be for both models and agencies as long as creativity, integrity and hard work are blended together.

And To: Models with the Spirit of Adventure Who Are Willing to Travel, Learn and Grow In Order To Succeed.

A Special Thanks To:

My Family, James, Jake, Morgane and Maddie – I love you all so much.

My In-Laws Reginald & Nell Moellers for "Hotel Moellers" and Jenni & Rick Shimek – couldn't have finished the book without you.

Karen and Brad Hertges – for the only DSL cable hook-up in Ossian, IA.

My Fabulous Researchers and Editors and Publisher:

The Brilliant Lynn DeLaney, Terri Busch, James Moellers, Janice and Gretchen Myers, David Dauffenbach, Diana Smith and Gregory James.

The Wonderful Agents for Your Interviews and Reviews:

Shane Aguanno, Matthew Anderson, Shoko Arai, Kathy Baxter, Alecia Bell, Jan Berendsen, Sylvia Berger, Robert Black, Gavin Boardman, Luc Brinker, Ger Brown, Michèle Brown-Miller, Brunella Casella, Christine Chan, James Charles, Mario Ciaz, Rui Colaco, Stephanie David, Deb Docherty, Marc Dochez, Falko Drews, Victoria Duruh, Sera Fong, Sharmin Foo, Chris Forberg, Christina Foussiani, Larissa Garcia, Claranz Geh, Ron Gerard, David Grilli, Justin Habel, Richard Hawley, Michelle Hendricks, Warren Johnson, Amy Leung, Karin Hendriks, May Jensen, Jill Joyce, Susan Kaleta, Justine Kirby, Pia Kohles, Kitty Lai, Tony Long, Santiago Lopez-Guix, Michel Lu, Kim Luret, Yasuo Maeda, Roberta Manganelli, Sal A. Marquez, Jr., Sergio Mattos, Marte Helene Mellbye, Ofelia Memoli, Emmanuelle Mercier, Gavin Miller, Julia Nitu, Anita Norris, Mimmi Olsson, Sonja Ostrowski, Tabitha Pagel, Jae Park, Kristy Petersen, Ofer Raphaeli, Desiree Richter, Marcie Robidart, Jeni Rose, Raphael Salvi, Susan Schwabinger, Elinor Shahar, Jean Song, Cherylann Stephens, Joseph Tenni, Sara Tetro, Lois Thigpen, Guido Toure, Pahul Vasbotten, Nina Wallin, Ellen Wasser-Hrin, Brandon Marilee Williams, Blake Wood, and Roman Young.

HOW TO USE THIS BOOK

This area is a general summation of the market with highlighted points, size of market, population and approximate number of fashion agencies.

■ MARKET PREFERENCES

❖ Models:
Includes what type models the market uses, heights, sizes, any statistical restrictions including largest bra cup size, runway height and sizes, market preferences, the importance of smiles, ethnic types used and the amount of work for models.

❖ Portfolios:
Includes the amount of direct bookings and the type of portfolios garnering these bookings, client preference with regard to viewing models, the level of experience/portfolios required for new faces as well as established models to enter the market.

❖ Agencies Preferences:
Includes the preferred personality traits, hair, make-up and dress for castings along with the duration required to work the market.

■ TYPICAL BOOKINGS

❖ Length of Work:
Includes how the market books - by the hour, half day, full day and/or multiple days.

❖ Type of Work:
Includes the work the market books - catalogue, campaign, editorial, athletic, swimwear, lingerie, runway, commercial print (including advertising), TV commercial, film, infomercial, trade show, store informal, showroom, and industrial.

❖ Busiest Seasons:
Includes the busiest and slowest times of the year.

■ TOP CLIENTS
Includes at least 10 top clients in the market.

■ COMPETITION
Includes how competitive the market is and how long casting lines can be.

■ PAY RATES
Includes rates by the hour, half day, full day, advertising/campaign, runway, and TV/film along with the amount of work that is union or non-union.

❖ Agency Cuts:
Includes the agencies' commission rate and any applicable taxes that can be deducted from the model's gross.

MODEL MARKETS OF THE WORLD
INTRODUCTION

❖ Agency Provides:
Includes information about advances for accommodations, airfare, laser copies of books, composites, tests and pocket money, as well as if agencies or clients offer money contracts.

■ LIVING

❖ Housing:
Includes information about models' apartments, the inexpensive and moderate pricing of accommodations, and the average price for cheap hotels.

❖ Transportation:
Includes the airports and the time it takes to travel from the city, modes of public transportation and costs, pricing for a short taxi ride, whether a car is a necessity and amount of traffic in the market.

❖ Food & Entertainment:
Includes pricing for cheap meals and what is available in the market in regards to food and entertainment.

■ REQUISITES
Includes information about the necessary visas to enter the market and if taxes are deducted from foreign models' wages.

■ WEATHER
Typical weather for each city.

■ CURRENCY
Includes conversions for (US Dollar) US$10 and (Canadian Dollar) C$10 to the market's currency.

■ MARCIA'S TIPS
Includes any last thoughts, must haves, the do's and don'ts and whether or not the market speaks English along with how easy or difficult it is to navigate the city.

NORTH AMERICA

Atlanta 8
Boston 11
Chicago 14
Dallas. 17
Greensboro/Charlotte 20
Houston 23
Los Angeles 26
Miami. 30
Milwaukee 33
Minneapolis 36
New York City. 39
Philadelphia 43
Phoenix 46
Pittsburgh 49
Portland 52
San Diego 55
San Francisco 58
Seattle 61
Tampa 64

Montreal 67
Toronto. 70
Vancouver 73

GEORGIA
ATLANTA

Southerners can be heard referring to Atlanta as "The City of the South". With a population nearing 5,000,000 in the metropolitan area, Atlanta is flourishing with beautiful parks, fabulous homes on tree-lined, clean roads filled with sophisticated city dwellers in high-end automobiles. It is a smaller medium size market with approximately 3 fashion agencies. Atlanta is a very good market for young talent to begin development with opportunities in catalogue and advertising along with a small amount of editorial to get a resume started. Packed into this Olympic city, Atlanta offers many diverse opportunities in the industry as well as beautiful weather and lots of culture.

MARKET PREFERENCES

❖ Models:

The market needs junior/teens (female and male), plus/full-size (5'9"-5'11", sizes 14-18), athletic, and adults. The market rarely uses big & tall or petite. Women are preferably looking the ages of 25-35, 5'8"-5'11", sizes 2-6 along with a few size 8's, no more than a C-cup, no more than a 36" hip; for runway 5'9"-5'11", sizes 2-6. Men are preferably looking the ages of 25-40, 5'11"-6'2", suit 40-42; for runway 6'0"-6'2", suit 40-42. All ethnicities are used in the Atlanta market. Smiles are important for catalogue and less so for editorial. Many models work full-time but Atlanta itself does not sustain them. Models fly in and out for bookings elsewhere. Agencies' main boards are composed of up to 70% women and about 45% of men working full-time.

❖ Portfolios:

Direct bookings take up about 45% of the market. In order to attain these bookings, women's portfolios need to be strong with plenty of tearsheets of editorial, catalogue and advertising/campaign. Direct bookings for men are usually garnered by those ages 35-40 with strong portfolios. When possible, clients prefer to see models in person. Experience is not necessary for new faces but development of the portfolio is crucial. The stronger the portfolio, the more opportunities available to the model. Models can enter Atlanta from a smaller market with a good beginning portfolio.

❖ Agencies Preferences:

Agencies prefer outgoing personalities because it is incredibly important in the Atlanta market. Models must be very professional and have strong communication skills. For bookings, models must be able to take direction well. Clients do not like to see models at castings with heavy make-up - they prefer a cleanly scrubbed, fresh look. Models need to look like

MARCIA ROTHSCHILD MOELLERS
GEORGIA ATLANTA

models. Runway and TV/film castings can be dress specific whereas print castings require a fashionable look that is complimentary to the body while not being overly done. Agencies prefer models to remain on stay a minimum of 2 weeks, dependent upon the model's level of development.

TYPICAL BOOKINGS

❖ Length of Work:
Hourly, half day and full day. Multiple day bookings do occur, but more often with commercial print/advertising than catalogue.

❖ Type of Work:
Catalogue, athletic, light editorial, lingerie, swimwear, runway, commercial print, TV commercial, film, infomercial, trade show, store informal, showroom, and industrial.

❖ Busiest Seasons:
Atlanta's busiest seasons are from late February to June and from August through the middle of November. The Atlanta market is slowest from Thanksgiving through New Year's.

TOP CLIENTS

Top clients include Macy's Central, Goody's, Neiman Marcus, Saks Fifth Avenue, Ford Motor Company, hotels/resorts, Home Depot, Women's Wear Daily, Seventeen Magazine, McCann-Erickson (ad agency) and Anheuser-Busch.

COMPETITION

The competition in Atlanta is pretty light in comparison to the larger markets. Casting lines are rarely long as most castings are time specific and spread out.

PAY RATES

Print averages $125-187.50 per hour. Half day $500-1,000. Full Day $1,250-2,500. Advertising/campaign $2,500-12,000. Runway $75 per hour with a 2 hour minimum or $400-1,000 per show. TV/film either follows SAG/AFTRA union scale rates or non-union, which varies with each job.

❖ Agency Cuts:
For commissions, agencies deduct 20% for print, runway, and non-union TV/film. 10% for union TV/film.

❖ Agency Provides:
Typically, Atlanta agencies do not advance accommodations, airfare, composites, laser copies of books or tests. If in conjunction with a confirmed booking, agencies may advance but it depends on the model and the situation. Agencies do not offer and only a rare few clients will offer money contracts.

LIVING

❖ Housing:
Agencies do not provide models' apartments. Inexpensive accommodations average $400-600 per month. Moderate $700-1200 per month. Cheap hotels average $69-139 per night.

MODEL MARKETS OF THE WORLD
10 ATLANTA GEORGIA

❖ Transportation:

The airport is 20-45 minutes from downtown, depending on traffic. The city's public transportation is not user-friendly for models because the shooting locations can be very distant from public transportation stops. A short ride in a taxi is $7-8. A car is a necessity for the Atlanta model. Traffic is horrible. On the upside, very few places charge for parking.

❖ Food & Entertainment:

Atlanta has amazing restaurants. An inexpensive lunch is $6-12 and an inexpensive dinner is $12-20. The city has lots to do with everything from museums to great shopping to restaurants and fun nightclubs.

REQUISITES

A work visa is not necessary unless a non-USA citizen. Agencies deduct taxes for all foreign models.

WEATHER

Atlanta weather is pleasant all year long with very mild winters.

CURRENCY

As of January 2005:
US$10 = C$12.34

MARCIA'S TIPS

Atlanta is a truly beautiful city. It is well known as "The City In The Trees" and is a warm and friendly big city with a small town flavor. Models with great smiles, good bodies that look the part while staying grounded work the best. Politeness and a sense of upwardly mobile fashion are paramount in this very Southern city. If models plan to work in Atlanta, they must be as the city is – happy, friendly, sophisticated and fashionable.

MASSACHUSETS
BOSTON

Boston is composed of a metropolitan area with a population of over 5,650,000, and is considered one of the larger small markets in the USA with approximately 5 fashion agencies. Boston is cosmopolitan and quite sophisticated, having many top level universities within its realm. There is diversity in consumers, ranging from a large group of young students from all over the world to an established, highly educated, family-oriented middle to upper class. Bostonians are more conservative than ultra modern, and it is obvious within the market as it is primarily commercial print/catalogue. The clients insist on models that are relatable but can also project a wide range of looks from lifestyle catalogue to high-end classic. A model should not expect to be "discovered" in Boston because state law does not allow agencies to solicit a model.

MARKET PREFERENCES

❖ Models:

The Boston market uses junior/teens, big & tall, plus/full-size (5'7"-5'11", sizes 12-24), athletic, adults, and very rarely petite. Women are preferably looking the ages of 18-45, 5'7"-6'0", sizes 2-8, no more than a full C-cup, no more than a 37" hip; for runway 5'9"-6'0", sizes 2-6. Men are preferably looking the ages of 18-40, 5'11"-6'3", suit 40-44; for runway 6'0"-6'2", suit 40-42. The Boston market uses all ethnicities and smiles are absolutely paramount for catalogue as well as editorial. A smaller section of models, about 25%, work full-time in Boston because the market is small and many combine school along with modeling.

❖ Portfolios:

About 40% of the market is from direct bookings. Direct booking portfolios must be very strong in catalogue and accompanied by a long resume of clients. Editorial is important but the consistent catalogue resume is more favorable. Clients prefer to see models in person for commercial print and TV commercial castings. Clients do not always insist on seeing models for catalogue bookings. New faces do not need experience, but will need 1 or 2 good tests to begin working. Established models must enter with portfolios that are strong with good testing or recent tearsheets with very nice smiles and good body shots.

❖ Agencies Preferences:

Agencies prefer models that are outgoing, super friendly, very approachable, interested in what they are doing, and demonstrate that they want to work. Personality is key. Hair and make-up needs to be very clean and natural. Dress can be casual, nothing over the top, with really simple, clean, body-conscious lines.

MODEL MARKETS OF THE WORLD
BOSTON MASSACHUSETS

Agencies prefer models to remain on stay for a couple days to see clients and direct book thereafter.

■ TYPICAL BOOKINGS

❖ **Length of Work:**

Hourly, half day, full day and rarely multiple days.

❖ **Type of Work:**

Catalogue, athletic, limited editorial, lingerie, swimwear, runway, commercial print, TV commercial, some film, trade show, store informal, showroom, and industrial.

❖ **Busiest Seasons:**

Boston is consistent with the market being busiest from March to June and from September to the very beginning of December. The slowest times are from January to February and from July to August.

■ TOP CLIENTS

Top clients include TJ Maxx (clothing), Marshall's, Filene's, Talbot's, advertising agencies Arnold and Hill Holliday, A.J. Wright (clothing), Bostonian Store, Bob's (clothing), Merck (pharmaceutical), Fleet Bank and Fidelity Investments.

■ COMPETITION

Boston is not a competitive market and because it is not flooded with modeling agencies, there is a fair amount of work. Every once in awhile, models will deal with long casting lines – an hour at the most.

■ PAY RATES

Print averages $75-200 per hour. Half day $600-750. Full day $1,000-2,000. Advertising/campaign $1,200-25,000. Runway $100 per hour or $500 per show. TV/film either follows SAG/AFTRA union scale rates or non-union, which varies with each job. The market is a 50% split between union and non-union.

❖ **Agency Cuts:**

For commissions, mandated by State law, agencies only deduct 10% for print, runway and TV/film.

❖ **Agency Provides:**

Agencies do not advance much due to the nature of a smaller market. They will advance on composites and laser copies of books, depending on the situation and marketability for immediate work. Neither agencies nor clients offer money contracts.

■ LIVING

❖ **Housing:**

Agencies do not provide models' apartments. Inexpensive accommodations average $500-800 per month. Moderate $1,000 per month. Cheap hotels average $80-200 per night.

❖ **Transportation:**

The airport is 10-15 minutes from downtown. Boston has public transportation, including train, subway and bus. They are not expensive and average $1.25 per ride. A short ride in a taxi is $5-$10, depending on traffic. Models do not need a car to work in Boston. If driving, street parking averages $8-$25 and the traffic in Boston is horrible.

❖ Food & Entertainment:

An inexpensive lunch is $5-$6 and an inexpensive dinner is $10. Boston is a cultural and historical city with lots to do: museums, great ballet, music venues, small clubs and restaurants.

REQUISITES

A work visa is not necessary unless a non-USA citizen. Agencies deduct taxes for all foreign models.

WEATHER

July and August is hot and humid. September through November is absolutely gorgeous with all the leaves turning colors.

CURRENCY

As of January 2005:
US$10 = C$12.34

MARCIA'S TIPS

Boston is not as modern as New York City or as "resort" as the Miami market. It is small and conservative. Models need to look a little more on the J. Crew side rather than Armani or Gucci. Boston is a very livable city and is easy to navigate. Models can walk the entire city, and it's a great market to combine modeling and school with wonderful universities nearby. Models can easily manage attending school and working because clients are very flexible about school schedules. Top models wanting to continue their education will enjoy the close proximity to New York City as direct bookings are more feasible with inexpensive, frequent and multiple transportation options between the cities.

ILLINOIS
CHICAGO

Chicago is a larger medium size market, with a population of almost 3,000,000 in the city itself – it is a smaller market than New York City and a larger market than Atlanta. Chicago has approximately 4 fashion agencies covering a metropolitan area of 9,650,000. The more diverse a model's look and personality, the more opportunity for work because Chicago has a bit of everything. It's easy to navigate, competition is not as intense as New York City, and clients have a pleasant Midwest mentality. Chicago is an easy place to get started for new faces.

MARKET PREFERENCES

❖ Models:

The Chicago market uses junior/teens, a good amount of plus-full size (5'8"-5'11", size 16 is perfect, 14 can work), athletic, and adults. Women are preferably looking the ages of 25-35, 5'7"-5'11", size 4-6, no larger than a C-cup, no larger than a 37" hip; for runway 5'9"-5'11", size 2-6, no larger than a B-cup. Men are preferably looking the ages of 25-35, 5'11"-6'2", suit 40-42; for runway 6'0"-6'2", suit 40-42. The market uses all ethnicities. Smiles are very, very important in the Chicago market. Most female models work full-time in Chicago, unless they are going to school, and male models balance modeling with either school or other employment.

❖ Portfolios:

About 35% of the market is from direct bookings. Direct bookings are usually garnered by either a model with the typical "girl or boy next door" look or of the New York star caliber. No experience is necessary for new faces as it is a good market for development. To work well in Chicago, new faces will have to enter with good testing in their portfolios. Established models should enter the Chicago market with an array of good testing, editorial and advertising throughout the portfolio. The stronger the book, the better the top client opportunities. Many models base in Chicago because there are a lot of castings.

❖ Agencies Preferences:

The agencies like approachable, nice, confident, and positive energy models. Personality is important for castings. Make-up needs to be minimal, clean and fresh. Hairstyles should be natural and well kept. Many castings are dress specific and the agency will advise the model what to wear. Agencies prefer casual, approachable, not overly done styles that are specific to a model. Agencies prefer new faces remain on to stay at least 1 month. Established models with strong books should plan to remain

MARCIA ROTHSCHILD MOELLERS
ILLINOIS CHICAGO — 15

on at least two weeks to see all the clients.

TYPICAL BOOKINGS

❖ Length of Work:
Hourly, half day, full day and rarely multiple days.

❖ Type of Work:
Runway, catalogue, light editorial, some campaign, lingerie, swimwear, athletic, commercial print, TV commercial, film, industrials, store informal, and trade show.

❖ Busiest Seasons:
Chicago is busiest from September or October to the middle of November; however, it is a good size market with work throughout the year. The Chicago market is slowest during the holidays and January through early March.

TOP CLIENTS

Top clients include department stores Kohl's and Carson Pirie Scott, Jockey (underwear & athletic), Quixtar (internet/catalogue order), Sears, Claire's Boutique (accessories), Kellogg's, Fitigues (clothing), Anheuser-Busch, Helene Curtis (hair care), and H20 Plus (beauty/skincare).

COMPETITION

The Chicago market is very competitive and casting lines can be as long as 20 minutes.

PAY RATES

Print averages $150-250 per hour. Half day $600-1,500. Full day $1,500-3,000. Advertising/campaign $500-6,000 in addition to the model's day rate considering usage. Runway $75-150 per hour. TV/film either follows SAG/AFTRA union scale rates or non-union, which varies with each job. There is very little non-union.

❖ Agency Cuts:
For commissions, agencies deduct 20% for print, runway and non-union TV/film. 10% for union TV/film.

❖ Agency Provides:
Some agencies will advance airfare, accommodations, testing and composites, depending on the situation and potential for work. Agencies do not offer money contracts. Some clients will offer money contracts although it is rare.

LIVING

❖ Housing:
Some agencies provide models' apartments. Inexpensive accommodations average $550-600 per month. Moderate $1,000 per month. Cheap hotels average $100-150 per night. It is not required to live in the city as housing can be cheaper outside the Chicago city limits.

❖ Transportation:
There are 2 major airports, O'Hare and Midway, and both are 30 minutes from downtown Chicago. Public

MODEL MARKETS OF THE WORLD
16 CHICAGO ILLINOIS

transportation is very inexpensive and includes excellent bus and subway/train. A short ride in a taxi is $5. A car is a luxury and parking can be expensive. Traffic is busy during rush hours.

❖ Food & Entertainment:

There is a lot of fast food; however, healthy alternatives can be found in Chicago. An inexpensive lunch is $5-10 and an inexpensive dinner is $6-12. Chicago is a great city for entertainment and is known for its great theater and comedy. Chicago is home to the renowned comedy troupe, Second City.

REQUISITES

A work visa is not necessary unless a non-USA citizen. Agencies deduct taxes for all foreign models.

WEATHER

Chicago has pretty typical seasons with the wind being very cold in the winter.

CURRENCY

As of January 2005:
US$10 = C$12.34

MARCIA'S TIPS

Chicago is a great place to live. People residing there will say it's the best! There is a lot of culture in Chicago, comparable to New York City without the heavy population and price tag. Chicago has lake beaches, great sports' teams and a lot of music. Models should be prepared for the cold winters – long johns are a necessity and prepare to bear the city's name of "The Windy City". Because it is centrally located, Chicago is great for models that have to fly throughout the USA. Chicago can be great for fresh new faces as agencies have more time for hand holding during the development stage in comparison to the larger markets.

TEXAS
DALLAS

Dallas is a larger medium size market – very similar to Chicago. It is a market that packs a big punch. The metropolitan area of Dallas (including Fort Worth) has a population of around 5,750,000, with approximately 4 fashion agencies catering to a good amount of bookings. It is a great place to make money because there are a handful of top, sought after retail clients based in Texas. Some of these retail clients are major revenue for modeling agencies because they book models frequently. These clients include well known JC Penney and Neiman Marcus. Dallas is also a great place to live with easy access to both of its airports. It's a top direct booking market that brings in models from all over the USA. Models that live in the market are either new faces or established models that choose to live there. Texas does everything big – from major clients and great direct bookings to consistently developing top models.

MARKET PREFERENCES

❖ Models:

The market uses junior/teens, big & tall (6'3"-6'4", size 44), petite (5'6"), plus/full-size (5'8"-5'10", sizes 12-14), athletic, and adults. Women are preferably looking the ages of 22-35, 5'8"-5'10", sizes 4-6, no more than a 34C, no larger than a 36" hip although most agencies prefer 34"; for runway 5'9"-5'11", sizes 4-6. Men are preferably looking the ages of 28-45, 5'11"-6'2", suit 40; for runway 6'0"-6'2", suit 40. Dallas mainly uses Caucasian, Black and Hispanic. Asian/Eurasian and Native American do not work so much. About 50% of the market is full-time, with some local models making over $200,000 a year.

❖ Portfolios:

The market is about 85% direct bookings. Models with portfolios that are strong with lots of advertising/campaign and editorial work best for direct bookings. Clients do not necessarily need to see models in person, unless a new face. No experience is needed to enter the market as models can be developed there. To enter as an established model, one must have advertising and editorial in the portfolio and/or a good resume of clients from another strong market along with top notch testing.

❖ Agencies Preferences:

Agencies prefer models with friendly, outgoing personalities. Clients want models they would enjoy spending the day with. For castings, models need to wear very simple, natural make-up and hair should not contain a lot of product. Clients prefer to see models that dress with a sense of style that is figure

MODEL MARKETS OF THE WORLD
DALLAS TEXAS

enhancing. Clients don't mind casual dress as long as it's fashion-conscious. Dallas does not have models that remain on stay. Models are mainly confirmed on a direct booking and then stay for other bookings. If a model wants work the market, a day or two will be needed for client appointments that are planned in advance with the agency.

TYPICAL BOOKINGS

❖ Length of Work:

Hourly, half day, full day and multiple days. Clients book models frequently and for all different lengths of work.

❖ Type of Work:

Catalogue, athletic, light editorial, campaign, lingerie, swimwear, runway, commercial print, TV commercial, film, infomercial, trade show, store informal, showroom and informal.

❖ Busiest Seasons:

The Dallas market is pretty consistent all year. It is definitely a little busier from May to October. As with most markets, it slows down around the Christmas holidays through New Year's.

TOP CLIENTS

Top clients include JC Penney, Foley's, Stage Stores (dept. store), Neiman Marcus, AAEFFS (Army/Navy/Airforce catalogue), Mary Kay, Beauty Control, Goody's (dept. store), Temerlin McClain (ad agency), and Dillard's.

COMPETITION

The competition in Dallas is fierce and is not a market where a model can immediately begin making a lot of money. Models must be prepared with a strong portfolio. Casting lines are pretty much obsolete for print. Models may deal with casting lines with TV commercial auditions.

PAY RATES

Print averages $187.50-500 per hour. Half day $1,000-2,500. Full day $2,000-8,000. Advertising/Campaign $2,500-10,000. Runway $85 per hour. TV/film either follows SAG/AFTRA union scale rates or non-union, which varies from job to job. 50% of TV/film is non-union because Texas is a "right to work" state.

❖ Agency Cuts:

For commissions, agencies deduct 20% for print, runway, and non-union TV/film. 10% for union TV/film.

❖ Agency Provides:

Agencies usually do not advance for airfare or accommodations unless for a confirmed booking, however, they will advance on composites, laser copies of books and tests, dependent upon the caliber of the model. Agencies sometimes advance weekly salaries depending on the situation. Neither agencies nor clients offer money contracts.

LIVING

❖ Housing:

The agencies do not provide models' apartments. Inexpensive accommodations average $500-1,000 per month. Moderate averages $1,000 and up. Cheap hotels average $89-150 per night.

❖ Transportation:

There are two airports near Dallas. DFW is about 35 miles from downtown. Love Field is about 10 miles from downtown. Dallas does not have very good public transportation. There are buses; however expect to need a car to get around because the city is very large and expansive. A short ride in a taxi for $4-5. Many models use car services to/from bookings, which average $50 via the airport one-way. Parking fees are pretty common downtown but not the norm throughout the city limits and many clients have parking available. Dallas' traffic is moderate. It flows well with the exception of rush hour.

❖ Food & Entertainment:

An inexpensive lunch is $5-10, with dinner averaging the same. Dallas is a lively town with Western cowboy influence as well as a good touch of Mexican culture. It has some of the best Mexican food in the USA.

REQUISITES

A work visa is not necessary unless a non-USA citizen. Agencies deduct taxes for all foreign models.

WEATHER

Dallas can get very warm in July and August. Otherwise, it's pretty mild with a small hint of all four seasons and a lot of summer.

CURRENCY

As of January 2005:
US$10 = C$12.34

MARCIA'S TIPS

Dallas is a very friendly city, and models will have to be just as friendly if they wish to succeed in the market. Appearance counts and a pretty, friendly smile can go a long way. Texans are known for their sense of style and sophistication. One of the greatest things about Dallas is that everything is done a large scale; therefore, a model will have to think the same way in order to achieve success.

SOUTH CAROLINA
GREENSBORO

Greensboro is a small market with a metropolitan area population of 1,125,000 with approximately 2 fashion agencies. Charlotte and Greensboro are combined as the market does expand to both of these cities. The market is similar to Atlanta in preferences whereas mainly booking catalogue and advertising. Greensboro is a money-making market but not a place to build a model's portfolio. Most models live out of state and are direct booked into the market.

■ MARKET PREFERENCES

❖ Models:

The market uses some junior/teens, petite (5'4"-5'8"), plus/full-size (5'8"-5'10", sizes 12-14), athletic, and adults. Women are preferably looking the ages of 25-40, 5'8"-5'10", sizes 4-6, no more than a C-cup, no more than a 36" hip; for runway 5'9"-5'11", sizes 4-6. Men are preferably looking the ages of 28-48, 5'10"-6'2", suit 40-42; for runway 6'0"-6'2", suit 40-41. The market uses all ethnicities. Smiles are important for catalogue. There is no editorial and models must have a very good body in order to work full-time. 30% of the market is composed of local models with only half working full-time.

❖ Portfolios:

50% of the market is from direct bookings. Direct booking models must have strong portfolios with campaigns and editorial work, as well as something unique that separates them from the average working model. Super edgy does not work in North Carolina. Clients do not insist on seeing models in person for print, but for TV/film it is a must. New faces will have opportunity, but not to the extent of an established model. Inexperienced teens will not work well. Established models must have strong portfolios with tearsheets if they want to earn money in the market.

❖ Agencies Preferences:

Agencies prefer models that are friendly and outgoing. Charlotte/Greensboro clients are extremely nice. If a model acts super worldly with an attitude, clients will not be interested. Personalities must stay very down to earth to succeed in this market. Clients prefer to see hair and make-up that is clean and fresh. Dress needs to be fashion forward and somewhat body conscious but not overboard. The agencies prefer to direct book models. To garner direct bookings, models send their portfolios in advance to agencies for client review. Local models do castings by client request only.

S. CAROLINA GREENSBORO

Marcia Rothschild Moellers

TYPICAL BOOKINGS

Length of Work:
Hourly, half day and full day. Greensboro/Charlotte has many multiple day bookings.

Type of Work:
Catalogue, athletic, lots of lingerie and swimwear, a small amount of runway using local models, commercial print, TV commercial, film, a little tradeshow using local models, very little informal, and a tiny amount of industrial.

Busiest Seasons:
Greensboro is consistent throughout the year. It's a little busier from August to November. The slowest time of the year is December to January.

TOP CLIENTS

Hanes, Bali, No Nonsense Hosiery, Wrangler, Timbercreek (clothing), Thomasville (furniture), Verizon Wireless, Lowe's Home Improvement, Rooms To Go, and Outer Banks (apparel).

COMPETITION

Locally, the competition is light. For direct bookings, it is as competitive as Chicago or Dallas. Models deal with long casting lines for TV/film only, and even those are usually with slotted times.

PAY RATES

Print averages $150-450 per hour. Half day $600-2,500. Full day $1,250-7,500. Advertising/campaign $1,500-25,000. Runway $85 per hour or $150 and higher per show. TV/film either follows SAG/AFTRA union scale rates or non-union, which varies with each job. 50% of TV/film is non-union as North Carolina is a right to work state.

Agency Cuts:
For commissions, agencies deduct 20% for print, runway, and non-union TV/film. 10% for union TV/film.

Agency Provides:
Depending on the situation, agencies will advance airfare and accommodations. They may advance on composites, laser copies of books and tests, dependent upon the caliber of the model. Some clients offer money contracts; however, agencies do not.

LIVING

Housing:
Agencies do not provide models' apartments. Inexpensive accommodations average $700-900 per month. Moderate $1,000-1,200. Cheap hotels average $50-85 per night.

Transportation:
The airport is 10 minutes from downtown. Public transportation is substandard in Greensboro with very little available. Taxis are usually used to and from the airport only. A short ride in a taxi is $5. If models are going to be

MODEL MARKETS OF THE WORLD
GREENSBORO S. CAROLINA

in the market for any length of time, they will need a car because the market is expansive. There are usually no parking costs and traffic isn't heavy.

❖ Food & Entertainment:

An inexpensive lunch is $7-12 and an inexpensive dinner is $15-20. Greensboro is a quiet, family-oriented town. It does have a fun downtown area with clubs and great restaurants. Models should plan to relax and take in the scenery while there.

REQUISITES

A work visa is not necessary unless a non-USA citizen. Agencies deduct taxes for all foreign models.

WEATHER

North Carolina has 4 seasons and a mild winter.

CURRENCY

As of January 2005:
US$10 = C$12.34

MARCIA'S TIPS

Greensboro/Charlotte is a great market to relocate to if models are already established and ready to reap the benefits of previous hard work. Established models with strong portfolios do well in the Greensboro/Charlotte market. It's a safe, clean city and easy to navigate. Native North Carolinians are really friendly and helpful. It's a Southern town with lots of hospitality. Models should always plan to bring a model bag with basic shoes, bras, hosiery, belts and lingerie in good shape because clients insist on it.

TEXAS
HOUSTON

Houston is a strong little market. The population of the city is near 2,000,000 with a metropolitan area population of 5,250,000. The market packs a great little punch because Texas is full of some fantastic catalogue clients. Houston has approximately 4 fashion agencies. It's a very catalogue market with a small amount of editorial. It's a great place to start a modeling career, get some experience while making some money, and then travel on to the bigger markets, such as its neighboring market, Dallas.

MARKET PREFERENCES

❖ Models:

Houston is a huge market for junior/teen – one of the best in the USA. The market also uses plus/full-size (5'8"-5'11", sizes 12-16) and adults. Women are preferably looking the ages of 20-50, 5'6"-5'11", sizes 2-8, no more than a C-cup, no larger than a 36" hip; for runway 5'9"-6'0", sizes 2-6. Men are preferably looking the ages of 18-53, 5'11"-6'2", suit 40-44; for runway 5'11"-6'2", suit 40-44. The market uses all ethnicities. Smiles are very important for catalogue and not as much for editorial. Models cannot work full-time in the Houston market unless in combination with other larger markets.

❖ Portfolios:

40% of the market is from direct bookings. Portfolios that work best have tearsheets and a resume of good repeat booking experience. Clients do not need to see models in person and usually book from composites. No experience is necessary as the agencies like to develop brand new faces while giving the opportunity to gain experience. Established models will need a portfolio with very good testing and preferably some editorial as well as a great composite to begin working.

❖ Agencies Preferences:

Agencies prefer models that are outgoing, a joy to spend the day with that follow direction well and are never late. Clients want to see hair and make-up that is natural, minimal and well-groomed. Dress for castings is upscale casual but not overly done. Agencies prefer models live in the market or to send their portfolios for review for direct bookings.

TYPICAL BOOKINGS

❖ Length of Work:

Hourly, half day and full day. Direct bookings are usually multiple days.

❖ Type of Work:

Catalogue, athletic, editorial, lingerie, swimwear, runway, commercial print, TV commercial, film, infomercial, trade

MODEL MARKETS OF THE WORLD
HOUSTON TEXAS

show, showroom, store informal and industrial.

❖ Busiest Seasons:

Houston's busiest times are from March to May and from August to November. Slower times are from June to July and around the Christmas holidays.

TOP CLIENTS

Top clients include department stores JC Penney, Foley's, Stage Stores, Neiman Marcus and Saks Fifth Avenue, Paper City (magazine), Academy (recreation), Laura Mercier (cosmetics), Tootsies (clothing), and Visible Changes (hair salon).

COMPETITION

Houston is pretty competitive because there is a large pool of good local talent and models have to come with experience in order to start working. Casting lines can be long and up to an hour so, especially with TV commercial castings.

PAY RATES

Print averages $150-300 per hour. Half day $750-1,000. Full day $1,500-3,000. Advertising/campaign $3,000-10,000. Runway $70-80 per hour. TV/film either follows SAG/AFTRA union scale rates or non-union, which varies with each job. The majority of TV/film is non-union as Texas is a "right to work" state.

❖ Agency Cuts:

For commissions, agencies deduct 20% for print, runway and non-union TV/film. 10% for union TV/film.

❖ Agency Provides:

Most agencies do not advance much of anything since it is a small market. They may advance with jobs already completed. Neither agencies nor clients offer money contracts.

LIVING

❖ Housing:

Agencies do not provide models' apartments. Inexpensive accommodations average $500-600 per month. Moderate averages $600-1,000. Cheap hotels average $65-150 per night.

❖ Transportation:

Houston has 2 airports. Hobby is 20 minutes from downtown and Intercontinental is 45 minutes from downtown. The city has buses for public transportation that are inexpensive but inconvenient for castings. Models must have a car in Houston because the market is expansive. Parking is almost always free but traffic is horrible.

❖ Food & Entertainment:

An inexpensive lunch is $5-10 and an inexpensive dinner is $15-20. Houston has great entertainment with a lot of nightclubs, wonderful music venues and cool coffee shops.

REQUISITES

A work visa is not necessary unless a non-USA citizen. Agencies deduct taxes for all foreign models.

WEATHER

Houston is very hot and very humid with the summer being the most uncomfortable.

CURRENCY

As of January 2005:
US$10 = C$12.34

MARCIA'S TIPS

Clients are very adamant about models being professional and definitely being on time. With traffic, models will need to plan ahead in order to have plenty of time to get to their castings and bookings. Houston is a very clean, friendly place and everyone loves to see a smile in a pretty package because appearance really counts.

CALIFORNIA
LOS ANGELES

Los Angeles is the second largest market in the USA with approximately 10 fashion agencies and a population of nearly 4,000,000. The city's metropolitan area, including Riverside and Anaheim, caters to a population of over 17,600,000. Los Angeles is a large market and has everything – commercial print, catalogue and editorial. Los Angeles is a great weather market that allows models to experience the best of both worlds. Not only do models have the opportunity to make money to invest in their careers, but they also have the opportunity for editorial that allows their careers to escalate to better day rates. Plus, new faces can be bigger fish in a slightly smaller pond than New York City, which allows for more opportunities all the way around. Los Angeles is an amazing development market as well as one that supports a full-time career. The market is obviously fantastic for models pursuing Hollywood. Models are always noting what celebrities they run into in their everyday lives in Los Angeles.

MARKET PREFERENCES

❖ Models:

The market uses junior/teens, plus/full-size (5'9"-5'11", sizes 14-16), athletic, and adults. Women are preferably looking the ages of 18-25, 5'8"-5'11", sizes 2-6, no more than a full C-cup, no more than a 36" hip; for runway 5'10"-5'11.5", sizes 2-6. Men are preferably looking the ages of 18-40, 5'11"-6'3", suit 39-42; for runway 6'0"-6'2", suit 40-42. The market uses all ethnicities. Smiles are definitely important for this large advertising and catalogue market, however not as important for editorial. Agencies' main boards have about 80% of their models working full-time.

❖ Portfolios:

Direct bookings make up about 65% of the bookings. Direct bookings are usually more all-American relatable types or top models of the New York City caliber that have established books with editorial and advertising/campaign. Clients prefer to see models in person, even when they are booking a model directly to a location shoot. The market prefers new faces with at least two good tests in their portfolios; unless Los Angeles is already home or a model plans on choosing Los Angeles for mother agency representation. For established models, the majority of the portfolio should be tearsheets from either very good advertising/catalogue jobs or editorial.

CALIFORNIA LOS ANGELES

MARCIA ROTHSCHILD MOELLERS

❖ Agencies Preferences:

Agencies prefer models that are outgoing, professional, attentive and friendly. Los Angeles is a great market for new faces to get started. Agencies prefer parents to be supportive; however, not so much in the forefront. These preferences are very important as the market has a lot of advertising/catalogue as well as many opportunities in the entertainment industry where personality and independence are paramount. In New York City, models can get away with jeans and a tank top and no make-up, but the clients in Los Angeles want to see models more put together. Models need to look neat with clean hair and light make-up (mascara & lip gloss), as well as nice neutral polish with a manicure/pedicure -- nothing overly done. Models should keep the clothing simple –jeans and a tank can work but with a sense of style. Think body-conscious clothing. A skirt to show legs is good for females. Agencies prefer models to remain on stay at least one month in Los Angeles.

TYPICAL BOOKINGS

❖ Length of Work:

Hourly (typically 2 hour minimum), half day, and full day. Multiple day bookings are common via the top clients.

❖ Type of Work:

The Los Angeles market has everything -- catalogue, athletic, editorial, campaign, lingerie, swimwear, runway, commercial print, TV commercial, film, infomercial, trade show, store informal, showroom, and industrial.

❖ Busiest Seasons:

Los Angeles is busy all year long. The busier times are from February to July and then from late September to early December. The market slows down in August to early September, and usually the Fridays through Mondays that fall around holidays.

TOP CLIENTS

Macy's, Neiman Marcus, magazines Flaunt, Shape, Teen, Women's Wear Daily, Vogue, Harper's Bazaar and Foam, Richard Tyler (designer), Sebastian (hair care), quite a few car companies (due to the great weather), Banana Republic, The Gap, Nordstrom, JC Penney, Dillard's, and Old Navy.

COMPETITION

Los Angeles is pretty competitive and is a market filled with internationally traveled models who want to act. This creates a large base of strongly established models in the market waiting for their "big break". A request casting can be a lobby full of models. General casting lines can be around the block.

PAY RATES

Print averages $187.50-350 per hour. Half day $750-1,500. Full day $1,500-8,000.

MODEL MARKETS OF THE WORLD
LOS ANGELES CALIFORNIA

Advertising/campaign $1,500-65,000. There are the rare campaign contracts of $1,000,000 and up. Runway $90-250 per hour. TV/film either follows SAG/AFTRA union scale rates or non-union, which varies with each job. 45% of the TV/film bookings are non union. Some non-union clients pay residuals and some pay buy-outs.

❖ Agency Cuts:

For commissions, agencies deduct 20% for print, runway and non-union TV/film. 10% for union TV/film.

❖ Agency Provides:

Dependent upon a model's situation, agencies may advance accommodations, airfare, composites, laser copies of books, tests and pocket money. Some agencies offer money contracts, usually through contests or due to the particular demand of a model. Clients occasionally offer money contracts.

LIVING

❖ Housing:

Most agencies do not provide models' apartments but they are very helpful in recommending accommodations. Dependent upon the amount of roommates, inexpensive accommodations average $500-800 per month. Moderate average $700-1,500. Cheap hotels average $85-225 per night. Most hotels in Los Angeles average $200-450.

❖ Transportation:

There are three airports in the vicinity of Los Angeles. Long Beach is about 30 miles from the city, Burbank is about 15 miles from the city, and LAX is about 25 miles from the city. City transportation is pretty close to non-existent. Los Angeles does have buses, but they are not very efficient for getting to castings. A short ride in a taxi is $5-7, depending on traffic. Some agencies use car services averaging $10-12 per hour. It is optimum to have a car, as castings and clients can be quite distant. The traffic in Los Angeles is heavy and horrible.

❖ Food & Entertainment:

An inexpensive lunch at any of the fast food establishments is $3-5 and a regular cheap lunch is $5-8. An inexpensive dinner is $7-15. Los Angeles is filled with lots of shopping, entertainment-based history and tourism, beaches nearby, mountains, ski resorts, and lakes in close proximity to the city. Restaurants are frequented by all the "power people" of the entertainment industry. Agents will say that some of the most lucrative deals have been made on napkins during a meal. Many models balance the beginning of their careers with night jobs in restaurants, bars and nightclubs. Los Angeles is a very trendy, "what is hot this week" environment.

CALIFORNIA LOS ANGELES

REQUISITES

A work visa is not necessary unless a non-USA citizen. Agencies deduct taxes for all foreign models.

WEATHER

The weather is very nice year-round. Some models that could be successful in New York City won't leave Los Angeles just because of the beautiful weather. One of the world's most famous photographers, Steven Meisel, recently moved to this fair weather city.

CURRENCY

As of January 2005:
US$10 = C$12.34

MARCIA'S TIPS

Los Angeles is a laid back market. Models should not expect it to be rushed and crazy. Los Angeles is actually one of the only markets that gives a model time to adjust. Since it is the second largest market in the USA, models anticipate their days to be filled with castings. Instead, Los Angeles is more even paced and goes with the flow of seasonal shooting schedules and castings. As relaxed as it can be, the entertainment world will remind models and actors that it is "THE Place To Be". This market is more youth-oriented and superficial than some of the other larger markets. There is a reason there are so many Los Angeles plastic surgeons. Models must remember to wear their sunscreen and find their gym right away. Every moment in Los Angeles is a possibility to be "discovered".

FLORIDA
MIAMI BEACH

Miami Beach is a large market with a metropolitan area population, including Fort Lauderdale and West Palm Beach, of nearly 5,500,000. There are approximately 10 fashion agencies located in the market. Everyone in the world comes to Miami Beach at one point in time within a 6 month period to shoot during "season" from October to April. It's a very strong location destination, as well as an opportunity for clients who want to escape the cold. Miami Beach is a great market to get started as long as models are ready to invest the time. It's a great market if models have been in the industry for a stretch and don't want to deal any longer with the hustle and bustle of Paris or New York City. Everything is easily accessible and in one basic geographical area. However, models should not think it's any less competitive. Miami Beach is just as tough as the other larger markets because of all of the strong clients choosing the location. If models have a great body, a charismatic smile and a drive to succeed, Miami Beach may be the place to escape the cold winter months.

■ MARKET PREFERENCES

❖ Models:

Miami Beach uses junior/teens, big & tall, petite (5'7"-5'8"), plus/full-size (5'9"-5'11", sizes 12-16), athletic, and adults. Women are preferably looking the ages of 18-50, 5'7"-5'11", sizes 2-6, no more than a C-cup, no larger than a 36" hip; for runway 5'10"-5'11", sizes 2-4. Men are preferably looking the ages of 18-50, 5'11"-6'2", suit 40-42; for runway 6'0"-6'2", suit 40-42. The Miami Beach market uses all ethnicities and loves great bodies. Smiles are important for catalogue but not as much for editorial. Models should not come to Miami Beach with chalk white skin or be prepared for their agency to tell them to get a tan. 70% of the market works full-time.

❖ Portfolios:

50% of the market is from direct bookings. Direct booking portfolios must be diversified with strong editorial to quality catalogue. Top of the line testing is important for new faces with clean, simple and fresh looks visible throughout the portfolios. No experience is necessary for new faces, but the models will need good polaroids/snapshots to start and then be prepared to test, test, and test. Established models should come with a strong portfolio with a range of tearsheets from editorial to catalogue.

❖ Agencies Preferences:

Agencies like models that are

FLORIDA MIAMI BEACH

MARCIA ROTHSCHILD MOELLERS

flexible. Junior/teens must have great personalities, lots of energy and be able to sell themselves to a variety of clients. Models have to be able to deal with diverse situations, because some clients do not speak English; therefore, models will have to sell themselves on energy alone, or even be prepared to wear furs in 90 F and not complain. For castings, hair and make-up should be simple and clean – less is definitely better. Dress is figure conscious because Miami Beach is a body market. Clothes should show off the figure but not in a vulgar way. Clients do not like models to look like they just came from the beach. Agencies prefer models to remain on stay a minimum of 3 months and a maximum of 6 months.

TYPICAL BOOKINGS

❖ Length of Work:

Hourly, half day, full day, and lots of multiple days.

❖ Type of Work:

Miami Beach has everything – catalogue, editorial, campaign, athletic, lingerie, swimwear, commercial print, TV commercial, film, runway, showroom, store informal, infomercial, trade show, and industrial.

❖ Busiest Seasons:

The busiest time is during "season" which is from October to April. The slowest time is June through July due to the extensive heat and humidity.

TOP CLIENTS

Top clients include department stores Bloomingdales, Burdines, Target, Sears and Kohl's, magazines Ocean Drive and Self, Boston Proper (catalogue), Avanti (catalogue house), resort, cruise & condominium companies, as well as clients from various parts of America, Europe and South America that have chosen the locations for its wonderful beaches.

COMPETITION

Agents will note that Miami Beach is more competitive than any other market in the world. A top client will come in once or twice during "season" with many models showing up for the casting, whether requested or not, as they are determined to meet the client. Casting lines can be as long as 3 to 4 hours.

PAY RATES

Print averages $187.50-312.50 per hour. Half day $1,000-1,250. Full day $2,500-3000. Advertising/campaign $10,000-60,000. Runway $100 per hour or $500 per show. TV/film either follows SAG/AFTRA union scale rates or non-union, which varies with each job. The market is split 50/50 between union and non-union TV/film bookings. Florida is a "right to work" state.

❖ Agency Cuts:

Agencies deduct 20% for print and non-union TV/film. 10-20% for runway. 10% for union TV/film.

MODEL MARKETS OF THE WORLD
MIAMI BEACH FLORIDA

❖ Agency Provides:

Agencies will advance almost anything, dependent upon the caliber of the model. Agencies prefer not to advance airfare, but may include accommodations, composites, laser copies of books, tests, and pocket money. Agencies do not offer money contracts; however some clients will.

LIVING

❖ Housing:

Most agencies provide model's apartments. It's a tropical area so be prepared for the insects. Inexpensive accommodations average $325-600 per month. Moderate $700-1,000. Cheap hotels average $50-200 per night with regular hotels averaging $300-600 per night.

❖ Transportation:

The airport is 15-20 minutes from Miami Beach and the market does not have a reliable public transportation system; however, almost everything is within walking distance. A short ride in a taxi is $3-4. Parking averages $1 an hour. Traffic is okay on the weekdays except at rush hour, but very heavy on the weekends.

❖ Food & Entertainment:

An inexpensive lunch is $4 and an inexpensive dinner is $8. There are fun things to do all day long in Miami Beach. The beach has many events, sidewalk cafes, outdoor malls, wonderful restaurants and a great nightlife including nightclubs, lounges and dancing that can go into the wee hours.

REQUISITES

A work visa is not necessary unless a non-USA citizen. Agencies deduct taxes for all foreign models.

WEATHER

Weather in Miami Beach is paradise and pretty much perfect all day and night long. Hurricane season lasts from late summer to early fall.

CURRENCY

As of January 2005:
US$10 = C$12.34

MARCIA'S TIPS

Models should try to obtain accommodations anywhere from 1st Street to 15th Street, which is the heart of Miami Beach and where everything is within walking distance. Models should bring lots of bathing suits as they will be on the beach everyday. They should also bring casual clothing and maybe 1 or 2 dressier outfits. Models should pack light since the weather is so consistent and have an umbrella on hand in case of a rainy day. Models will need to bring comfortable shoes because they will be walking a lot.

WISCONSIN
MILWAUKEE

Milwaukee is considered a small market with a metropolitan area population of 1,725,000. There are approximately 3 fashion agencies based in the city, and even though it's small, people are always surprised by the fact that it can be just about as busy as Chicago only on a slightly smaller scale. The market has lots of great locally based clients and some very good photographers who receive national bids from top clients. Milwaukee caters to a very relatable lifestyle fashion clientele and is open to booking models with edgy editorial looks for their higher end clients. Clients have a good work ethic with a Midwestern mentality. Friendly smiles and being in a good mood are paramount to working well in Milwaukee.

MARKET PREFERENCES

❖ Models:

The market uses junior/teens, big & tall, petite (5'5"-5'7"), plus/full-size (5'8"-5'10", sizes 10-14), occasionally athletic, and adults. Women preferably are looking the ages of 20-40, 5'8"-5'11", sizes 2-6, no more than a C-cup, no larger than a 37" hip; for runway 5'9"-5'11", sizes 2-6. Men are preferably looking the ages of 20-40, 5'11"-6'2", suits 40-42; for runway 6'0"-6'2", suits 40-42. The market uses all ethnicities. Smiles are important for catalogue and editorial. About 5% of the market works full-time. Most models work other full-time jobs, attend school or depend on various markets to supplement their incomes.

❖ Portfolios:

10% of the market is from direct bookings. Direct booking portfolios must have good tearsheets with an array of clients showing consistent work. The portfolios can range from edgy to lifestyle fashion. Clients do not necessarily have to see models in person. No experience is necessary for new faces as they can be developed there. Established models will need to enter the market with good testing and a couple of tearsheets; however, their portfolios do not have to be extensive.

❖ Agencies Preferences:

Agencies like models that are down to earth with great energy and an outgoing, vibrant and confident attitude. For castings, models should have minimal make-up and natural hair. Dress should be classic, relaxed, neat and not overly done. Agencies prefer models to remain on stay for at least a month.

TYPICAL BOOKINGS

❖ Length of Work:

Hourly, half day, full day and there are not many multiple days.

MODEL MARKETS OF THE WORLD
MILWAUKEE WISCONSIN

❖ Type of Work:

Milwaukee has a wide range of work. Catalogue, a small amount of editorial and athletic, lingerie, swimwear, runway, commercial print, TV commercial, film, rarely infomercial, trade show, store informal, showroom, and industrial.

❖ Busiest Seasons:

The busiest time is from May to the end of October. The slowest time is in the winter from November to the end of February.

TOP CLIENTS

Top clients include department stores Kohl's, Fleet Farm and Carson Pirie Scott, Jockey, Kohler (bath systems), Shopko, Info Magazine, Oshkosh B'Gosh, Lands End, Harley Davidson, Holoubek (clothing), and SAB Miller Brewing Company.

COMPETITION

The Milwaukee market is less competitive than Chicago. Casting lines can be as long as 15 minutes.

PAY RATES

Print rates average $125-250 per hour. Half day $500-750. Full day $1,000-2,500. Advertising $500-$3,000. Runway $135 per show. TV/film either follows SAG/AFTRA union scale rates or non-union, which varies with each job. The market is about 70% union.

❖ Agency Cuts:

For commission, the agencies deduct 20% for print, runway and non-union TV/film. 10% for union film/TV.

❖ Agency Provides:

Dependent upon the situation or the caliber of the model, most agencies will advance accommodations, airfare, composites, laser copies of books, tests and pocket money. Neither agencies nor clients offer money contracts.

LIVING

❖ Housing:

Agencies do not provide models' apartments. Inexpensive accommodations average $500-650 per month. Moderate $750-1,000 per month. Cheap hotels average $99-150 per night.

❖ Transportation:

The airport is 15 minutes from downtown. Milwaukee has inexpensive public transportation including bus and Amtrak. A short ride in a taxi is $5. A car is not necessary to get to castings. Parking is usually free or metered. Traffic is decent except during rush hour.

❖ Food & Entertainment:

An inexpensive lunch is $5-8 and an inexpensive dinner is $8-10. Milwaukee is known for its great culturally-based festivals. The area has lots of great concerts in the summer including Summerfest, the largest in the USA. Models should also check out the Milwaukee County Zoo and the Botanical Domes. Milwaukee has some of the best German restaurants in the USA. The historic district of Old Third Ward Street has numerous restaurants, bars and jazz clubs. Milwaukee is renowned for its bratwurst!

REQUISITES

A work visa is not necessary unless a non-USA citizen. Agencies deduct taxes for all foreign models.

WEATHER

Winters are hard. It gets very cold starting at the end of November through end of March.

CURRENCY

As of January 2005:
US$10 = C$12.34

MARCIA'S TIPS

Milwaukee is a very friendly working city with good family ethics and it's an easy place to make friends. Models can make connections that will last a lifetime. It's pretty difficult to succeed in Milwaukee if models don't have a good smile. A model bag with basic shoes, hose, belts, t-shirts, bras and underwear is a must. Summers are the best in Milwaukee with lots of activities and bookings. One of the most unique things to see at the Milwaukee Art Museum is the Calatrava Wings.

MINNESOTA

MINNEAPOLIS

Minneapolis is a medium size market parallel with Chicago and has a metropolitan area population of 3,350,000. The market has approximately 10 fashion agencies. Minneapolis has Fortune 500 companies based locally as well as some strong retail clients. The primary market in Minneapolis is lifestyle fashion along with relatable commercial print and advertising. It is a very livable city with a good quality of life. The city is surrounded by lush greenery, beautiful lakes and it is truly gorgeous. The city's agents say that if it wasn't for the inclement weather, more people would live and work there.

MARKET PREFERENCES

❖ Models:

The Minneapolis market uses junior/teens, big & tall, petite (5'2"-5'5"), plus/full-size (5'8"-5'11", sizes 12-16), athletic, and adults. Women are preferably looking the ages of 20-45, 5'8"-5'11", sizes 2-6, no more than a C-cup (occasional a D-cup), and no larger than a 37" hip; for runway 5'9"-5'11", sizes 2-6. Men are preferably looking the ages of 20-50, 5'11"-6'2", suit 40-42; for runway 6'0"-6'3", suit 40-42. The Minneapolis market uses all ethnicities and smiles are important for catalogue and editorial. 30% of the market works full-time during season. During slower periods, models combine work with other markets.

❖ Portfolios:

20-25% of the market is from direct bookings. Clients mainly direct book from composites that have a very standard, relatable, commercial look with maybe one high fashion shot on the back of the card. Clients prefer to see models in person, if possible, and no experience is necessary for new faces with at least one good test. Established models should enter the market with really fresh and clean shots, good beauty/skin shots, lots of smile shots, some high fashion editorial and lifestyle fashion either in the form of good testing or tearsheets.

❖ Agencies Preferences:

Agencies like models that are very laid back because the culture of Minneapolis lends itself to this. Models should also be nice, easy going, and very organized. For castings, hair and make-up should be light and natural. Dress for castings should be trendy and casual. Agencies prefer that models remain on stay at least two weeks; however, longer would be preferred.

TYPICAL BOOKINGS

❖ Length of Work:

Hourly, half day and full day. 25% of

MARCIA ROTHSCHILD MOELLERS
MINNESOTA MINNEAPOLIS

bookings are multiple days.

❖ Type of Work:

Minneapolis has it all – catalogue, athletic, editorial, lingerie, swimwear, campaign, runway, commercial print, TV commercial, film, infomercial, trade show, store informal, showroom, and industrial.

❖ Busiest Seasons:

The market is busiest from May to September and the slowest time is from November to the end of January.

TOP CLIENTS

Top clients include Minneapolis-based department stores Target and Marshall Field's, Sportsmen's guide (catalogue), Neiman Marcus, Best Buy (tech store), H& R Block (accounting), Parenting Magazine, and powerhouse ad agencies Carmichael Lynch, Campbell Mithun, Fallon and Martin Williams.

COMPETITION

The competition can be as tough as Chicago from May until September. Castings are usually appointed times and lines are never longer than 20 minutes.

PAY RATES

Print averages $150-250 per hour. Half Day $600-750. Full day $1,200-1,700. Advertising/campaign $500-$10,000. Runway $0-700 per show. A lot of runway is pro bono because it is considered an opportunity to gain experience. TV/film either follows SAG/AFTRA union scale rates or non-union, varying with each job. 75% is non-union.

❖ Agency Cuts:

For commissions, agencies deduct 20% for print and runway. 10% for union TV/film and non-union TV/film.

❖ Agency Provides:

Minneapolis agencies rarely advance airfare, accommodations, laser copies of books or pocket money. Depending on the situation, they may advance composites but never tests. Neither agencies nor clients offer money contracts.

LIVING

❖ Housing:

Agencies do not provide models' apartments. Inexpensive accommodations average $350-500 per month. Moderate $500-600 per month. Cheap hotels average $80-120 per night.

❖ Transportation:

The airport is 15 minutes from downtown. Minneapolis has inexpensive public transportation including train and bus. A short ride in a taxi is $8-10. Models need a car to get to castings and bookings as they tend to be very long distances. Parking downtown is $8-10. Some studios are outside of the city limits and the parking is free. Traffic is moderate.

❖ Food & Entertainment:

An inexpensive lunch is $5-8 and an inexpensive dinner is $8-15. Minneapolis

MODEL MARKETS OF THE WORLD
MINNEAPOLIS, MINNESOTA

has every kind of food and all the shopping one can imagine. The market is home to the world renowned Mall of America. Most of the city's bars and restaurants are centrally located and there are lots of nightclubs. The atmosphere is very Midwest.

REQUISITES

A work visa is not necessary unless a non-USA citizen. Agencies deduct taxes for all foreign models.

WEATHER

The biggest drawback to living in Minneapolis is the brutal winters. The springs and falls are beautiful. Summers can be very warm and humid with lots of mosquitoes.

CURRENCY

As of January 2005:
US$10 = C$12.34

MARCIA'S TIPS

Minneapolis is not a snooty market so haughty models will need to keep their attitudes in check or they will not succeed in Minneapolis. Clients won't hire snotty models no matter what they've done or where they've been. Models should be very open to anything regarding bookings and should not feel above anything. Many bookings lead to other bookings because it is a repeat booking market. Models want to keep in touch with the clients, keep them happy, and be very easy to work with. Minneapolis is all about securing and pleasing the client base.

NEW YORK
NEW YORK

New York City is the largest and most lucrative modeling market in the world. It has a city population of just over 8,000,000 in a very small area with a metropolitan area population of over 21,750,000. There are approximately 25 varying levels of fashion agencies. New York City is the most pivotal market for a model's career but at the same time can be the most difficult to break into. All the top editorial and commercial models will at some time base themselves in New York City. All the major clients of the world will at some time come to New York City to shoot. New Yorkers are fast paced, success-oriented, hard working and very, very blunt. The best of the best flocks to the city with aspirations of making it to the top. The cost is high on every level. If models choose to stick it out, it has been noted, the greater the risk, the greater the reward.

MARKET PREFERENCES

❖ Models:

The New York City market needs everything – junior/teens, big & tall, petite (5'4"-5'7"), plus/full-size (5'9"-5'11", sizes 10-22), athletic, and adults. Women are preferably looking the ages of 22-35, 5'9"-5'11", fashion sizes 4-6, couture sizes 2-4, no more than a C-cup, no larger than a 36" hip; for runway 5'9"-6'0", sizes 2-4, no more than a B-cup. Men are preferably looking the ages of 18-35, 6'0"-6'2", suit 40-42; for runway 6'0"-6'2", suit 40-42. All ethnicities are sought after and smiles are very important for catalogue; however, not so for editorial. About 75% of the women work full-time, especially those in high fashion. For men, probably more than half model and have something on the side – a part-time or flexible job, parenting, or school.

❖ Portfolios:

20% of the market is from direct bookings that are usually garnered by established models with high-end editorial and strong advertising/campaign, or from repeat bookings. Clients prefer to see models in person and no experience is necessary to start; however, it helps. If models plan to arrive as a new face, they should be prepared to listen and learn. The New York experience is a lot to take in and new faces should not expect to immediately start booking, but instead see their first time there as a learning process for what will ultimately be required of them to succeed. If models plan to arrive marketed as an established model, they will need to have good catalogue tears and advertising/editorial tearsheets. To enter as a top model, a strong portfolio with international tearsheets, advertising/campaigns, and a strong resume of European top market experience is re-

MODEL MARKETS OF THE WORLD
NEW YORK NEW YORK

quired.

❖ Agencies Preferences:

Agencies prefer models be ambitious and motivated as well as humble and polite with good interpersonal skills and a determined work ethic. A lanky, in shape body is a must in New York City. The overall look is the "less is more" approach – natural beauty, flattering jeans, fitted basic tank tops with expensive, good shoes. Models should be a clean canvas – think along the lines of the client as an artist wanting the image they envision. Agencies prefer models to remain on stay at least two months.

TYPICAL BOOKINGS

❖ Length of Work:

Hourly (usually showroom & catalogue), half day and the majority of bookings are full day. Multiple days happen more often when the economy is in an upward swing.

❖ Type of Work:

Every type of work is available in New York City – catalogue, athletic, editorial, campaign, lingerie, swimwear, runway, commercial print, TV commercial, film, infomercial, trade show, store informal, showroom and industrial.

❖ Busiest Seasons:

New York City is busy year-round. The absolute busiest times fluctuate year to year. The market usually slows just before the Christmas holidays through New Year's and then again right after the runway shows, with castings beginning two times a year in September and January. The shows cause the market to slow down in mid-February and at the end of September because many clients follow the runway shows on to Milan and Paris.

TOP CLIENTS

New York City has it all – the top magazines such as Vogue, W, GQ, Harper's Bazaar, and Sports Illustrated, as well as the top international magazines due to the amount of top models and photographers based in the city. New York City has the top ad agencies, a great deal of designers including Ralph Lauren, Tommy Hilfiger, Calvin Klein, and other clients including Revlon, Victoria's Secret, L'Oreal, Macy's, Neiman Marcus, J. Crew, Abercrombie & Fitch, The Limited Corporation, Lane Bryant and Bebe.

COMPETITION

New York City has the fiercest competition in the world on all levels. Casting lines can be as short as a minute or as long as several hours.

PAY RATES

Print averages $free-1,500 per hour. Half day $1,000-5,000. Full day $2,500-25,000. Advertising/campaign $500-1,000,000 and up. Editorial is from free to $1000 per day. Runway $free-50,000 per show with the average $500-1,000 per show (top models sometimes pull 5 figures to walk exclusively for a designer). TV/film either follows SAG/AFTRA union scale rates or non-union, which varies with each job. Agencies receive lots of calls for music videos which fall under the non-union category. The market is primarily split 50/50 between union and non-union.

❖ Agency Cuts:

For commissions, agencies deduct 20% for print, runway and non-union TV/film. 10% is deducted for union TV/film.

❖ Agency Provides:

Agencies will advance accommodations, airfare, testing, composites, laser copies of books and website. On very rare occasions, agencies will advance weekly pocket money, dependent upon the caliber of the model and the agency. Agencies do offer money contracts; however, usually through contests. Some clients offer money contracts, but it is rare. In New York City, it is very important for new faces to save their money before arriving, as most agencies do not advance pocket money. Models should be prepared to get a night job if planning on staying. Agencies have been known to note that new faces working at night tend to be more patient and relaxed with the process because they aren't as worried about money.

LIVING

❖ Housing:

Some New York City agencies provide models' apartments. Depending on how many roommates, a model's accommodations can be had for as cheaply as $400-2,000 per month. Moderate averages $2,000-3,500 per month. Cheap hotels average $99-200 per night. Most New York City hotels average $300-600 per night.

❖ Transportation:

There are 3 airports in the vicinity of New York City – JFK, LaGuardia and Newark – and all are under 1.5 hours with traffic from downtown. The city has excellent public transportation including train, subway and bus, and it is extremely effective and inexpensive. A short ride in a taxi is $5-10, depending on traffic. Many agencies use car services and they average $50-100 each way to the airports. The traffic in New York City is formidable.

❖ Food & Entertainment:

New York City has every type of food imaginable. An inexpensive lunch is $5-7 and an inexpensive dinner is $12-14. On a limited budget, one can be very creative in the city regarding entertainment. There is so much to do and see – the best museums, concert halls, art galleries, and all sorts of nightclubs, coffee shops and restaurants.

REQUISITES

A work visa is not necessary unless a non-USA citizen. Agencies deduct taxes for all foreign models.

MODEL MARKETS OF THE WORLD
NEW YORK NEW YORK

WEATHER

The weather in New York City can be extreme. It can snow in October and be warm in December. New York City follows the seasons but is always unpredictable.

CURRENCY

As of January 2005:
US$10 = C$12.34

MARCIA'S TIPS

New Yorkers will say it's a myth that they are unfriendly. New York City is a walking city, statistically the safest, large city in America, which is an equalizer among the diverse types of people mingling together. Models should stay positive and friendly, which can be difficult in one of the most go, go, dog-eat-dog, success-oriented cities in the world. It's tough and that means models have to be strong and smart but that doesn't mean they can't have a heart.

PENNSYLVANIA
PHILADELPHIA

Philadelphia is a very small, lifestyle-oriented fashion market. There are approximately 5 agencies catering to a metropolitan area population of 2,450,000. The market is geared toward an older, more relatable model. The market has diminished due to the slowing economy over the past 10 years. Some clients have left permanently and some have chosen to shoot in nearby New York City. Still, it is a valid fashion market and can be a very plausible addition to models anywhere from the Midwest to the east coast who are seeking additional market representation and have a reason to visit Philadelphia other than for modeling.

MARKET PREFERENCES

❖ Models:

The market uses junior/teens, petite (5'3"-5'5"), plus/full-size (5'9"-5'10", sizes 16-20), very few athletic, and adults. Women are preferably looking the ages of 24-35, 5'8"-5'10.5", sizes 4-8, no more than a C-cup, no larger than a 36" hip; for runway 5'9"-5'11", sizes 4-6. Men are preferably looking 24-45, 5'11"-6'2", suit 40-42; for runway 6'0"-6'2", suit 40-42. Smiles are very important for catalogue but not always for editorial. The market uses most ethnicities, leaning towards Light Black but not as many Native American or Black models. 30% of the market works full-time.

❖ Portfolios:

About 50% of the market is from direct bookings. Portfolios for direct bookings must be composed mainly of tearsheets and be internationally developed. The bulk of direct bookings go to New York City models, former Philadelphia models now living elsewhere, and models that are being rebooked. Clients absolutely prefer to see models in person. No experience is necessary for new faces. Clients never book brand new faces until they have tested and have been to a larger market for experience. Once new faces have garnered some editorial, the clients will then consider for bookings. This is solely because of the amazing amount of top models available to them on the east coast. Established models must enter the market with good tearsheets and strong tests.

❖ Agencies Preferences:

Agencies like models that are outgoing, friendly and easy to get along with. Hair and make-up should be natural, clean and well-groomed. Dress is completely dependent upon the casting and agencies will advise. One client could prefer a more casual look – jeans, good shoes, and a nice body conscious top; whereas, another client may prefer a more upscale dressy look

MODEL MARKETS OF THE WORLD
PHILADELPHIA PENNSYLVANIA

(especially for runway) – along the lines of a more corporate Saks Fifth Avenue image. Philadelphia is not a client appointments only market. Agencies prefer models live there. If models are eager to expand into Philadelphia or come in and out of the market for various reasons, they can contact the agencies and send their portfolios for review.

TYPICAL BOOKINGS

❖ **Length of Work:**

Hourly (minimum 2 hours), half day, full day and rare multiple days.

❖ **Type of Work:**

Catalogue, some editorial, a small amount of athletic, lingerie, swimwear, runway, commercial print, TV commercial, very few film, trade show, promotional work, showroom, and industrial.

❖ **Busiest Seasons:**

The busiest times are late January through July and the slowest times are the summer and from December to the middle of January.

TOP CLIENTS

Top clients include Revlon, QVC Home Shopping, Boscov's (dept. store), Saks Fifth Avenue, Bloomingdales, advertising agencies Lorel Marketing and Portfolio Marketing, Deb Shops (junior catalogue), USMP (promotional work), and lots of trade show.

COMPETITION

The market is extremely competitive as there are fewer and fewer accounts left. At times, casting lines can be long as long as 2 hours.

PAY RATES

Print averages $125-150 per hour. Half day $500-750. Full day $1,000-1,500. Advertising/campaign $1,500-3,000. Runway $350 per show. TV/film either follows SAG/AFTRA union scale rates or non-union, which varies with each job. Philadelphia is about 98% non-union for TV/film. Typical non-union rates are $350 per half day and $650 per full day.

❖ **Agency Cuts:**

For commissions, agencies deduct 20% for print, runway, and non-union TV/film. 10% for union TV/film.

❖ **Agency Provides:**

Due to the very small nature of the market, agencies do not advance on anything. Neither agencies nor clients offer money contracts.

LIVING

❖ **Housing:**

Agencies do not provide models' apartments. Inexpensive accommodations average $900-1,000 per month. Moderate $1,800-2,500. Cheap hotels average $125-250 per night.

❖ Transportation:

The airport is 35 minutes from downtown. The market has inexpensive public transportation including train, subway and bus. A short ride in a taxi is $7. A car is pretty essential for models as castings are time specific and far apart. Most parking is meter ($2 in quarters for 2 hours). Other parking averages $8-25, depending on the time of day. Traffic is horrible at rush hour.

❖ Food & Entertainment:

An inexpensive lunch is $6-7 and an inexpensive dinner is $10-20. Philadelphia is a great city for entertainment. It has wonderful museums extolling the history of the USA, lots of good theater, major sports arenas, nightclubs, great restaurants and jazz bars.

REQUISITES

A work visa is not necessary unless a non-USA citizen. Agencies deduct taxes for all foreign models.

WEATHER

Philadelphia has very typical weather for a market with 4 seasons.

CURRENCY

As of January 2005:
US$10 = C$12.34

MARCIA'S TIPS

The cool thing about Philadelphia is how many different locations and cultures there are throughout the city. There is Chinatown, Little Italy, South Street where the hippies hang out, and Manyunk where the upscale yuppies socialize. With all the different areas, it is easy for a model to find a nitch. Philadelphia is an extremely cynical town with a "prove it to me" attitude. Models sometimes have to see the same clients 4 or 5 times before they even consider booking and then clients have a lot of model loyalty once the product is tried and true.

ARIZONA
PHOENIX

Phoenix is a small market with a metropolitan area population, including Scottsdale and Tempe, of just under 3,000,000. Phoenix is a market where models relocate, not because of the work but because of their own personal lifestyle choices. Modeling is a secondary income for the majority of models in Phoenix. It is an easy market to fly in and out of to the other larger markets. Clients come to Arizona in the winter months, between November and May, as the climate is warm and dry, and the chances of losing a day of work to cold weather or rain is almost obsolete. Phoenix is a good opportunity market for models that want a slower pace, some extra income, and want to remain out of the cold during the busier months in the industry.

MARKET PREFERENCES

❖ Models:

The market uses junior/teens, plus/full-size (5'8"-5'10", sizes 12-20), a lot of athletic and adults. Women are preferably looking the ages of 18-40, 5'8"-6'0", sizes 4-8, no more than a C-cup, no larger than a 36" hip; for runway 5'9"-5'11", sizes 2-6. Men are preferably looking the ages of 20-45, 5'11'-6'2", suit 40-42; for runway 6'0"-6'2", suit 40-42. The market uses all ethnicities. Smiles are very important for catalogue and not as much for editorial. Most models cannot work full-time in Phoenix. A small percentage does, but they rely on direct bookings from other markets to supplement their incomes.

❖ Portfolios:

10% of the work in the Phoenix market is from direct bookings. For direct bookings, portfolios must have lifestyle fashion and clean shots along with current tests and tearsheets. Composites are essential as clients mainly book from them. Experience is not necessary for new faces. To enter the market, established models should have at least a good test book that is not outdated and reflects a good, fresh look. Models with tearsheets and editorial along with a relatable, lifestyle fashion look do very well in Phoenix.

❖ Agencies Preferences:

Agencies prefer models that are friendly, outgoing and approachable. Hair and make-up needs to be clean and simple for castings. Clients prefer to see a model as is, rather than one's interpretation of fashionable. It is best for models to dress casual; however, upscale – think Banana Republic. Agencies don't require models to come to the market to see clients. Instead, models may send their portfolios for review, if it is direct booking caliber, or models may visit the market if they are considering moving there. It's a great market for models to reside shortly, travel and get more experience, and then come back to enjoy life and the slower pace.

TYPICAL BOOKINGS

❖ Length of Work:
Hourly, half day, full day and occasional multiple days.

❖ Type of Work:
Catalogue, athletic, some editorial, lingerie, swimwear, runway, commercial print, TV commercial, film, infomercial, trade show, store informal, and showroom.

❖ Busiest Seasons:
Phoenix is busiest from mid-January through May and then again from mid-September to mid-December. June, July and August are the slowest months due to the unbearably dry, hot weather.

TOP CLIENTS
Top clients include Dillards, Macy's, Neiman Marcus, Petsmart, Saks Fifth Avenue, Albertson's (grocery store), catalogues Antigua, Bon A Parte and Wearguard, as well as St. John (designer).

COMPETITION
Phoenix is competitive because it is so small and models occasionally deal with long lines, but more often than not, castings are done on a request basis. Models may have to wait as long as a half hour at a casting.

PAY RATES
Print averages $150-187.50 per hour. Half day $600-1,000. Full day $1,200-2,000. Advertising averages 1,200-$4,000. Runway $200 per show with rehearsals and fittings at $50 per hour. TV/film either follows SAG/AFTRA union scale rates or non-union, which varies with each job. 75% of TV/film is non-union as Arizona is a "right to work" state.

❖ Agency Cuts:
For commissions, agencies deduct 20% for print, runway and non-union TV/film. 10% for union TV/film.

❖ Agency Provides:
Agencies do not advance much of anything due to the nature of it being a small market. They will advance airfare, depending on the situation with an advanced booking. Neither agencies nor clients offer money contracts.

LIVING

❖ Housing:
Agencies do not provide models' apartments. Inexpensive accommodations average $350-500 per month. Moderate $500-700 per month. Cheap hotels average $125-250 per night.

❖ Transportation:
The airport is 10-15 minutes from most of the metropolitan areas of Phoenix and there is no public transportation. A short ride in a taxi is $5-$10, depending on

MODEL MARKETS OF THE WORLD
PHOENIX ARIZONA

the time of day. Models find having a car optimum. Parking is not an issue because the majority of it is free. Traffic is not a problem with rush hours being less typical than most major cities.

❖ Food & Entertainment:

An inexpensive lunch is $5 and an inexpensive dinner is $5-$10. The Phoenix/Scottsdale/Tempe area has a huge nightlife scene with lots of restaurants and nightclubs, as well as very good theater. Models should definitely check out all the locales of Arizona, which offers anything from an Indian reservation to beautiful Sedona, which is located in the northern mountains.

REQUISITES

A work visa is not necessary unless a non-USA citizen. Agencies deduct taxes for all foreign models.

WEATHER

From the first of November to May, it is a beautiful 80 F with sunshine, sunshine, sunshine. From June to the end of October, it is extremely hot with temperatures averaging over 100 F.

CURRENCY

As of January 2005:
US$10 = C$12.34

MARCIA'S TIPS

Models should always remember to use sunscreen. Phoenix is a fantastic place to live, and it is a friendly community. Haughty attitudes need not apply. If models can travel outside of the Phoenix market for bookings, they can have a successful career while putting down roots. Many models love how close the market is to the busy Los Angeles market and airfares are inexpensive between the two. Models have been known to live in laid back Arizona and commute to Los Angeles for bookings and even castings. Models choose to relocate to Phoenix because it is a great place to raise a family and because the weather is so consistently warm.

PENNSYLVANIA
PITTSBURGH

Pittsburgh is a small market with approximately 2 agencies covering a metropolitan area population of 6,000,000. The market is a relatable lifestyle market where models get started, have their hand held, learn the basics of the business, and then move onto a medium size market. There is a little bit of everything from catalogue to TV commercial as well as a small amount of editorial. Pittsburgh provides a smaller view of the industry with easier access than the larger markets. Nearby markets feel the market is growing because models are traveling there for bookings. The local agencies feel it is still more of a locally based market than a market where models may travel in and see clients then leave. Either way, if models are based in a surrounding market, it may be worth their while to check out Pittsburgh, if they have an appropriate portfolio for direct bookings or if they are seeking a new city in which to base.

MARKET PREFERENCES

❖ Models:

The market uses junior/teens, plus/full-size (5'9"-5'11", sizes 12-20), athletic, and adults. Women are preferably looking the ages of 18-30, 5'7"-5'11", sizes 2-8, no more than a D-cup, no more than a 38" hip; for runway 5'9"-5'11", sizes 2-6. Men are preferably looking the ages of 18-35, 5'11"-6'3", suit 40-42; for runway 5'11"-6'4", suit 40-42. The market uses all ethnicities. Smiles are equally important for catalogue and editorial. Models do not work full-time in Pittsburgh. Most go to school or supplement their income via other markets or a part-time job.

❖ Portfolios:

About 25% of the market is from direct bookings. Clients prefer to direct book from portfolios that have tearsheets consisting of commercial print, catalogue and advertising with a diverse appeal from relatable to high end classic. No experience is necessary for new faces but they must have very good recent polaroids/snapshots and a great smile. Established models should enter the market with a good portfolio of tearsheets from relatable editorial and catalogue/advertising along with a very good composite exemplifying these categories.

❖ Agencies Preferences:

The Pittsburg agencies do not like divas. They want friendly models with great energy. Hair and make-up needs to look natural. Dress for castings should be simple, sophisticated and form fitting. Pittsburgh is not an appointment market. Established models from outside the market will be direct booked only. Models must base in the market in order to obtain long-term, consistent work.

MODEL MARKETS OF THE WORLD
50 PITTSBURGH PENNSYLVANIA

■ TYPICAL BOOKINGS

❖ Length of Work:
Hourly (2 hour minimum), half day, full day (usually with usage attached), and very rare multiple days.

❖ Type of Work:
Catalogue, a small amount of editorial, athletic, runway, commercial print, TV commercial, film, a few infomercial, trade show, store informal, and industrial.

❖ Busiest Seasons:
The busiest times are from February to March and from July to November. The slowest time is from April to June.

■ TOP CLIENTS
Top clients include Dick's Sporting Goods, American Eagle (clothing), Marc USA (ad agency), Value City (clothing), GNC (nutrition), Saks Fifth Avenue, Nordstroms, Whirl (magazine), Pittsburgh Magazine, and Victoria's Secret.

■ COMPETITION
The market has very little competition. Casting lines are long only for TV commercials with the wait being as long as an hour.

■ PAY RATES
Print averages $100-175 per hour. Half day $400-650. Full day 1,000-1,200. Advertising $1,000-8,000. Runway $100 per show, $25 for fitting and $300 for bigger shows. TV/film either follows SAG/AFTRA union scale rates or non-union, which varies with each job. About 40% of the market is non-union.

❖ Agency Cuts:
For commissions, agencies deduct 20% for print, runway and non-union TV/film. 10% for union TV/film.

❖ Agency Provides:
Due to the small nature of the market, the agencies generally do not advance anything. They may advance airfare with a confirmed booking from a client. Neither agencies nor clients offer money contracts.

■ LIVING

❖ Housing:
Agencies do not provide models' apartments. Inexpensive accommodations for $350 per month. Moderate $550 per month. Cheap hotels average $49-99 per night.

❖ Transportation:
The airport is 20 minutes from downtown. Pittsburgh does have public transportation including train, subway and bus. It is moderately expensive and not recommended for use by the agencies. A short ride in a taxi is $5-8. Models must have a dependable car due to the widespread nature of bookings and castings. Parking in the city can be pricey and traffic is moderate.

❖ Food & Entertainment:
An inexpensive lunch is $5 and an inexpensive dinner is $12. Entertainment

in Pittsburgh is good with a fabulous community theater scene, good nightclubs, interesting coffee shops, and lots of nightclubs and restaurants.

REQUISITES

A work visa is not necessary unless a non-USA citizen. Agencies deduct taxes for all foreign models.

WEATHER

Winters are tough.

CURRENCY

As of January 2005:
US$10 = C$12.34

MARCIA'S TIPS

The market and the city itself are very friendly with a welcoming community. Pittsburgh is a city of immigrants with lots of different cultures. Everyone tries to help everyone. The architecture is beautiful. Models will not work as much as they would in larger markets but there are a good handful of money clients. Models must be willing to travel in their cars to get to clients as they are spread throughout the state and can go as far as into Ohio.

OREGON
PORTLAND

Portland is a small market with a metropolitan area population of 2,100,000. There are approximately four fashion agencies based in the city. The Portland market mainly books athletic and fashion. This is definitely an outdoor market and it is growing, growing, growing. Portland is one of the markets paving the way for athletic and sportswear retail gaining ground in the USA as consumers continue to buy more of these products. Portland can't go wrong with Nike right in its backyard. Models cannot be petite in frame size and must be in excellent shape. If models have a relaxed, laid-back mentality blended with an outgoing attitude and a love for fitness, then Portland is a great market choice.

MARKET PREFERENCES

❖ Models:

The market uses junior/teens, big & tall, plus/full-size (5'8.5"-5'11", sizes 14-20), lots of athletic, and adults. Women are preferably looking the ages of 21-45, 5'8"-5'10", sizes 4-6, no more than a C-cup, no larger than a 37" hip; for runway 5'9"-5'11", sizes 4-6. Men are preferably looking the ages of 25-50, athletic 5'10"-6'1", fashion 5'11.5"-6'2", suit 40-42; for runway 6'0"-6'2", suit 40-42. The market needs all ethnicities; however, there is very little opportunity for Native American models. Good smiles are a must for catalogue and editorial. About 10% of the market works full-time. Most models have other employment or attend school.

❖ Portfolios:

Portland books about 10% direct. Direct booking models must have strong portfolios with diverse editorial/advertising and have very good testing. No experience is necessary for new faces, but it helps with garnering work. Established models should enter the market with very good testing and at least several tearsheets.

❖ Agencies Preferences:

Agencies like models that are outgoing and friendly. Clients like both trendy (especially the athletic clients) to traditionally commercial looks. Dress should be casual, outdoorsy and put together nicely. Some castings are dress specific.

TYPICAL BOOKINGS

❖ Length of Work:

Hourly, half day, full day and some multiple day bookings.

❖ Type of Work:

Catalogue, athletic, light editorial, campaign, swimwear, lingerie, runway, film, TV commercial, commercial Print, tradeshow, infomercial, showroom and

MARCIA ROTHSCHILD MOELLERS
OREGON PORTLAND

industrial.

❖ Busiest Seasons:

The busiest times are from January to February, June and then from September to November. The market is slow during holidays and December.

TOP CLIENTS

Top clients include Nike, Adidas America, Columbia Sportswear, Norm Thompson (catalogue), Pendleton (clothing), Jantzen (swimwear/sportswear), Fred Meyer (comparative to Wal Mart), computer tech companies including Intel, Hewlett-Packard and Tektronix, and Wieden + Kennedy (ad agency).

COMPETITION

Portland is very competitive due to having the third largest infusion of 18-25 year olds in the USA. Lines can be as long as an hour at the larger castings.

PAY RATES

Print averages $100-187.50 per hour. Lingerie is time and a half. Half day $600-1,000. Full day $1,250-2,000. Advertising/campaign $3,000-15,000. Runway $125 per hour. TV/film either follows SAG/AFTRA union scale rates or non-union, which varies with each job. About 80% of the Portland market is non-union.

❖ Agency Cuts:

For commissions, agencies deduct 20% for print and runway. 15% for non-union TV/film. 10% for union TV/film.

❖ Agency Provides:

Some agencies will advance on testing and composites, dependent upon the caliber of the model. Agencies do not offer money contracts. Some clients will offer money contracts; however, to professional athletes only.

LIVING

❖ Housing:

Agencies do not provide models' apartments. Inexpensive accommodations average $500 per month. Moderate $750 per month. Cheap hotels average $50-250 per night.

❖ Transportation:

The Portland International Airport is 15 minutes from downtown or 30 minutes during rush hour. Portland has public transportation including train, subway and bus. The Rapid Transit is inexpensive and comes into the city from all directions, but is not always dependable with client scheduling. A short ride in a taxi is $3-4. It's a smart move for a model to have a car in Portland. Parking is $8-12 per day and traffic is busy at rush hour.

❖ Food & Entertainment:

An inexpensive lunch is $4-6 and an inexpensive dinner is $5-8. Models who love the outdoors and like to ski, mountain bike, kayak, snowboard, mountain climb, run or just walk, will absolutely love Portland. Forest Park is mere minutes from downtown and is the largest unde-

MODEL MARKETS OF THE WORLD
PORTLAND OREGON

veloped park within the bounds of a major metropolitan city with miles of trails to run, walk or mountain bike. Portland has an abundance of nightlife, boasting more brew-pubs per capita than any city in the USA. Indie-rock dominates the club scene. The Pearl District boasts numerous art galleries and upscale retailers. Theatre options abound. Portland is also one of the nation's top experimental film markets. Portland is a college town with a lot of hip neighborhoods.

many bike commuters. The city is located one hour from Mt. Hood, which boasts a handful of ski resorts, and three hours from the desert region of Bend, a mecca for skiers and outdoor enthusiasts. Athletic models can really thrive in this market if they fit the criteria.

REQUISITES

A work visa is not necessary unless a non-USA citizen. Agencies deduct taxes for all foreign models.

WEATHER

Rainy season is November to April. Winters are wet. It can be hot from June through October.

CURRENCY

As of January 2005:
US$10 = C$12.34

MARCIA'S TIPS

Models will need to carry an umbrella anytime from late fall to spring. Clients e xpect a great level of professionalism. Models should make sure to bring a model bag to all bookings. Clients appreciate real people, not fake, poser types. The mentality is casual, very liberal and well educated. People are extremely nice and polite. Portland is very bike-friendly, and has

CALIFORNIA
SAN DIEGO

San Diego is a small market in comparison to the large market of New York City and the medium market of Chicago. The San Diego market has a metropolitan area population over 3,000,000 with approximately 3 fashion agencies. What separates San Diego from other markets is that it is a destination location; however, on a smaller scale than that of Miami. More than half of San Diego's clients are from elsewhere. This seaside city is a beautiful, great weather, body-oriented catalogue and commercial print market. Great skin, a beautiful smile, a fabulous shape and good attitude are all a must. Models who base in San Diego love that it is just a short distance from the larger market of Los Angeles.

MARKET PREFERENCES

❖ Models:

The market uses junior/teens, petite (5'4"-5'7"), athletic, and adults. Women are preferably looking the ages of 18-35, 5'8"-5'11, sizes 2-8, no more than a C-cup, no larger than a 36" hip; for runway 5'9"-5'11", sizes 2-6. Men are preferably looking the ages of 18-35, 5'11"-6'2", suit 40-42; for runway 6'0"-6'3", suit 40-42. The San Diego market uses all ethnicities. Smiles are important for catalogue as well as editorial. Models do not work full-time in the market unless combining it with the other local markets.

❖ Portfolios:

About 30% of the San Diego bookings are direct. The direct booking portfolios must possess a strong blend – not too editorial, not too relatable lifestyle – because neither extreme works well. Most clients prefer to see the models at castings. No experience is necessary for new faces as it is an approachable market for development. Established models must enter the market with at least solid, good testing throughout the portfolio to garner bookings.

❖ Agencies Preferences:

Agencies like models that are professional and approachable. Hair and make-up is dependent upon the client's preference – agencies will advise. Models must wear appropriate make-up for TV castings whereas catalogue clients prefer to see very light, simple and neat make-up. Most clients prefer models to wear casual clothes. Jeans are okay as long as the look is clean and body conscious. Models need to be versatile in dress; however, it is advised to check with the agency before going to a casting. Agencies prefer models to remain on stay in the San Diego market for at least 2 months.

MODEL MARKETS OF THE WORLD
SAN DIEGO CALIFORNIA

TYPICAL BOOKINGS

❖ Length of Work:
Hourly, half day, full day and a few multiple days.

❖ Type of Work:
Catalogue, editorial, athletic, lingerie, swimwear, runway, commercial print, TV commercial, very little film, infomercial, trade show, store informal, showroom, and industrial.

❖ Busiest Seasons:
San Diego is busiest from January through April and September to December. The market slows down from May through August.

TOP CLIENTS
Top clients include Sebastian (hair care), department stores Mervyn's, Gottschalk's, Saks Fifth Avenue, Nordstrom and Fuller, catalogues Eddie Bauer and Lands End, Riviera Magazine, and Fruit of the Loom.

COMPETITION
Competition is minimal because the San Diego market has a very specific nitch clientele. Castings can be as little as a minute to as long as an hour.

PAY RATES
Print averages $100-250 per hour. Half day $400-1,250. Full day $800-3,500. Advertising/campaign $1,000-15,000. Runway $250 per show. TV/film either follows SAG/AFTRA union scale rates or non-union, which is 15% of the market.

❖ Agency Cuts:
Agencies deduct 20% for print and runway. 15% for non-union. 10% for union.

❖ Agency Provides:
San Diego agencies may advance on airfare, composites, laser copies of books and tests, dependent upon the caliber of the model, but never on accommodations or pocket money. Agencies do not offer money contracts; however some clients will..

LIVING

❖ Housing:
Agencies do not provide models' apartments. Inexpensive accommodations average $750-1,000 per month. Moderate $1,000-2,000. Cheap hotels average $100-200 per night.

❖ Transportation:
The airport is 10 minutes from downtown. The San Diego market has public transportation in the form of buses, which are inexpensive but not dependable for castings. A short ride in a taxi is $5. Models must have a car to get to their castings and bookings. Parking is $2-10. Traffic is moderate.

❖ Food & Entertainment:
An inexpensive lunch is $5 and an inexpensive dinner is $10. San Diego is growing and the city has multiple young

and upcoming consumers flocking to the area which has led to a lot of development geared toward entertaining. San Diego is a fun, little hot spot with people from Los Angeles coming for weekends to enjoy the beaches and the nightlife.

REQUISITES

A work visa is not necessary unless a non-USA citizen. Agencies deduct taxes for all foreign models.

WEATHER

San Diego is one of the best and most consistent climates one can find in the USA. The average temperature is about 72F.

CURRENCY

As of January 2005:
US$10 = C$12.34

MARCIA'S TIPS

The most important element for models to remember about San Diego is that it is a supplemental market. When models choose to live in San Diego, they have to survive a good duration of inconsistent highs and lows and be prepared to commute to Los Angeles for additional work and castings. San Diego is definitely a market where maintaining a good shape is paramount. Many clients come to shoot outdoors and are booking with spring/summer apparel in mind. To be successful, models need to keep it fresh, clean and friendly while enjoying the beautiful locations of San Diego.

CALIFORNIA
SAN FRANCISCO

San Francisco is a smaller medium size market with a metropolitan area population, including Oakland and San Jose, of 7,200,000 and can really be considered a larger medium size market in client power. Heavy hitting clients, including the Gap, Levi's, Old Navy and Banana Republic, are serviced by only 3 fashion agencies catering to the needs of the entire market. Clients are geared toward advertising/campaign that has a casual lifestyle fashion look. It's a great market for new faces to develop, considering these top clients are in their back yard along with catalogue and editorial as well. San Francisco is also a great market for models to come back to after they have established a good portfolio to enjoy less frenzy in a casually sophisticated city.

MARKET PREFERENCES

❖ Models:

San Francisco uses junior/teens, big & tall, petite (5'4"-5'7"), plus/full-size (5'10", sizes 12-20), athletic, and adults. Females are preferably looking the ages of 18-50, 5'8"-5'11", sizes 4-6, no more than a C-cup, no larger than a 36" hip but preferably 35"; for runway 5'9"-5'11, sizes 2-6. Men are preferably looking the ages of 18-50, 5'10"-6'2", suit 40-42; for runway 6'0"-6'2", suit 40-42. The market uses all ethnicities, with a strong base of Asian and Eurasian consumers. Only about 5% of the market currently works full-time due to the fluctuating economy. This figure rapidly expands along with upward swings in the economy.

❖ Portfolios:

25% of San Francisco is from direct bookings and the portfolios must reflect 100% well-seasoned, internationally traveled models with an accumulation of advertising/campaign and editorial tearsheets. Clients will pay well to secure top level models. Still, clients actually prefer to see models in person. New faces must have a great test book to work but agencies are willing to develop and test. Established models must enter with a book full of advertising and editorial tearsheets that reflect consistent work.

❖ Agencies Preferences:

Agencies prefer models that are nice, sweet and outgoing because these are the type clients always choose. Hair and make-up should be simple and clean for castings. Clothes should be very simple along the lines of Banana Republic. Dependent upon the caliber of the model, agencies prefer models to remain on stay for 2 or more weeks. Top models can come to see clients and then be available for direct bookings.

MARCIA ROTHSCHILD MOELLERS
CALIFORNIA — SAN FRANCISCO

▸ TYPICAL BOOKINGS

❖ **Length of Work:**
Hourly (2 hour minimum), half day, full day and rare multiple days.

❖ **Type of Work:**
Catalogue, editorial, campaign, athletic, lingerie, swimwear, runway, commercial print, TV commercial, film, infomercial, trade show, store informal, showroom, and industrial.

❖ **Busiest Seasons:**
San Francisco has consistent work. The busiest time is typically from April to November, and the slowest time is from December to March.

▸ TOP CLIENTS

Top clients include The Gap, Levi's, Banana Republic, Old Navy, Discovery (specialty store), magazines 7x7 and Soma, Mervyn's, Macy's, and Jessica McClintock (day/evening wear).

▸ COMPETITION

The competition is fierce due to the high level of clients pursued by all the top level USA markets. Fashion and TV commercial castings can be as long as 45 minutes.

▸ PAY RATES

Print averages $187.50-225 per hour. Half day $750-2,000. Full day $1,200-5,000. Advertising / campaign $7,000-15,000. Runway $125-150 per hour. TV/film either follows SAG/AFTRA union scale rates or non-union, which varies with each job. The market is 65% non-union.

❖ **Agency Cuts:**
For commissions, the agencies deduct 20% for print and runway. 10% for union TV/film. Commissions vary for non-union TV/film.

❖ **Agency Provides:**
Agencies do not advance much of anything. Direct booking clients usually pay airfare and accommodations. Agencies do not offer money contracts; however some clients will.

▸ LIVING

❖ **Housing:**
Agencies do not provide models' apartments. Inexpensive accommodations average $500-700 per month. Moderate $1,000-1,500. Cheap hotels average $30-75 per night.

❖ **Transportation:**
The airport is 20 minutes from downtown. San Francisco has excellent and inexpensive public transportation including train and bus. A short ride in a taxi is $5. Models do not need a car for castings; however if models choose to rent, parking is pricey. Traffic in the market is very light.

❖ **Food & Entertainment:**
An inexpensive lunch is $5-8 and an inexpensive dinner is $8-10. The city has

MODEL MARKETS OF THE WORLD
SAN FRANCISCO, CALIFORNIA

amazing restaurants with world renowned chefs; however, be willing to pay the tab. The entertainment is great but not as good as other larger cities. San Francisco has excellent music venues.

REQUISITES

A work visa is not necessary unless a non-USA citizen. Agencies deduct taxes for all foreign models.

WEATHER

Indian summers can last as long as September through October with temperatures soaring as high as 90 F.

CURRENCY

As of January 2005:
US$10 = C$12.34

MARCIA'S TIPS

When coming to visit the San Francisco market, it is important for models to keep a very open mind as it is a multi-cultural melting pot of various clients and individuals. Business trips can be enhanced if models keep an open mind and do not assume it should be just like Chicago or Dallas. The city is very friendly with an upscale approach and can be rather casual as well as elegant at the same time.

WASHINGTON
SEATTLE

Seattle is a smaller middle size market with a metropolitan area population of 3,650,000 and has approximately 3 fashion agencies. Primarily, Seattle is a relatable lifestyle and fashion/catalogue market with very little film or TV. It's an excellent market to begin modeling because models can get their feet wet with some very good clients that pay well. Some of Seattle's clientele is so prestigious in the industry that Los Angeles and New York City try to book these top clients as well. The wonderful thing about Seattle is that the competition is not as stiff as these larger markets and the atmosphere is much more relaxed.

MARKET PREFERENCES

❖ Models:

The market uses junior/teens, big & tall, petite (5'4"-5'8"), plus/full-size (5'9"-5'11", size 14-18), athletic, and adults. Women are preferably looking the ages of 18-40, 5'9"-5'11", sizes 2-8, no more than a C-cup, no larger than a 37" hip; for runway 5'9"-6'10", sizes 2-6. Men are preferably looking the ages of 25-40, 5'11"-6'2", suit 40-42; for runway 6'0"-6'2", suit 40-42. The market uses all ethnicities and the demographics of the city are strong in Asian and Eurasian. Smiles are very important for catalogue and not as important for editorial. 25-30% of the market works full-time – more women than men. Models who intend to work full-time in the market must make investments in their career by traveling and / or taking modeling seriously.

❖ Portfolios:

The market is made up of approximately 50% direct bookings. For direct bookings, portfolios must have strong editorial with a catalogue feel because it is very important for models to show relatable lifestyle in their books. Even though half of Seattle's bookings are direct, clients prefer to see models in person. Experience is not necessary for new faces. Established models must have a portfolio full of tearsheets from catalogue, editorial and advertising.

❖ Agencies Preferences:

Agencies prefer models that are professional, friendly and interact well with others. For castings, models should have a very clean face, very light make-up and hair pulled away from the face. Clients want to book a model that looks like a model. If models are a very earthy, they will have to appear very put together – think Banana Republic, not jeans and Birkenstocks. If models are coming to Seattle to check out the market, summer is the recommended time and agencies prefer models to remain on stay 2-3 weeks.

MODEL MARKETS OF THE WORLD
SEATTLE WASHINGTON

■ TYPICAL BOOKINGS

❖ **Length of Work:**

Hourly, half day, full day and a good amount of multiple days.

❖ **Type of Work:**

Catalogue, athletic, editorial, lingerie, swimwear, runway, minimal TV commercial and film, commercial print, trade show, very little infomercial, store informal, showroom, and very little industrial.

❖ **Busiest Seasons:**

The busiest time is from April through October. The market is slower from November to March.

■ TOP CLIENTS

Top clients include Nordstrom (dept. store), Eddie Bauer, Bon/Macy's, Boeing (aircraft), Microsoft, REI (recreation/outdoor sports), Nike, Pacific Trail (outdoor clothing), and catalogues Norm Thomson and LL Bean.

■ COMPETITION

The Seattle market is less competitive than New York City, Miami and Los Angeles. The competition level is very similar to Chicago, Dallas and Atlanta. There are never long casting lines.

■ PAY RATES

Print averages $150-200 per hour. Half day $750-1,500. Full day $1,200-3,000. Advertising/campaign $3,000-15,000, plus an additional day rate or frequently, a negotiated buy-out. Runway $150 per show with prestigious shows paying more. TV/film either follows SAG/AFTRA union scale rates or non-union, which varies with each job.

❖ **Agency Cuts:**

Agencies deduct 20% for print, runway and non-union TV/film. 10% for union TV/film.

❖ **Agency Provides:**

Most agencies do not advance anything, unless a voucher is presented for a job completed. Agencies do not offer money contracts; however, some clients will.

■ LIVING

❖ **Housing:**

Models' apartments are not provided by the agencies. Inexpensive accommodations average $300-500 per month. Moderate $600-800 per month. Cheap hotels average $50-75 per night.

❖ **Transportation:**

The airport is located 15 miles from the city. Buses are the main source of public transportation and are not expensive. A short ride in a taxi is $3. A car is important to get to castings and parking is inexpensive, averaging $2 per hour. The city's traffic is pretty bad.

❖ **Food & Entertainment:**

An inexpensive lunch is $5 and an inexpensive dinner is $8. The city is known for its strong music base with lots to do in the evenings from wonderful international restaurants to lounges, nightclubs and great music venues.

REQUISITES

A work visa is not necessary unless a non-USA citizen. Some Canadian models will go through Seattle agencies to acquire their USA work visas. Agencies deduct taxes for all foreign models.

WEATHER

The Seattle weather affects work. There is lots of rain in the winter. Clients flock to the market in the summer because of its beautiful weather lasting until the beginning of October.

CURRENCY

As of January 2005:
US$10 = C$12.34

MARCIA'S TIPS

Models should be prepared to layer clothing because temperatures can drop drastically in the evening. When sightseeing Seattle, models should make sure to see the Space Needle, experience the EMP (the Jimi Hendrix museum), and ride a ferry. Seattle is surrounded by lakes, mountains, fabulous culture and a renowned music scene. Seattle is truly a wonderful place for young, active people.

FLORIDA
TAMPA

The Tampa market is the second largest market in Florida. Tampa is a small to medium size market with a metropolitan area population of 2,600,000. Approximately 2 fashion agencies service Tampa as well as St. Petersburg, Clearwater, Bradenton and Sarasota. Tampa covers a lot of ground and is primarily a print market that is less competitive throughout the year. The area offers many different scenic locations which are very attractive to clients – gorgeous beaches, great historical areas, fabulous estates, and beautifully restored hotels. Tampa has everything to offer except the mountains. The weather is gorgeous and clients come to shoot in this warm weather locale to book models that exemplify the mood of the market. It's a relatable, healthy body, beauty and fashion market.

■ MARKET PREFERENCES

❖ Models:

The market uses teens, plus/full-size (5'9"-5'11", sizes 12-14 and 18-20), athletic (using fashion models in great shape), and adults. Women are preferably looking the ages of 20-39, 5'7"-5'11", sizes 2-8, no more than a full C-cup, no larger than a 36" hip; for runway 5'9"-5'11.5", sizes 2-4. Men are preferably looking the ages of 20-45, 5'11"-6'2", suit 40-44; for runway 6'0"-6'2.5", suit 40-42. Freckles and moles can be a problem for certain beauty or lingerie/swimwear jobs, dependent upon the client. The market uses all ethnicities. Smiles are important for editorial and catalogue. 10% of the market works full-time with most models having an additional career, school or children.

❖ Portfolios:

95% of the market is from direct bookings which are garnered by either models with strong portfolios or from repeat bookings. Clients do not need to see models in person as the majority of clients will book from composites. No experience is necessary for new faces. In order to obtain bookings, new faces must have good testing that is more relatable/lifestyle fashion than it is high fashion. Established models must enter the market with a strong portfolio with tearsheets along with a very good composite that reflects beauty, body and lifestyle fashion.

❖ Agencies Preferences:

Agencies prefer models that are outgoing, vivacious and professional. Hair and make-up should be light and natural. For castings, clients prefer models wear something simple that shows off the body. Established models can send portfolios in advance to gauge the market response. Then, if direct booked into the market, the models can see the clients for bookings and remain on stay at least a month or longer. Agencies would prefer appropriate models base out of the market for at least a couple of months.

TYPICAL BOOKINGS

❖ Length of Work:
Primarily hourly bookings, some half day and full day, and very few multiple days.

❖ Type of Work:
Catalogue, athletic, light editorial, lingerie, lots of swimwear, runway, commercial print TV commercial, film, infomercial, trade show, store informal, and industrial.

❖ Busiest Seasons:
The market is busy all year long. Tampa is busiest from September to May. The slowest time of the year is August due to the heat and humidity.

TOP CLIENTS

Top clients include department stores Beall's, Dillard's, Neiman Marcus, and Saks Fifth Avenue, Home Shopping Network, VF Imagewear (catalogue), Uniform City, Momentum (theme parks), Publix (grocery), and *Sarasota Magazine*.

COMPETITION

The competition in the market is light if models have a great look and decent pictures in their portfolios that are appropriate for the market. There are never any long casting lines.

PAY RATES

Print averages $75-125 per hour. Half day $400-500. Full day $800-1,000. Advertising/campaign $3,500-5,000. Runway $75 per hour or $200 per show. TV/film either follows SAG/AFTRA union scale rates or non-union, which varies from job to job. 80% of the market is non-union for TV/film as Florida is a "right to work" state. Non-union work averages $100-125 per hour.

❖ Agency Cuts:
For commissions, agencies deduct 20% for print, runway and non-union TV/film. 10% for union TV/film.

❖ Agency Provides:
Agencies sometimes advance on composites and airfare, depending on the situation. Neither agencies nor clients offer money contracts.

LIVING

❖ Housing:
Agencies do not provide models' apartments. Inexpensive accommodations average $500-700 per month. Moderate $1,000-1,500. Cheap hotels average $45-250 per night.

❖ Transportation:
The airport is located in the city and is only 5 minutes from downtown. Tampa has public transportation including train,

MODEL MARKETS OF THE WORLD
TAMPA FLORIDA

subway and bus. Agencies do not advise public transportation for castings. A car is an absolute necessity in the market and parking is easy and usually free. A short ride in a taxi is $10. Traffic in the market is terrible.

❖ Food & Entertainment:

An inexpensive lunch is $5 and an inexpensive dinner is $5-10. Tampa's entertainment is good and includes theater, nightclubs, big name concert venues, professional sports, movie theaters, fabulous restaurants, nice resorts, and great shopping.

REQUISITES

A work visa is not necessary unless a non-USA citizen. Agencies deduct taxes for all foreign models.

WEATHER

The weather is gorgeous most of the year. It can be a little too hot in August. Hurricane season lasts about 6 months from the end of June to the beginning of November.

CURRENCY

As of January 2005:
US$10 = C$12.34

MARCIA'S TIPS

To secure work in Tampa, models absolutely must have a driver's license or someone that can drive them to their castings and bookings. Models must have very good shoes if they plan to do runway because show clients require models to bring their own. Many clients require some model wardrobe to be brought to bookings as well. Definite essentials include khakis, white and dark polo shirts, button down shirts, basic skin colored lingerie/underwear, nice black slacks/skirt, shoes in black/brown, white tennis shoes and sandals.

CANADA
MONTREAL

Montreal is a medium size market with a metropolitan area population of 3,600,000. Montreal is almost but not quite as large as the market in Toronto and has approximately 7 fashion agencies. Montreal is a very sophisticated and fashionable city and has been rated one of the top 3 trendiest cities in the world. This city loves fashion and everything about it. The market is also known for developing top models that travel on to great international careers. Montreal has a nice, small client base to support the development of these careers and some good direct bookings for internationally established models as well.

MARKET PREFERENCES

❖ Models:

The market uses junior/teens, petite (rarely), plus/full-size (5'8"-5'11", size 14), athletic, and adults. Women are preferably looking the ages of 18-35, 5'9"-5'11", sizes 2-6, no more than a B-cup, no more than a 36" hip; for runway 5'9"-5'11", sizes 2-4. Men are preferably looking the ages of 18-34, 5'11"-6'2", suit 40; for runway 6'0"-6'2", suit 40. The market will book models with freckles but models that have a lot of moles do not fare as well. Montreal uses all ethnicities. Smiles are very important for catalogue and editorial. Most models work part-time in the market with only 25% working full-time.

❖ Portfolios:

10-15% of Montreal is direct bookings. Direct booking portfolios must be really strong due to the market's small demand and will need to be top of the line with lots of editorial, advertising and campaigns from strong, international markets. Clients seldom repeat book models. The clients prefer to see models in person and they use a lot of local talent. Experience is not necessary for new faces. Canadian models can be developed and then move onto bigger markets. Established models will need catalogue and commercial print as well as editorial tearsheets along with really good testing. Portfolios must reflect experience and international tearsheets are strongly recommended. Non-Canadian models are welcome to come to Montreal; however, the market is small so work can sometimes be limited. Clients are always seeking new models with great books.

❖ Agencies Preferences:

Agencies prefer models that are outgoing individuals, nice, polite, with good interpersonal skills, ambitious and focused on modeling as a career. For castings, hair and make-up should be very clean and natural, no make-up is preferred. Clothing should be basic and neat. For men, t-shirts, dress pants or jeans, and a

MODEL MARKETS OF THE WORLD
MONTREAL CANADA

nice pair of shoes. For women, clean, neat hair, a nice tank top, and a skirt to show the legs along with nice shoes. Agencies recommend established models remain on stay in the market for a minimum of two months in order to become familiar with the local clients.

TYPICAL BOOKINGS

❖ **Length of Work:**

Hourly, half day and full day. Montreal rarely has multiple day bookings.

❖ **Type of Work:**

Catalogue, athletic, editorial, campaign, lingerie, swimwear, runway, commercial print, TV commercial, film, trade show, store informal, showroom, and industrial.

❖ **Busiest Seasons:**

Montreal is busiest in the warmer months from the end of March to the middle of August and from September to November. The slowest time is from December to the first part of March.

TOP CLIENTS

Top clients include clothing companies Buffalo, Dubuc and Parasuco, Holt Renfrew (dept. store), Lise Watier (cosmetics), Aldo (shoes), La Senza (lingerie), and magazines *Fashion*, *Flair* and *Elle*.

COMPETITION

Competition is tough in Montreal due to the small base of clients. Castings can vary in length from 5-15 minutes with approximately 10-15 models per casting. Runway can have 20-25 models per casting.

PAY RATES

Print averages (CANADIAN DOLLAR) C$120-250 per hour. Half day C$300-1,200. Full day C$800-5,000. Advertising/Campaign C$2,500-15,000 including usage. Runway C$300-1,200 per show. All of Montreal's TV/film is done on union pay scale.

❖ **Agency Cuts:**

For commissions, agencies deduct 20% for print and runway. For TV/film 10%. Agencies deduct taxes for Canadian models and they deduct 15% for taxes for foreigners. Foreign models are subject to the withholding tax which is forwarded to the CCRA (Revenue Canada), where models may reclaim their taxes in their own country.

❖ **Agency Provides:**

Agencies may advance accommodations, airfare dependent upon the job, composites, laser copies of books, and tests. Neither agencies nor clients offer money contracts.

LIVING

❖ **Housing:**

Some agencies provide models' apartments. Inexpensive accommodations average C$450-570 per month. Moderate

MARCIA ROTHSCHILD MOELLERS
CANADA MONTREAL

C$600-700. Cheap hotels average C$135-250 per night.

❖ Transportation:

The airport is 20-30 minutes from downtown. Montreal has excellent, inexpensive public transportation including metro and bus. Models can take the metro or bus for about C$2.50, or purchase a one-week pass for C$18.00 or a monthly pass for C$61.00. A short ride in a taxi is C$10. Models do not need a car in Montreal and if they do have a car, parking is expensive depending on the location in the city. Traffic is moderate.

❖ Food & Entertainment:

An inexpensive lunch is C$6 and an inexpensive dinner is C$15. Entertainment in Montreal is wonderful with fabulous restaurants, shopping and nightclubs. Nightlife is very popular in Montreal.

REQUISITES

Work visas are required for many non-Canadians. Depending on which country a model is from, a visa may be required to even enter as a visitor. Work visas are on a per booking basis. The client sponsors the visa/work papers. The visa documents are confirmed prior to the model arriving in Montreal. The model is required to take the documents to immigration at the port of entry where they are authorized and stamped. There are very few non-resident models that remain on stay in Montreal.

WEATHER

Montreal has a very cold climate with up to 6-8 months of snow – sometimes even in August. Summer lasts for about 2 months and although it is short, it is very beautiful.

CURRENCY

As of January 2005:
US$10 = C$12.34

MARCIA'S TIPS

Montreal is split between French and English speaking; however, if models can only speak English, it should not be a problem for them to navigate the city. The great thing about Montreal is the variety of diverse cultures. It is a great city to live in. Attitude is very important and models have to be very self-assured because the people of Montreal like a sense of self-confidence. Perfectly clear skin is imperative as Canadian consumers revere beautiful skin.

CANADA
TORONTO

Toronto is the largest market in Canada and it has a metropolitan area population of 5,100,000 with approximately 10 fashion agencies. Toronto is a great place for Canadian models to start their career because the market has fabulous editorial, great creative people and a good amount of money clients to boot. It's a wonderful, stylish, cool, hip, young city with so much to do. Toronto is also a great place to base whether models stay there for their entire career, or travel internationally first and then decide to settle down and have a family, or join the millions of Toronto citizens who just love the city. It's a busy, diversified market with everything. The market insists that models be as top notch as Toronto is. If models have the Toronto look as well as can be smart and dedicated, they just can't lose.

■ MARKET PREFERENCES

❖ Models:

The market uses junior/teens, petite (rarely), plus/full-size (5'9"-5'10", sizes 14-16), athletic, and adults. Females are preferably looking the ages of 18-35, 5'8"-5'11", sizes 2-6, no more than a C-cup, no more than a 36" hip; for runway 5'9"-5'11", sizes 2-6. Men are preferably looking the ages of 18-50, 6'0"-6'3", suit 40-42; for runway 6'0"-6'3", suit 40-42. Moles and freckles may present a problem if they are dense and dependent upon the location on the body, as the market reveres perfect skin. The market uses all ethnicities. Smiles are important for catalogue and editorial. 70% of the market works full-time.

❖ Portfolios:

About 20% of the market is from direct bookings. Direct booking portfolios must be strong with lots of tearsheets that are the caliber of New York City or from another top market. Clients prefer to see models in person unless it is a model with a great book. No experience is necessary for Canadian new faces because it is a strong development market. Established models must have great pictures that are marketable to Toronto – more fashion-oriented and modern with diversity including lifestyle fashion as well as high fashion.

❖ Agencies Preferences:

Agencies prefer models that are outgoing, happy, confident and exude positive energy. For castings, hair and make-up should be simple and very natural. Dress should be stylish and hip without going overboard. Agencies prefer models that live nearby, commute into the market to meet clients and then return home. If models live further away, they prefer for them to establish themselves and remain on stay in the market for at least 2 weeks.

TYPICAL BOOKINGS

Length of Work:
Hourly, half day, full day and some multiple day bookings.

Type of Work:
Catalogue, editorial, campaign, athletic, lingerie, swimwear, runway, commercial print, TV commercial, film, trade show, store informal, showroom, and industrial.

Busiest Seasons:
The market is truly consistent throughout the year with Christmas and other big holidays being slower.

TOP CLIENTS

Top clients include *Flare Magazine*, *Canadian Elle* and *Fashion Magazine*, department stores Holt Renfrew and The Bay, Roots (sportswear), Sears, clothing companies Boutique Jacob and Winners, and Aldo Group (shoes).

COMPETITION

Competition is very intense in Toronto. Casting lines can be as long as 2-3 hours.

PAY RATES

Print averages (CANADIAN DOLLAR) C$110-350 per hour. Half day C$750-1,500. Full day C$1,500-3,500. Advertising/campaign C$2,000-75,000. Runway C$150-750 per show. The market has a union for TV/film which is booked at union scale rates. About 30% of the market is non-union with rates varying with each job.

Agency Cuts:
For commissions, agencies deduct 20% for print and runway and 15-20% for TV/film. Agencies deduct 15% for taxes for foreigners. Foreign models are subject to a withholding tax which is forwarded to the CCRA (Revenue Canada), where models may reclaim their taxes in their own country.

Agency Provides:
Agencies usually advance airfare and accommodations on direct bookings. Dependent upon the caliber of the model, most agencies will advance laser copies of books, composites and tests. Neither agencies nor clients offer money contracts.

LIVING

Housing:
Agencies do not provide models' apartments. Inexpensive accommodations average C$500-800 per month. Moderate C$900-1,200 per month. Cheap hotels average C$65-300 per night.

Transportation:
The airport is 30 minutes from downtown, dependent upon traffic. Toronto has inexpensive public transportation including train, subway and bus. A short ride in a taxi is C$6. Models do not need a car in the market to get to castings. Parking is expensive and traffic is

MODEL MARKETS OF THE WORLD
TORONTO CANADA

moderate.

❖ Food & Entertainment:

An inexpensive lunch is C$8-10 and an inexpensive dinner is C$10-20. Entertainment is excellent including theater, museums, galleries, bars, coffee shops, restaurants, night clubs, sports events, as well as many beautiful lakes in the area for those who love the outdoors.

■ REQUISITES

Work visas are required for many non-Canadians. Depending on which country a model is from, a visa may be required to even enter as a visitor. Work visas are on a per booking basis. The client sponsors the visa/work papers. The visa documents are confirmed prior to the model arriving in Toronto. The model then takes the documents to immigration at the port of entry where they are authorized and stamped. There are very few non-resident models that remain on-stay in Toronto.

■ WEATHER

The winters are harsh; however, the summers are quite beautiful and warm.

■ CURRENCY

As of January 2005:
US$10 = C$12.34

■ MARCIA'S TIPS

Personality is essential in the Toronto market. It is also very important for models to be exceptionally groomed and stylish. Toronto is a very sophisticated city and the clients consistently work with top models from Canada, New York City and other top international markets. It's important that models realize Toronto understands fashion and is exposed to this level of professionalism everyday. To succeed in Toronto, models will have to be the best of everything.

CANADA
VANCOUVER

Vancouver is a medium size market in comparison to Toronto. There are approximately 7 fashion agencies with a fast growing metropolitan area population of 2,150,000. As Vancouver grows, more and more clients are coming for the fabulous locations, not to mention, lots of top models who started their careers in the city, still consider Vancouver home. A lot of Americans are buying into Vancouver because it is a nice, safe, exciting developing city. Vancouver may not be as large as Los Angeles, Toronto or New York City, but models enjoy nice advertising/campaign and runway pay rates comparable with those in larger markets.

MARKET PREFERENCES

❖ Models:

The market uses junior/teens, plus/full-size (very rarely), athletic, and adults. Women are preferably looking the ages of 18-40, 5'7"-5'11", sizes 2-8, no more than a B-cup, no larger than a 37" hip; for runway 5'9"-5'11, sizes 2-8. Men are preferably looking the ages of 18-50, 5'11"-6'3", suit 40-42; for runway 5'11"-6'3", suit 40-42. The market uses all ethnicities. Smiles are important for catalogue and editorial. About 5% of the women's market works full-time. Men cannot work full-time and must supplement their incomes with another career or school.

❖ Portfolios:

10% of the market is from direct bookings. Strong portfolios with international tearsheets and campaigns are a must for direct bookings. Clients prefer to see models in person. New faces do not need experience but agencies prefer to see good snapshots initially. For established models to enter the market, they will need a good resume of experience and repeat clients along with a portfolio of either very good, current testing or tearsheets from editorial, advertising and catalogue. Either way, the portfolio must have an already proven appeal.

❖ Agencies Preferences:

Agencies prefer models that are able to easily understand the clients' needs, those that can make the day go quicker, can be flexible, pleasant, professional, and easily adaptable with no ego problems. For castings, clients prefer to see models clean, fresh, with minimal make-up and well put together. Attire should have a slightly more west coast appeal – athletically fit, outdoor sophisticated and body conscious. Females should have a little black dress for specific appointments and males should have a nice pair of black trousers and a black t-shirt. Agencies prefer for new faces to arrive and test first. To work consistently in the

MODEL MARKETS OF THE WORLD
VANCOUVER CANADA

market, new faces will need to be based there. Established models can be based there or elsewhere if they are a top model and are available for direct bookings.

■ TYPICAL BOOKINGS

❖ Length of Work:

Hourly (2 hour minimum), half day and full day. Vancouver has a fair amount of multiple day bookings.

❖ Type of Work:

Catalogue, athletic, editorial, campaign, lingerie, swimwear, runway, commercial print, TV commercial, film, trade show, store informal, showroom, and industrial.

❖ Busiest Seasons:

There is consistent work in Vancouver throughout the year. June through October is the busiest season and the market's slowest season is from November through April.

■ TOP CLIENTS

Top clients include Holt Renfrew (high-end dept. store), AG Hair Products, menswear clients Brinell and San Mar (menswear), Kenan (lingerie), Kohl's (dept. store), Grapheme Koo (ad agency for Oakridge Centre, West Edmonton Mall, King Optical, and Hangers), JFC (ad agency for Guess, Mac & Jac, Kenzie, Aritzia, Leone, Plum Clothing, Park Royal Shopping Centre) Whistler catalogues, as well as many Canadian, American, Asian and European crews shooting in Vancouver regularly.

■ COMPETITION

Competition is moderate. Models usually do not deal with long casting lines, but occasionally they can be as long as 30 minutes.

■ PAY RATES

Print averages (CANADIAN DOLLAR) C$125-250 per hour. Half Day C$500-1,000. Full day C$1,000-2,000. Advertising/campaign C$500-50,000. Runway C$150-200 per hour. TV commercials are 66% non-union and the rest fall under union pay scale. Film is practically all union, starting union scale session rate for a principal role is approximately C$600. Overtime occurs often, and adds considerably to the bottom line. Pay rates above scale can be negotiated depending on the budget, the size of the role and the importance of the artist. There are usage fees on top of all of this as well, which generally range from 85% to 130%.

❖ Agency Cuts:

For commissions, agencies deduct 20% for print and runway, 15% for TV/film. Vancouver agencies are not required to deduct taxes if the model is Canadian. Agencies deduct 15% for taxes for foreigners. Foreign models are subject to a withholding tax which is forwarded to the CCRA (Revenue Canada), where models may reclaim the taxes in their own country.

MARCIA ROTHSCHILD MOELLERS
CANADA VANCOUVER

❖ Agency Provides:

Agencies seldom advance on anything. They may on airfare or accommodations if in sync with a booking. They sometimes advance on composites, and rarely on laser copies of books or tests. Agencies do not and very few clients offer money contracts.

LIVING

❖ Housing:

Agencies do not provide models' apartments. Inexpensive accommodations average C$400-500 per month. Moderate C$600-800 per month. Cheap hotels average C$90-150 per night.

❖ Transportation:

The airport is 20 minutes from downtown. Vancouver has inexpensive public transportation including sky train, bus and sea bus. A short ride in a taxi is C$5. Models do not need a car to get around in Vancouver. Parking is pricey downtown and traffic is heavy.

❖ Food & Entertainment:

An inexpensive lunch is C$5 and an inexpensive dinner is C$10. There is a lot to do in Vancouver with everything within a short distance. Wonderful skiing, sailing and golf can all be achieved in the same day. Vancouver is great for outdoor sports and the city is packed with theatres, galleries, museums, and great restaurants that cater to a huge international population. It's one of the most multi-cultural cities in the world.

REQUISITES

Work visas are required for many non-Canadians. Depending on which country a model is from, a visa may be required to even enter as a visitor. Work visas are determined on a per booking basis. The client sponsors the visa/work papers. The visa documents are confirmed prior to the model arriving to Vancouver. The model then takes the documents to immigration at the port of entry where they are authorized and stamped. There are very few non-resident models that remain on stay in Vancouver.

WEATHER

A lot of rain from November to May.

CURRENCY

As of January 2005:
US$10 = C$12.34

MARCIA'S TIPS

The attitude of people living in Vancouver is quite often criticized by their Eastern counterparts as being too relaxed and laid back. Vancouver people do not take themselves or life too seriously. They are generally very into health and fitness because it is a healthy outdoor place, but models should not let this attitude overtake them. Vancouver clients are quite particular and they prefer to work with professionals. Models must be prepared to be in shape, with perfect skin, on time, cell

MODEL MARKETS OF THE WORLD
VANCOUVER CANADA

phones off during bookings, with up-to-date portfolios, with a good understanding of the clients' needs and a great attitude. It could be said that those in Vancouver are laid back as long as those that work there don't lean back too far.

AFRICA

Capetown. 78
Johannesburg 82

SOUTH AFRICA
CAPE TOWN

Cape Town is the largest market on the continent of Africa with a population of 3,250,000 and approximately 10 fashion agencies stationed in this most well-known city of South Africa. The market is comparable to the German markets, primarily composed of commercial print and catalogue. Cape Town is the competitor to Miami – vying for big clients looking for fabulous locations. Working models have raved about the beauty of Cape Town, and have said that the locations are some of the most spectacular they have ever seen. Many European models jet to Cape Town during the cold months of Europe to catch the wave of catalogue and editorial clients doing the same.

MARKET PREFERENCES

❖ Models:

The market uses plus/full-size (1.76-1.80 cm/5'9.5"-5'11", Continental sizes 42-48/American sizes 10-16) and definitely needs athletic, and adults. Women are preferably looking the ages of 22-30, 1.74-1.80 cm (5'8.5"-5'11"), Continental sizes 36-38 (American 4-6), no more than a C-cup, no larger than a 95cm/37.5" hip; for runway 1.75-1.80 cm (5'9.5"-5'11"), Continental sizes 34-36 (American 2-4). Men are preferably looking the ages of 25-40, 1.83-1.88 cm (6'0"-6'2"), Continental suit 50 (American 40); for runway 1.85-1.90 cm (6'1"-6'3"), Continental suit 50 (American 40). The majority of models have blonde or light brown hair. Caucasian and Light Black models work best. If models are too African Black, they don't work as much because of the existing strong base of that type. Of course, this may not apply to Black models that are established and relatable for catalogue. Hispanic will work but more for the females booking swimwear. Smiles are absolutely important for catalogue, but not for editorial. About 40% of the market works full-time.

❖ Portfolios:

5% of the market is from direct bookings. To garner these bookings, portfolios need to be very lifestyle catalogue, definitely outdoorsy with great smiles, have strong testing and be in sync with the market. Most of the time, direct bookings are repeat bookings. Cape Town clients prefer to see models in person and agencies bring in a lot of new models, particularly for female editorial which is always looking for something fresh and new. New faces must have one or two very good tests (top photography level) and established models must have lots of catalogue pictures along with relatable editorial. Models that work best are those that are established and can project anything from high end to relatable. It is best if a portfolio shows a lot of diversity

MARCIA ROTHSCHILD MOELLERS
SOUTH AFRICA CAPE TOWN

and is composed of great body and smile shots.

❖ Agencies Preferences:

Cape Town is very laid back and agencies prefer models that arrive with a great attitude, a very good smile and the ability to sell themselves. The clients work very long hours; therefore, prima donnas need not apply. The clients are looking for flexible models with a better attitude and personality than a model with a better book and bad attitude. Clients like to see hair done simply with very little make-up – a true depiction of a model. The weather is really hot in Cape Town so models may dress quite casually as long as they appear neat and tidy. Clients don't want to see models that look like they just came from the beach. Agencies prefer for models to remain on stay for at least 6-8 weeks. It is not in a model's best interest to remain on stay for a shorter period of time.

TYPICAL BOOKINGS

❖ Length of Work:

Half day, full day and lots of opportunities for multiple days.

❖ Type of Work:

Catalogue, athletic, editorial, lingerie, swimwear, minimal runway, enormous amounts of TV commercial, a lot of commercial print, store informal and very little industrial.

❖ Busiest Seasons:

Cape Town is busiest from the beginning of November to mid-April with the slowest time from June to July.

TOP CLIENTS

Top clients include international *Vogue* magazines, catalogues Otto Versand, Debenhams, J.D. Williams, Marks & Spencer, Garnier (hair care), May Clothing (department store), *Wallpaper* (magazine), 60 (clothing), and Opel Europe (automotive).

COMPETITION

Competition is fierce because the major part of the high season is the European winter, so most of the models and clients come to South Africa to enjoy the warm climate. Because of the influx of work, agencies bring in many models and clients will try to forego long casting calls and arrange appointments instead. Still, casting lines can be up to an hour or more at times.

PAY RATES

Print averages (RAND) R 4,000-12,000 per half day. Full day R 8,000-24,000. Advertising/campaign R 8,000-100,000. Runway R 1,300 per show. TV commercials are all non-union and wages are based on a set rate averaging R 46,000 per day. Usage and buy-outs are additional based on a percentage per country and average R 12,000-50,000 extra.

MODEL MARKETS OF THE WORLD
CAPE TOWN SOUTH AFRICA

❖ Agency Cuts:

For commissions, agencies deduct 20% for print, runway and TV. Agencies deduct 25% taxes from all foreign models.

❖ Agency Provides:

Most agencies will advance accommodations, composites and laser copies of books. They very rarely advance airfare and tests. Neither agencies nor clients offer money contracts.

LIVING

❖ Housing:

Most agencies provide models' apartments. Inexpensive accommodations average R 2,000 per month. Moderate R 3,500 per month. Cheap hotels are quite pricey at R 850-2,000 per night.

❖ Transportation:

The airport is 25 minutes from downtown. Cape Town does not have a public transportation system. Navigating is difficult and models use rikkis – little miniaturized buggies that are pedal powered by rikki drivers. A short ride in a taxi is R 50 and a short ride in a Rikki is R 10. Agencies prefer that models rent cars because it is a safer option, particularly at night. Models are encouraged to divide the expenses of renting a car as a group. Parking is expensive around the center of the city. Traffic is moderate all year with the exception of Christmas and New Year's when it becomes quite heavy.

❖ Food & Entertainment:

An inexpensive lunch or dinner is R 30. Cape Town is known as party central – lots of clubs, restaurants, the beach and many water sports. Anything fun to do in a warm climate can be found in Cape Town.

REQUISITES

Work visas are not necessary for foreign models. They can work on a tourist visa obtained upon arrival at the airport and it allows for 60-90 days of work, provided models pay 25% tax on all jobs. For longer stays, agencies obtain a 2 year extension for R 3,000. Agencies do not advise models to obtain their work visa in advance as the red tape can be incredible.

WEATHER

The sun shines most of the year which is why the clients choose the location. The weather is dependable during any season in South Africa. However, the seasons are different in Cape Town from those in North America, with summer being from October to April.

CURRENCY

As of January 2005:
US$10 = R 60.74
C$10 = R 48.23

MARCIA'S TIPS

Cape Town's pace is quick. A model can go to a casting at 6 p.m., the client can put the model on hold for a job at 8 p.m., and then confirm the booking at 9

SOUTH AFRICA CAPE TOWN

p.m. with a starting time of 6 a.m. the next morning. Cape Town has the same safety issues and isolated incidences as any other large city. As in any city, models need to watch where they are going and who is around them. The city has a beach culture with everything revolving around outdoor activities. Lots of celebrities visit throughout the summer and it's easy to get around as everyone speaks English. Most models think Cape Town is loads of fun.

SOUTH AFRICA
JOHANNESBURG

Johannesburg is one of the largest markets in the world for Black models even though the market is small in comparison to other international markets. There are approximately 10 fashion agencies in the city with a metropolitan population area, including Soweto, East Rand and West Rand, of over 8,000,000. The market books local catalogue, TV commercial, fashion and beauty advertising as well as editorial, all catering to one of the largest demographics of Black consumers. The city houses many internationally recognized fashion magazines and advertising companies. Johannesburg is great for runway models and hosts a big Fashion Week in July. This city is a wonderful place for international Black models to build their portfolios while gaining experience.

MARKET PREFERENCES

❖ Models:

The market uses junior/teens (girls from ages 15 and up), athletic (slightly more muscular than regular fashion models) and adults. Women are preferably looking the ages of 18-30, 1.75-1.80 cm (5'9"-5'11"), UK sizes 6-10 (American 4-8), preferably a B-cup but no more than a C-cup, no larger than 93 cm/37" hip; for runway 1.78-1.80 cm (5'10"-5'11"), UK sizes 6-8 (American 4-6). Men are preferably looking the ages of 18-40, 1.83-1.88 cm (6'0"-6'2"), suit 40-42; for runway 1.83-1.89 (6'0"-6'2.5"), suit 40-42. Freckles are not a problem in the market, but moles can be, depending on where and the quantity. The market uses primarily Black models and a small portion of all of the other ethnicities. It is imperative that Black models have good skin and skin tone because there are a lot of bookings for beauty products. Smiles are important for catalogue but not for editorial. About 45% of the market works full-time.

❖ Portfolios:

30% of the market is from direct bookings. Clients mainly direct book lifestyle fashion catalogue models that have numerous tearsheets, including advertising/campaign, throughout their portfolios along with an equally strong composite. Clients prefer to see the models in person. New faces can begin working with 1 or 2 good tests, although they will need to have more experience before booking campaigns. Established models will have to enter with good beauty shots, commercial print, catalogue, lifestyle fashion, swimwear, lingerie, and editorial fashion throughout their portfolios.

❖ Agencies Preferences:

Agencies prefer models with a

S. AFRICA JOHANNESBURG

MARCIA ROTHSCHILD MOELLERS

professional attitude that are punctual, confident and polite. Clients prefer models with natural hair colors in a natural style. The style is not as important as the length. Hair below the shoulder can be considered too long. Minimal to no make-up is preferable for castings. Dress should be trendy and edgy. Jeans are fine as long as the look is put together with some panache. Agencies prefer models to remain on stay for 2-3 months.

TYPICAL BOOKINGS

❖ Length of Work:

Half day, full day, and not many multiple days.

❖ Type of Work:

Catalogue, athletic, lingerie, swimwear, runway, commercial print, TV commercial, film, infomercial, store informal, and industrial.

❖ Busiest Seasons:

The busiest time in Johannesburg is from June to September. The market is slowest from December to March. All Johannesburg agencies close around December 15th to January 10th for the Christmas holidays.

TOP CLIENTS

Top clients include L'Oreal, Garnier, Standard Bank, telecommunication companies Vodacom and MTN, clothing companies Jet and Edgars, magazines *Elle* and *FHM*, Dark + Lovely (hair care), Lux, and advertising agencies TBWA Gavin Reddy and Jupiter Drawing Room.

COMPETITION

The market is less competitive than the London, New York City and Cape Town markets. Still, casting lines can be as long as 30 minutes to 2 hours, depending on the job.

PAY RATES

Local clients usually work from set rates. Print rates average (RAND) R 550-1,600 per half day. Full day R 1,300-3,600. Advertising/campaign R 4,000-20,000 (the market only does local campaigns). Runway R 2,200 per show (includes fitting and rehearsal). South Africa does not have a union for TV/film, but rates are usually approved by either NAMA (National Association for Model Agencies) or AAA (Advertising Standard Authority). TV commercial rates average R 3,000-15,000 plus usage.

❖ Agency Cuts:

For commissions, agencies deduct 20% for print, runway and TV/film. Agencies deduct 25% in taxes for foreign models.

❖ Agency Provides:

Most agencies will advance with a 10% fee on accommodations, airfare, composites, laser copies of books, and tests. Models get paid monthly, and in extreme cases, agencies will advance money upon arrival. Neither agencies nor clients offer money contracts.

MODEL MARKETS OF THE WORLD
JOHANNESBURG S. AFRICA

LIVING

Housing:

Agencies do not have models' apartments but outsource options via private owners and companies. Inexpensive accommodations (1 roommate) average R 1,600 per month. Moderate (single room) R 2,500 per month. Model accommodations are scarce in Johannesburg. Cheap hotels average R 350 per week or R 1,500 per month. Hotels are very expensive.

Transportation:

The airport is about 1 hour from downtown. Johannesburg has public transportation including train and bus, but the agencies do not recommend models use it. If absolutely necessary, it is inexpensive at R 5-20. The agencies advise using agency model transport. The majority of agencies have their own drivers and they are available during work hours, and sometimes even after hours. A short ride in a taxi is R 100. Johannesburg is made up of highways which are the best way to get to castings. Taking shortcuts through the suburbs can actually take longer. The roads are extremely busy between 7:00 a.m. and 6:30 p.m. Models should plan to leave at least an hour before their scheduled arrival times.

Food & Entertainment:

An inexpensive lunch (fast food) is R 24 and an inexpensive dinner (an appetizer, chicken or steak and 2-3 glasses of wine) is R 100. Johannesburg has a wide variety of cultures and is more of a bar/lounge kind of place with Hip Hop and House music everywhere. The more upscale venues are located in Sandton and Rivonia and attract most of the model industry. For something completely different, models can head off to the Melville area, which has upscale restaurants, trendy Rasta bars and book cafes. Agencies advise models to stay away from central Johannesburg because it is not safe.

REQUISITES

Work visas are not necessary for foreign models. They can work on a tourist visa obtained upon arrival at the airport. This allows for 60-90 days of work provided models pay their 25% taxes on all jobs. For longer stays, agencies can obtain a 2 year extension for R 3,000. Agencies do not advise models to obtain their work visa in advance as the red tape can be incredible.

WEATHER

Johannesburg is normally dry and humid around November through April. Sun screen is highly advised. The temperature can go up to 35 Celsius. Johannesburg normally has a rainy season around September and winter starts in May. The coldest month is June with temperatures dropping to - 0 Celsius in the evenings.

CURRENCY

As of January 2005:
US$10 = R 60.74

S. AFRICA JOHANNESBURG

MARCIA ROTHSCHILD MOELLERS

C$10 = R 48.23

MARCIA'S TIPS

Even though Johannesburg caters to a high fashion clientele, these clients prefer portfolios to have more catalogue and natural beauty pictures. Editorial selections for the portfolio should not be adventurous. The market is basically lifestyle and relatable and, if pictures are too artistic or edgy, they can scare clients away. Near Johannesburg, models can enjoy day trips to see wild animals or go on a safari. Africa has many different roots and the cultures are diverse throughout the countryside. It is very easy to navigate Johannesburg as 90% of the market speaks English.

ASIA

Bangkok 87
Dubai 91
Hong Kong 95
Istanbul 99
Kuala Lampur 102
Osaka 105
Seoul 109
Shanghai 113
Singapore 116
Taipei 119
Tel Aviv 123
Tokyo 126

THAILAND
BANGKOK

Bangkok is a medium size market in Asia and is definitely growing. The metropolitan area has a population of over 8,000,000 and there are approximately 5 fashion agencies for foreign models. Bangkok is a developing market and is progressing along a lot quicker than some of the other Asian markets that still have third world economies. In the past 5 years, fashion has become one of Thailand's major exports. The Thai government recently initiated "Fashion City" in Bangkok and is investing a tremendous amount of money into the market to make it internationally acclaimed as a fashion city. The money is predominantly spent in marketing which adds up to more fashion shows, more grants for fashion schools and a lot more opportunities for fashion designers. Bangkok is one of the best markets for new faces who have not been able to invest greatly in testing. Thai clients and agencies are eager to work with new faces and assist with development. Bangkok is also known for having more work for male models than the other Asian markets.

MARKET PREFERENCES

❖ Models:

The Bangkok market uses physically fit models – professional athletes as well as fashion models that are super fit. The market primarily uses adult models. Women are preferably looking the ages of 18-24, 1.70-1.80 cm (5'7"-5'11"), strictly by measurements which must be bust 31-34/waist 23-25/hips 34-36, no more than a C-cup; for runway 1.75-180 cm (5'9"-5'11"), bust 31-34/waist 23-25/hips 34-36. Men are preferably looking the ages of 18-30, 1.75-1.85 cm (5'9"-6'1"), suit 38-40; for runway 1.75-1.85 cm (5'9"-6'1"), suit 38-40. A great, physically toned shape is essential for male models. The market prefers dark brown or black hair with a darker eye color. Blonde hair or freckles do not work well in the Thai market. Bangkok uses Caucasian, Eurasian, Pan Asian, and Asian models, but not Chinese looking. Skin tones run from light to olive. The agencies encourage models not to be tan on top of their natural skin color. 100% of the foreign models work full-time. About 50% of the local market does.

❖ Portfolios:

5% of the market is from direct bookings. Usually, these jobs are very highly paid. Direct bookings are rare due to the larger influx of models coming into the market lately. Models directly booked are either returning on a repeat booking, or have dropped by to see the client beforehand, or have a specific look

MODEL MARKETS OF THE WORLD
BANGKOK THAILAND

for a beauty/hair client. Clients definitely prefer to see a model in person. No experience is necessary for new faces except for at least one good test to show the clients. Established models must have portfolios with a diverse selection of tearsheets from high end to relatable fashion representing their face, smile and body well.

❖ Agencies Preferences:

Bangkok agencies prefer models that are professional, friendly, easy going, patient and warm hearted. Thai culture is very Buddhist and if a model does not possess any of these traits, it will be difficult to work well in Bangkok. Hair should be very natural, clean and straight with no hair products. Make-up must be very, very light. Dress should be fashionable, trendy and appropriate for the weather. Bangkok is always hot and humid. The key point is to look like a model and not a tourist because there are a lot of back packers in the city. Clients don't want to spend money on booking a model that looks like they were just pulled off the streets. Agencies prefer models to remain on stay 2-3 months with many new faces staying as long as 6 months. Models who want to stay longer than a 30 or 60 day visa allows make a day trip "visa run" to Cambodia, Laos, or Malaysia, before the visa expires. The cost is THB 2,000 for a 30 day extension, including travel expenses for the day trip.

TYPICAL BOOKINGS

❖ Length of Work:

No hourly, very rarely half day, almost all full day, and occasional multiple days.

❖ Type of Work:

Catalogue, a lot of editorial and TV commercial, campaign, athletic, lingerie, swimwear, runway, commercial print, trade show, store informal, and industrial.

❖ Busiest Seasons:

The city is busy all year long. The busiest times are from January to April and from September to December. The slowest times are April due to Thai New Year, and from Christmas to the end of the year.

TOP CLIENTS

Top clients include hair care clients Sunsilk, Clinique and Rejoice, Nivea, Sony, Magazines *Elle*, *Lips*, *Madame Figaro*, *Cleo*, Thai Men's Magazine and *FHM*, Thai Airways, beer companies Singa and Heineken, property companies, as well as ad agencies J. Walter Thompson and Saatchi & Saatchi.

COMPETITION

The competition is getting tougher but it is still lighter than most markets. Casting lines can be as long as 2-3 hours because casting companies prepare every model completely, almost imitating the job exactly, and then videotape each model so the client will have an easier time choosing.

MARCIA ROTHSCHILD MOELLERS
THAILAND BANGKOK

PAY RATES

Print averages (Thai Baht) THB 4,000-5,000 per half day. Full day THB 20,000-40,000. Advertising/campaign THB 30,000-50,000. Runway THB 8,000-10,000 per show (8-10 hours). Magazines THB 8,000-10,000. Thailand is all non-union for TV/film. A day rate averages THB 50,000-100,000 with additional fees for usage or buy-outs, depending on the product. The usage can make the rates as high as THB 1,000,000. Many Indochinese TV commercials are shot in Bangkok.

❖ Agency Cuts:

For commissions, the agencies deduct 30% and they are required to deduct 10% taxes from foreign models.

❖ Agency Provides:

Dependent upon the caliber of the model, most agencies advance accommodations, airfare, composites, tests and weekly pocket money. Neither agencies nor clients offer money contracts.

LIVING

❖ Housing:

Agencies provide models' apartments. Inexpensive accommodations average THB 5,000-10,000 per month. Moderate THB 10,000-15,000 per month. Cheap hotels average THB 500-1,000 per night.

❖ Transportation:

The airport is 30 km/30 minutes from downtown. Bangkok has inexpensive public transportation including train, metro/subway and bus. Since they are very inexpensive, models take taxis everywhere – a short ride is THB 60. Traffic is bad in the city.

❖ Food & Entertainment:

An inexpensive lunch is THB 100 and an inexpensive dinner is THB 200. Bangkok is the city that never sleeps. There are entertainment districts for local and foreign people as well as districts where the two mix. New nightclubs are opening up monthly. Thai food is amazing and very cheap, fresh and spicy. The culture is primarily Buddhist and there are many temples and monasteries. There are few parks in the city and models should visit beyond the city boundaries to appreciate the nature of Thailand.

REQUISITES

A work visa is not required but models will need to apply for a tourist visa before they arrive. Models can arrive without a visa and stay for 30 days in Thailand. If models apply beforehand at the Thai Consulate, they will be granted 60 days. See Agency Preferences for visa extension details.

WEATHER

Bangkok is very constant – always hot and humid. The market has 2 seasons – rainy and not rainy. Umbrellas are a necessity between March and October during the monsoon/storm season. There is no rain at all and it is very dry from November to February.

CURRENCY

As of January 2005:
US$10 = THB 384.25
C$10 = THB 312.60

MARCIA'S TIPS

Bangkok speaks the language of Thai. About 5% of the city speaks English. In the city itself, everyone can speak a small amount of English. In the industry, most people speak English relatively well. Models must learn some basic Thai to navigate the city and it is easy to learn. A very open mind and patience are essential in Bangkok. It is an underdeveloped country and things don't happen as quickly or properly as one may be used to. Thailand will not feel like home. Models need to be patient, helpful and understanding. A cell phone will be a model's best friend. Models can either bring one with international access or they can buy one cheaply in the city. Models must maintain a good attitude and be professional. Arrogance, impatience and an "I'm above it all" attitude will not work in Bangkok.

UNITED ARAB EMIRATES
DUBAI

Dubai is a cosmopolitan city and is one of the wealthiest per capita in the United Arab Emirates (UAE) as well as the world. Dubai has a metropolitan area population of over 2,000,000 with approximately 5 fashion agencies located in the city. The population is made up of many different nationalities, mainly European, Middle Eastern and Indian. Dubai resembles the Riviera with its bikini-clad women on the beaches, beautiful people at the nightclubs and many designer-clad shoppers in the city's huge malls. Dubai is gaining a reputation in the industry and is definitely a growing fashion business with new magazines, new designers, and many models flocking to this expanding market. Advertising is big business in Dubai with many international top advertising agencies based in the city representing top clients. With all the glamour and glitz, it is still a new market and should only be tried by the savvy and strong.

MARKET PREFERENCES

❖ Models:

The market uses some athletic, and primarily adults. Women are preferably looking the ages of 20-30, 1.75-1.80 cm (5'9"-5'11"), UK sizes 8-12 (American 6-10), no more than a C-cup, no larger than a 96 cm/38" hip; for runway the requirements are the same and strictly enforced. Men are preferably looking the ages of 20-33, 1.80-1.88 cm (5'11"-6'2"), suit 40-42 (with 42's requested more often); for runway the requirements are the same and strictly enforced. Mediterranean looks are favored. All ethnicities do work, especially for projects that require an international look, although not nearly as often as models with Mediterranean looks. The look for Dubai is sexy, beautiful bodies, great skin, but not edgy or extreme. Smiles are very important for catalogue and editorial. Although the market is still developing, most local models do not work full-time. Most foreign models on stay in Dubai are focused 100% on work. This makes the full-time work ratio about 20%.

❖ Portfolios:

About 5% of the market is from direct bookings. Clients direct book when they are looking for something very specific – composed of models that have caught their attention or from ethnic looks not available in the market at the time of the casting. Direct bookings are garnered by established models with good portfolios. Clients prefer to see models in person. No experience is necessary for new faces. The agencies will train models with potential in all aspects of the business. For established models to enter the market, agencies prefer tearsheets from

MODEL MARKETS OF THE WORLD
DUBAI UNITED ARAB EMIRATES

Europe with both relatable commercial print and editorial. Swimwear shots are very important but models with pictures that are overly sexy or nude need not apply.

❖ Agencies Preferences:

Agencies like models with a positive attitude that are polite, open-minded and sensitive to the local culture. Even though Dubai is very open minded, models may have to go to a casting in an office where skimpy clothing is frowned upon. Agencies advise models to wear casual clothing that is a bit trendy, body conscious, but not too revealing. As it is very hot in Dubai, this can pose a problem. Hair must be well groomed and make-up must be minimal and natural.

TYPICAL BOOKINGS

❖ Length of Work:

Half day and full day. TV commercials usually are multiple days.

❖ Type of Work:

Catalogue, a lot of editorial and TV commercial, campaign, athletic, lingerie, swimwear, runway, commercial print, trade show, store informal, and industrial.

❖ Busiest Seasons:

Dubai is consistent year round. Dubai is busiest from September to April (except during Ramada, the holy month when Muslims fast and most businesses close early in the afternoons). Summer tends to be slower from July to August.

TOP CLIENTS

Top clients include Saks Fifth Avenue, Emirates Airlines, Jumeirah International (Luxury building company owning Madinat, Jumeirah, Emirates Towers and Burj Al), Arab BBC, Wella, Clarins, Moet & Chandon, Cartier, Saatchi & Saatchi (ad agency), Radius Leo Burnett (ad agency), Fortune Promoseven (ad agency), and Gargash (Mercedes distributor).

COMPETITION

The competition in Dubai is less than with the larger markets of Europe and the USA. Casting lines are usually short, except for TV commercials which can last up to an hour.

PAY RATES

For international models, print averages (UAE DIRHAM) AED 1,500-2,000 per minimum 2 hour booking. Half day AED 2,000-2,500. Full day AED 3,000-3,500. Advertising/campaign AED 3,000-6,000. Runway AED 1,500-2,500 per show. TV commercials are all non-union. TV commercial rates are very low compared to Europe's, averaging AED 3,500-5,000 per day, Dubai TV commercials do not include all the usage that models are used to accruing in larger European markets.

❖ Agency Cuts:

For commissions, agencies deduct 20% for print, runway and TV and taxes are never deducted as Dubai is tax free.

❖ Agency Provides:

Most agencies advance visas, accommodations and airfare. Dependent upon the caliber of the model, agencies may advance composites, laser copies of books, tests and weekly pocket money. Neither agencies nor clients offer money contracts.

LIVING

❖ Housing:

Models stay in apartments/villas which are privately owned and sourced out by the agencies. Inexpensive accommodations average AED 2,000-2,800 per month. Moderate AED 3,000-3,500. Hotels range from AED 150 (very beautiful, hostel type) to AED 2,000 (5 star) per night.

❖ Transportation:

Dubai International Airport is located on the periphery of the city center, and is approximately 5 - 30 minutes by taxi, depending on the traffic. Dubai has buses but they are not used by the middle class as they are overly crowded. There is no metro/subway system yet; however, plans are underway to construct a sky track. A short ride in a taxi is AED 20. Taxis are inexpensive and the traditional means of transportation for most models. Traffic can be pretty bad in certain areas of Dubai during lunch time and at the end of the work day, otherwise, traffic usually flows.

❖ Food & Entertainment:

An inexpensive lunch is AED 25 and an inexpensive dinner is AED 35, excluding alcoholic drinks. Models comment about the lack of cultural activities in Dubai. However, there are many nightclubs playing everything from jungle and house to R&B and salsa. The restaurant scene is extensive and one can become very spoiled by all the different choices of food. Dubai also garners its share of top international entertainers.

REQUISITES

To enter Dubai, models do not need a work visa. Models must have a tourist visa which is valid for three months and costs approximately AED 600. Some nationalities can obtain a visa on arrival at the airport while others have to apply beforehand. Most modeling agencies arrange for the visa to be ready to be obtained by the model upon arrival. Alternatively, a tourist visa can be arranged through the UAE Embassy, and it usually takes about 7 business days to receive. In emergency cases, Models can pay AED 750 and receive the tourist visa in as little as 2 days.

WEATHER

The climate in Dubai is very hot during the summer, with temperatures climbing to 45 C although this rarely poses problems as all buildings are air-conditioned. During the cooler months from November to February, the weather is pleasant, with temperatures ranging between 20 C - 25 C.

CURRENCY

As of January 2005:
US$10 = AED 36.73
C$10 = AED 29.77

MARCIA'S TIPS

Models should possess an open mind, a beautiful smile, a bikini, good sunscreen, and be ready for a new adventure! Dubai is a young, hip, growing city, with a great social scene, and it is perfect for outgoing souls who love to experience different cultures. The Arab population is hospitable and friendly as long as the culture is respected. As with agents and clients everywhere, punctuality is greatly appreciated although in Dubai, it is demanded along with a great attitude. The common language of UAE is English and is widely spoken.

CHINA
HONG KONG

Hong Kong is the largest market in China and has approximately 6 fashion agencies in the city with a metropolitan population area, including Kowloon, of 7,250,000. Hong Kong handles bookings from all over China, as well as Taiwan and other parts of Asia. The majority of the Chinese fashion market is still in its early development stages with Hong Kong leading the way. This is due to Hong Kong having already developed into a sophisticated urban city under British reign before China regained control. Hong Kong has a high demand for Eurasian new faces as well as experienced Caucasian models. Many Eurasian models come back to Hong Kong several times a year due to the demand for their look. There is also a high supply of editorial which is mainly for models heading to other Asian markets.

MARKET PREFERENCES

❖ Models:

The Hong Kong market uses junior/teens (females starting at age 16), petites (5'7", Continental size 6/American 4), and adults. Women are preferably looking the ages of 18-25, 1.73-1.80 cm (5'8"-5'11"), Continental sizes 36-38 (American 4-6), preferably an A or B-cup and no more than a C-cup, no larger than a 36" hip: for runway 1.76-1.79 cm (5'9.5"-5'10.5"). Men are preferably looking the ages of 18-30, 1.83-1.85 cm (6'0"-6'2"), Continental suit 48-50 (American 38-40), occasionally Continental suit 52 (American 42) if the look is perfect for the market; for runway 1.83-1.88 cm (6'0"-6'2"), Continental suit 48-50 (American 48-50). The market prefers men that have really beautiful features and not rough and rugged looks. The market very rarely books redheads. Freckles do not work well in Hong Kong and beauty moles do not work at all. Hong Kong does not take on models that only work for editorial, as the magazines do not pay well enough and the models cannot break even after expenses. The market primarily books Eurasian, Asian (mainly local Chinese models), Caucasian, Hispanic, Native American Indian, and very rarely Light Black (1 Light Black female per season). Beautiful smiles are imperative for catalogue and editorial. Catalogue clients book both relatable/lifestyle and stronger fashion models for catalogue. 100% of the foreign models work full-time.

❖ Portfolios:

About 70% of the market is from direct bookings. Hong Kong books a lot of TV commercial work for all of China and Taiwan, as the clients are looking to this larger market for higher quality models. Direct bookings for TV commercials

MODEL MARKETS OF THE WORLD
HONG KONG CHINA

are booked from videotapes, polaroids/snapshots and the model's composite. For these direct bookings, the model's portfolio is not as important and a few good tests are fine. Hong Kong clients prefer to see models in person. New faces must be prepared for very demanding clients and models may need to build up their books before making money. Clients prefer established models with portfolios full of tearsheets because they choose the models based on the merits of the portfolio and a presentable composite card.

❖ Agencies Preferences:

Agencies prefer models that are independent, cheerful, polite, confident, open-minded, modern, and positive with a healthy lifestyle. Models must present themselves professionally. Clients prefer to see models with simple, clean hair and natural make-up – foundation, blush, mascara, with no eyeliner or eye shadow. Models must look fashionable, but not too edgy, while showing their body shape. Clients prefer smart and casual – jeans, tight tank top or t-shirt, nice shoes or high heels. Agencies prefer models to remain on stay for 2 to 3 months, or longer if the client response is good.

TYPICAL BOOKINGS
❖ Length of Work:

Hourly, half day, full day and multiple days. TV commercials are a minimum of 4 hours and can take as long as 3 to 4 days.

❖ Type of Work:

Catalogue, editorial, campaign, lingerie, swimwear, commercial print, runway and lots of TV commercial.

❖ Busiest Seasons:

The busiest times of the year are from December to March and from July to October for catalogue. Runway is busiest from January to March and from June to October. Fashion Week is every January and July for shows. Editorial is consistent all year long. The slowest times of the year are Chinese New Year and from Christmas to the end of the year.

TOP CLIENTS

Top clients include clothing companies Giordano and Sparkles, advertising agencies Saatchi & Saatchi and Leo Burnett, Gucci, skin care products Oil of Olay and Pond's, hair care companies Pantene, Rejoice (shower gel) and VS, and electronic/mobile companies Nokia, Motorola, Samsung and Sony Ericsson.

COMPETITION

As the Chinese market grows, Hong Kong's competition is getting tougher. Show castings can have long lines up to an hour or more. Most castings average 10-30 minutes.

PAY RATES

Print averages (HONG KONG DOLLAR) HK$1,000-1,800 per hour. Half day HK$4,000-7,000. Full day HK$8,000-

15,000. Advertising/campaign HK$3,000-200,000. Runway HK$3,000-4,500 per show (including a half day fitting, half day rehearsal and show date). Hong Kong does not have unions for TV/film and they are quoted at regular rates ranging from hourly to a package deal.

❖ Agency Cuts:

For commissions, Hong Kong agencies deduct 40-45%. Agencies do not deduct taxes for foreigners.

❖ Agency Provides:

Agencies advance airfare, accommodations, and composites. Depending on the model's caliber, agencies advance pocket money, testing, and mobile phone charges. Occasionally agencies will offer money contracts; however, clients will not.

LIVING

❖ Housing:

Most agencies provide models' apartments. Inexpensive accommodations average HK$2,000-3,000 for a shared room per month. Single rooms average HK$5,000 per month. Cheap hotels average HK$500-1,200 per day.

❖ Transportation:

The airport is 25 minutes from downtown via the easy and convenient Airport Express (train). Hong Kong has all forms of public transportation. Agencies usually advise their models to travel by the inexpensive metro (the MTR) which is HK$4-13. A short ride in a taxi is HK$15; however, they are not recommended by the agencies. Traffic is bad during business hours.

❖ Food & Entertainment:

An inexpensive lunch is HK$10-15 and an inexpensive dinner is HK$15-20. Hong Kong has all sorts of food with Asian cuisine ranking at the top. There are a lot of bars and restaurants that cater to Caucasian customers, and models frequent these places which usually offer free drinks and provide the models with a good place for entertainment and leisure.

REQUISITES

A work visa is necessary for legal status in Hong Kong and must be obtained before arrival in the market. Models cannot enter Hong Kong with a fever.

WEATHER

The weather is quite warm throughout the year. January to March is cold and dry, 5 C - 20 C; April to June is typhoon season and is rainy and humid, 20 C - 28 C; July to October is humid with occasional tropical rainstorms, 25 C – 32 C; and November to December is dry, 10 C – 20 C.

CURRENCY

As of January 2005:
US$10 = AED 36.73
C$10 = AED 29.77

MODEL MARKETS OF THE WORLD
HONG KONG CHINA

MARCIA'S TIPS

The catalogue clients in China are very demanding and shoot models in more than 50 outfits in a half-day booking. This experience is an asset for models working throughout Asia. Females need to bring black high heels, boots, sandals, white and skin colored lingerie, tube tops, tank tops, t-shirts, cosmetics and accessories. Males need to bring black and brown leather shoes, business suit, sneakers, white shirts, pants, sunglasses and accessories. Models should bring their alarm clock, date book and be prepared to get a mobile phone upon arrival. 90% of Hong Kong speaks English so it is easy to navigate. Mainland Chinese clients speak simple English or use a translator, if necessary.

TURKEY
ISTANBUL

Istanbul is a large market and the city is gaining attention as it is rapidly growing and not as well known on the international scene. The competition is still light in comparison to the other top markets of Europe. Istanbul has a metropolitan area population of over 11,000,000 and approximately 6 fashion agencies booking a large amount of work. Istanbul is known as one of the best markets in the world for immediate cash bookings in US$ currency. The market is also gaining a reputation as a great place to develop portfolios without all the intense competition of the stronger, well known markets. The market has many Turkish magazines, and international flagships such as Elle, Marie Claire and Harper's Bazaar, all shot by the country's top photographers.

MARKET PREFERENCES

❖ Models:

The market uses junior/teens (starting at age 16 and dependent on the time of the year), plus/full-size (Continental sizes 42-48/American 12-18), and adults. Women are preferably looking the ages of 18-27, 1.73-1.80 cm (5'8"-5'11"), Continental size 38 (American 6), no more than a B-cup, and no larger than a 93cm/37" hip. The market has very little runway for women or men. Men are preferably looking the ages of 18-35, 1.83-1.90 cm (6'0"-6'3"), Continental suit 48-54 (American 38-54). The market prefers colorful eyes in shades of blue and green. The market mainly books Caucasian. The market does use all other ethnicities, preferably Asian and Eurasian, but very little work is available to them. Smiles are important for catalogue and editorial. 80% of the market works full-time.

❖ Portfolios:

7% of the market is from direct bookings. The bulk of these are repeat bookings by models that have already been to the market. Clients definitely prefer to see models in person. This is not a market for new faces with no experience. New faces must enter with very good testing and some tearsheets in hand. Established models will need to enter with a portfolio with strong editorial throughout.

❖ Agencies Preferences:

Agencies prefer models that are professional, fun, confident, open-minded, polite and focused. Istanbul is quite elegant and fashionable for castings compared to other European markets. Females should wear high heel shoes and some make-up to castings. Agencies prefer models to remain on stay for at least one month or longer.

MODEL MARKETS OF THE WORLD
ISTANBUL TURKEY

■ TYPICAL BOOKINGS

❖ **Length of Work:**
Full day and multiple days.

❖ **Type of Work:**
A lot of campaign, catalogue and TV commercial, editorial, lingerie, swimwear, commercial print, and showroom.

❖ **Busiest Seasons:**
Istanbul is busy throughout the year and the busiest seasons are from January to March and from July to August. The slowest times of the year are national and religious holidays.

■ TOP CLIENTS

Top clients include departments stores Beymen, Network, Sarar, Home Store, and Vakko, Levi's, Red Apple, Diesel, and magazines Marie Claire and Elle.

■ COMPETITION

The competition is light because there are only 6 agencies handling a market with a large workload. Casting days are full with around 10 castings per day. Casting lines can be as long as 2 hours.

■ PAY RATES

Print averages (US DOLLAR) US$400-2,000 per day (10 hours). Advertising/campaign US$2,000-7,000. Runway US$400-700. Turkey does not have unions for TV/film. TV commercials average US$1,000-2,000 per booking.

❖ **Agency Cuts:**
For commissions, agencies deduct 40% for print and TV commercial. Depending on a model's home country, agencies may deduct 23% for taxes for foreign models.

❖ **Agency Provides:**
Most agencies advance for accommodations and composites. Dependent upon the caliber of the model, they may advance airfare and pocket money. Neither agencies nor clients offer money contracts.

■ LIVING

❖ **Housing:**
Most agencies provide models' apartments. Inexpensive accommodations average 550-1,350 YTL (NEW TURKISH LIRA) per month. Moderate average 1,350-2,000 YTL per month. Cheap hotels average 20-35 YTL per night.

❖ **Transportation:**
The airport is 30km/30 minutes from downtown. Istanbul has inexpensive public transportation including train, metro/subway and bus. A short ride in a taxi is 4-4.5 YTL. Traffic is crazy in Istanbul.

❖ **Food & Entertainment:**
An inexpensive lunch is 14 YTL and an inexpensive dinner is 20 YTL. The entertainment in the market is very expansive with many different types of the cuisines of Europe; however, the Turkish dishes

are very delicious. The market has lots of nightclubs and music – everything from underground to jazz. The city stays up all night long and has some wonderful little coffee shops.

REQUISITES

A work visa is not necessary to enter the market and models may enter as tourists through customs. Foreign models should check with their agencies in advance in regard to any medical shots they may need.

WEATHER

Turkey's weather is usually warm with a few spells of rain and cold weather.

CURRENCY

As of January 2005:
US$10 = 13.40 YTL
C$10 = 10.70 YTL

MARCIA'S TIPS

Clients work the models very hard and they should be prepared for long days with many outfit changes. The country is full of wonderful adventures with many diverse cultures and historical monuments. Agents say the Bosphorus is amazing and a must see. It should be relatively easy for models to navigate as 50% of the city speaks English. Still, it would be smart for models to ask their agency in advance for a list of basic Turkish words to learn because it pays to respect the culture and language, especially in a market with so much work.

MALAYSIA
KUALA LUMPUR

Kuala Lumpur, with a population of about 4,100,000, is fast becoming one of the newest, hip, talked about tourist hangouts in Malaysia. It is a smaller medium size market with about 15 fashion agencies. With great tourism and fabulous locations usually come clients and models. The market is not as fashion-oriented as Singapore or Bangkok. Clients can run from product to fashion clothing. The market is very slow paced and it takes a couple months' stay for a model to see the return. The market is not based on castings except for TV commercials where models must have the ability to act. For print jobs, clients book from models' composites or portfolios. Kuala Lumpur has a lot of magazines and wonderfully creative people shooting great editorial, which makes it a worthwhile market for tearsheets. Kuala Lumpur also has a lot of runway which is choreographed by the agencies. This market is one of the new frontiers for foreign models and apparently one of the best kept secrets in the Asian market.

MARKET PREFERENCES

❖ Models:

The market uses junior/teens, plus/full-size (only locally based), athletic, and adults. Women are preferably looking the ages of 18-25, 5'9"-5'11", sizes 2-6, no more than a B-cup, C-cup only for beer advertising, no larger than a 36" hip; for runway 5'9"-5'11.5", sizes 2-4. Men are preferably looking the ages of 20-30, 5'11"-6'3", suit 40; for runway 6'0"-6'3", suit 40. The market does not like models with freckles or beauty marks. All ethnicities are used except Black. Smiles are important for catalogue but not as much for editorial. About 50% of the female models work full-time. For men, full-time modeling is not possible.

❖ Portfolios:

80% of the market is from direct bookings. Direct booking portfolios must show experience and have more relatable fashion than edgy looks. Clients do not need to see models in person and will book from composites / portfolios. New faces are welcome as long as they come with good testing. Kuala Lumpur is a good place to help new faces build their portfolios, but they must be patient. Established models must come with good testing and/or tearsheets that are more relatable fashion. Good beauty shots reflecting excellent skin as well as great body shots are important. Kuala Lumpur welcomes established models from catalogue markets to build their books with tearsheets in the market.

❖ Agencies Preferences:

Agencies like models that are cheerful and confident. Hair should be in any style that is easily manageable. The market does not book models with plaited hair, dreads or an afro. For castings, minimal make-up that is very natural is preferred. Dress should be clean and casual. Agencies prefer models to remain on stay for 2 months.

TYPICAL BOOKINGS

❖ Length of Work:

Half day and full day.

❖ Type of Work:

Catalogue, athletic, editorial, campaign, lingerie, swimwear, runway, commercial print, TV commercial, infomercial, trade show, store informal, showroom, and industrial.

❖ Busiest Seasons:

Work is unpredictable. The middle of the year around June is very busy. It slows down around holidays.

TOP CLIENTS

Top clients include Padini Holdings (clothing), Isetan (dept. store), Docker's, Levi's, magazines Bazaar, Marie Claire and FM, beer companies Tiger and Carlsberg, and many advertising agencies.

COMPETITION

The market is very non-competitive and relaxed. When there are castings, lines are never longer than 30 minutes.

PAY RATES

Print averages (RINGGIT MALAYSIA, also known as the Malaysian Dollar) RM150-3,000 per half day. Full day RM300-8,000 or more depending on usage. Advertising/campaign RM3,000-15,000. Runway RM300-1,000 per show. TV commercial RM2,000-10,000. All TV is non-union in Malaysia.

❖ Agency Cuts:

For commissions, agencies deduct 20%. They do not deduct taxes for foreigners.

❖ Agency Provides:

Most agencies advance airfare, accommodations and pocket money for models, dependent upon the situation. Neither agencies nor clients offer money contracts.

LIVING

❖ Housing:

Most agencies provide models' apartments. Inexpensive accommodations average RM400-600 per month. Moderate average RM700-800 per month. Cheap hotels are high, averaging RM300-500 per day.

❖ Transportation:

The airport is a 28 minute ride by train to downtown and is RM35 one way. By taxi, it takes 45 minutes to reach the city and is RM60. The market has inexpen-

MODEL MARKETS OF THE WORLD
KUALA LUMPUR MALAYSIA

sive public transportation including train, subway/metro and bus. A short ride in a taxi is RM3-10. Traffic is bad in the early morning and after work. Otherwise, it is light.

❖ Food & Entertainment:

An inexpensive lunch and dinner is RM5 for a traditional plate with rice or noodles. Kuala Lumpur is developing a very cool night scene with fancy nightclubs, hip bars, and the entertainment is fantastic.

REQUISITES

A work visa is not required for foreign models. Models come in on a tourist visa and work.

WEATHER

It is always hot and humid. Monsoon season is from October to February where it is a little bit cooler and very rainy.

CURRENCY

As of January 2005:
US$10 = RM38
C$10 = RM30.81

MARCIA'S TIPS

The culture in Malaysia is so fascinating. They have 4 different types of religion and along with each are amazing temples, festivals, holidays and unique cuisines. People are very friendly and nice in Kuala Lumpur. 80% of the population speaks English so it is easy to navigate. The city has some wonderful architecture, including the famous Petrona Towers which is the second tallest building in the world.

JAPAN
OSAKA

Osaka is a medium size market in Asia. There are approximately 3 fashion agencies covering the market with a metropolitan area population of over 8,000,000. It is strictly a catalogue market with a small portion of commercial print. The market does not have editorial magazines nor do they have runway. Osaka's catalogue tears can be used in other markets in Asia and in some of the smaller markets in the USA. Osaka is very safe and easy to navigate. If a new face is perfect for the market, it is a great place to start. One of the best advantages to Osaka is that if a model does well there, they can work throughout Asia with success assured.

MARKET PREFERENCES

❖ Models:

The market uses junior/teens (girls starting at age 16), athletic, and adults. Women are preferably looking the ages of 16-25, 5'7"-5'10", sizes 2-4, no more than a C-cup, no larger than a 90cm/35" hip. Men are preferably looking the ages of 25-35, 6'0"-6'2", suit 40R. Redheads will occasionally work in the market but it is very, very rare. Freckles are not acceptable nor are models with lots of moles. The market books only Caucasian with medium toned skin. Spanish models can work well as long as they are not too olive. A model with the lightest essence of Eurasian may work as well. 100% of the models work full-time as they come on contract. Smiles and perfect body shape are absolutely essential. In order to work the market, models must learn the catalogue poses provided by the agencies before arrival. These are very important as many of the clients do not speak English, and it is very difficult for the clients to work with the models if they cannot move well for the bookings.

❖ Portfolios:

Only 1% of the market is from direct bookings, and they are very rare. For direct bookings, models must have already worked with the client. Clients prefer to see models in person and the agencies drive models around in vans with a manager who speaks to the Japanese clients for them. Established models must arrive with tearsheets in order to ensure work and contract guarantees. Clients do not want to see high fashion models. Instead, they prefer a very relatable Sears catalogue type.

❖ Agencies Preferences:

Agencies prefer models that are polite, communicate well, and are cooperative and patient. For castings, hair and make-up should be very neat, straight and simple, almost unnoticeable. Dress should be clean and jeans are okay but they have to be very nice. The look has to be put to-

MODEL MARKETS OF THE WORLD
OSAKA JAPAN

gether but not too dressy. Agencies prefer models to come on a guaranteed money contract for 2 months.

TYPICAL BOOKINGS

❖ Length of Work:

Full days are the norm with multiple days being very rare – maybe 10%.

❖ Type of Work:

Lots of Catalogue and wedding, athletic, lots of lingerie, swimwear, commercial print, local TV commercial (very little), store informal, showroom, and industrial.

❖ Busiest Seasons:

Osaka is busy all year long. It is busiest from September to Christmas holidays. The slowest months are February and August.

TOP CLIENTS

Top clients include department stores Daimaru, Isetan and Takashimaya, lingerie/underwear clients Cecile, Senshukai, Nissen and Wacoal, Panasonic and Sony.

COMPETITION

The competition in Osaka is fierce. There are many models vying for the same jobs and models must know their catalogue moves to compete because clients shoot anywhere from 20-30 outfits per day. Clients expect everything to be perfect – from movement to good facial expression. Casting lines can be as long as one hour.

PAY RATES

Print averages (YEN) ¥130,000-200,000. Advertising ¥300,000-800,000. There are no unions in Japan for TV commercials, which usually only run locally. TV commercials average ¥400,000-1,000,000.

❖ Agency Cuts:

For commissions, agencies deduct 30-40% for print and TV. USA models must submit the IRS Tax Form 8802 to request the IRS Tax Form 6166 and Canadian models must bring the Fiscal Attestation in order to avoid having 20% deducted for taxes.

❖ Agency Provides:

Models arrive on guaranteed money contracts. These contracts advance accommodations, airfare, composites, laser copies of books, tests, occasionally van transportation and a weekly salary. These expenses are deducted from the contract of the model's guaranteed earnings. New faces usually go on minimum contracts that only cover these expenses. More experienced models have extra wages attached to their contracts for incentive. The contract price only reflects the guarantee and models can make much more if they exceed their contract in bookings. Contracts include a two-week period to see if the model will work. If the model does not work, they can be sent home and they will not owe monies back from their expenses covered on the contract or their contract can be renegotiated. Some clients in the market offer money contracts as well.

LIVING

❖ Housing:

Agencies provide models' apartments. Inexpensive accommodations average ¥130,000 per month. Moderate ¥150,000-160,000 per month. Cheap hotels average ¥180,000 per month (for 2 occupants), or ¥5,000-10,000 per night.

❖ Transportation:

The airport is one hour by bus from downtown. Osaka does have public transportation including train, metro/subway and bus. It is expensive compared to other cities. A short ride in a taxi costs ¥650. Traffic is heavy.

❖ Food & Entertainment:

An inexpensive lunch is ¥400 and an inexpensive dinner is ¥600. Osaka is famous for its noodles and sushi. The city has great restaurants and nightclubs; however, everything closes down at midnight. Japan is filled with amazing tourist spots including Kyoto, city of the world treasure, and Nara.

REQUISITES

Models must have a visa to work in Osaka. Models must work this out with the agency and the Japanese Consulate prior to arrival. The entire process can take up to 3 weeks. USA models must submit the IRS Tax Form 8802 to request the IRS Tax Form 6166 and Canadians need the Fiscal Attestation upon arrival in order to avoid having taxes deducted.

WEATHER

The weather is the same as Tokyo. Winter is from November to February and is very cold. Summer is June to September and very hot and humid. Models should carry an umbrella (costs ¥100) for the rainy season from the end of June to the end of July.

CURRENCY

As of January 2005:
US$10 = ¥1027.90
C$10 = ¥835.31

MARCIA'S TIPS

Models should travel with their own pillows, bed sheets and towels. They should make sure to follow the agency's list of requested items to be included in the model bag because that is very important for bookings. Females need to bring neutral and black pantyhose to each job. Females should bring their own line of products for personal hygiene as the products are different in Japan. Catalogue moves are paramount! Models must be confident and not shy in order to work in Osaka. It is important to read body language and gestures as only 10% of the clients speak English. Japanese people are willing to help, and models should keep trying to communicate if they need assistance. Only about 5% of the Japanese population speaks English – they are very cooperative and will feel badly if they can't understand someone.

KOREA
SEOUL

Seoul is a large market in Asia and it is the capital city of Korea having a metropolitan area population of 21,950,000. This modern city is great for its local models because the clients prefer Korean stars and top Korean models. It is beginning to open up more and more for foreign models. There are approximately 5 fashion agencies for foreign models in the market catering to a client base including over 600 fashion clients, 30 magazines that book foreign models, and a good amount of advertising/campaign. TV commercials are starting to become very lucrative. As Seoul continues to grow and cater to Korea's 1.02 billion consumers, the market will definitely continue to grow for models because there is plenty of work and money to be made.

MARKET PREFERENCES

❖ Models:

The market uses junior/teens, athletic (same size as fashion models but a bit more muscular), and adults. Women are preferably looking the ages of 18-22, 5'8"-5'11", Korean sizes 55-66 (American 2-6), no larger than a B-cup, no larger than a 90 cm/35.5" hip. The market does not book runway for foreigners because it is not profitable at this point. Men are preferably looking the ages of 19-25, 6'1"-6'2" and height is strictly enforced, Korean suit 100 (American 40). The market prefers brown hair and brown eyes due to their demographics. Blondes work but redheads do not. Freckles and moles do not work well due to the culture's reverence for perfectly clear skin. The market mainly books Caucasian, Eurasian and Hispanic/Latin. Smiles are very important for catalogue and editorial. 100% of the models work full-time in Seoul.

❖ Portfolios:

40% of the market is from direct bookings and they are usually for very good money. Clients prefer higher quality models that have at least some editorial and a few campaigns from top international markets. Portfolios must be job specific with each case being slightly different. Clients prefer to see models in person. New faces that have been modeling for 6 months or more and have made 1 prior trip overseas are welcome. New faces must have at least 30 usable pictures from either testing or editorial and established models should bring all their pictures, present as well as past, even ones other markets may deem as too old, as Seoul wants to pick what is right for the Korean market.

❖ Agencies Preferences:

Agencies like models that are professional, polite and open-minded. For castings, women should have hair that is past shoulder length, able to be straightened easily if it is naturally curly and make-up should be minimal and natural. Men need to make sure their hair is neatly groomed. Dress should be trendy as clients love it. Agencies prefer models remain on stay for money contracts from 45-60 days.

TYPICAL BOOKINGS

❖ Length of Work:

Half day (5 hours including make-up) and full day (9 hours including make-up and meal). Editorial is booked in 5 hour and 9 hour increments.

❖ Type of Work:

The market has lots of catalogue and editorial as well as athletic, lingerie, swimwear, commercial print, TV commercial, and very rarely film.

❖ Busiest Seasons:

The market has 4 catalogue seasons with up to 10 castings per day. The busiest times are from November to December (a relatable catalogue look with good proportions for lingerie and underwear), and from mid-December to February (highly established editorial and trendy looks and also relatable catalogue looks). March is fashion advertising time. April to May is TV commercial season. From June to August, everything is needed. September to October is fashion advertising and TV commercial season. The only slow times are somewhat around the holidays but even then the market is busy.

TOP CLIENTS

Top clients include Samsung Electronics, Samsung Motors, Cheil Textile (20 brands of clothing), E-Land (10 brands of clothing), Try (5 lingerie brands), department stores Lotte and Hyundai, Fila (sportswear), licensed clothing companies Elle and Marie Claire, Chevinon (jeans), and Body Shop (skincare).

COMPETITION

Competition is tough, frenetic and very much like the Tokyo market. Models are driven around to their castings with a promotion manager speaking to the Korean clients. There are never long casting lines.

PAY RATES

Jobs are paid in (US DOLLAR) $US. Print averages $300 for the rare hourly booking. Half day $500-1,500. Full day $1,000-3,000 (top models make much more with some garnering money contracts with clients for up to a month at $10,000 per day). Advertising/campaign averages $3,000-50,000. Direct bookings average $20,000-45,000. TV/film is all non-union in Korea and the rates vary job to job.

❖ Agency Cuts:

For commissions, agencies deduct 10-15% and 20% for taxes for foreigners.

❖ Agency Provides:

Models arrive on guaranteed money contracts. These contracts advance expenses including airfare, accommoda-

MODEL MARKETS OF THE WORLD
SEOUL KOREA

tions, composites, transportation and a weekly salary of $100 for pocket money. Beginners usually contract for 60 days for $12,000 and leave with around $1,000-2,000 in pocket. Clients offer money contracts but only to top models and celebrities.

LIVING

❖ Housing:

Agencies provide models' apartments. Inexpensive accommodations average (SOUTH KOREAN WON) 880,000KRW per month. Moderate 1,100,000KRW per month, including utilities and phone. Agencies do not recommend that models stay in hotels as they can be risky or very expensive.

❖ Transportation:

The airport is located in the city Incheon which is about 1 hour from Seoul. The city does have a very well-organized subway system but the agencies provide all transportation to/from castings and jobs. The subway and bus cost less than 800KRW. A short ride in a taxi is 3,000-4,000KRW. Traffic can be intricate.

❖ Food & Entertainment:

An inexpensive lunch and dinner is 5,000KRW. If models insist on eating American or European food, they will pay more -- 11,000-22,000KRW at the least. Korea has both historical/culturally-based restaurants as well as modern. Korea is strongly based in culture. Models can visit historical palaces, botanical gardens, museums, amusement parks and folk villages. There is a very full nightlife with clubs in the Itaewon area, and shopping malls are open 24 hours. Models can go to the nearby islands for a weekend holiday for 250,000KRW and agencies are very helpful arranging holiday/weekend excursions.

REQUISITES

Models must have work visas and they can arrange to have this before or after arrival. Once the agencies have a signed contract, they arrange the appropriate work confirmation papers and send them to the Korean embassy nearest the model's location where the model applies to pick up the visa. Many agencies find it easier for a model to come into Seoul as a tourist and then take a 1 day trip to Osaka to do the paperwork for the visa.

WEATHER

Temperatures can be anywhere from as low as -5 Celsius to as high as 30 Celsius, depending on which of the 4 seasons Korea is in.

CURRENCY

As of January 2005:
US$10 = 10,290.9KRW
C$10 = 8,380.57KRW

MARCIA'S TIPS

When in Korea, models should be ready to work and not think it's going to be a vacation. Korean agencies specifically bring foreign models into work their massive list of clients and they also want models to fulfill their money contract. So, if models aren't busy working, they will be busy on castings. Most models comment on how much they enjoy Korean people and how inappropriately they are characterized via the media. About 50% of the clients can speak some English. Models should be careful what they say in English in front of Korean clients and agencies as most understand a lot more than they say. On the streets in Seoul, not as many people speak English. Models should ask their agency what words to learn in order to better navigate the city.

CHINA
SHANGHAI

Shanghai is a new market for international models, but it has great potential in comparison to other cities opening up throughout mainland China. The city has approximately 10 fashion agencies with a metropolitan area population of 13,250,000. Many Chinese foresee Shanghai becoming the future Asian center of fashion and advertising. At this point it is a small market but definitely growing. Right now, the market is mainly a relatable commercial print and catalogue market. Shanghai is for the true model adventurer who is ready to travel uncharted waters. Models rave about the amazing bookings to incredible locations throughout China – truly The *National Geographic* of the fashion industry.

MARKET PREFERENCES

❖ Models:

The market uses primarily adults. Women are preferably looking the ages of 18-25, 5'7"-5'9" for catalogue, sizes 4-6, no more than a B-cup, no larger than a 35.5" hip; for runway 5'9"-5'11", sizes 4-6. Men are preferably looking the ages of 20-35, 6'0"-6'2", suit 40-42; for runway 6'0"-6'2", suit 40-42. The market prefers Caucasian models for catalogue. For commercial print and TV commercials, the market uses both Caucasian and Eurasian. Smiles are important for catalogue and editorial. Freckles do not work well in the market. Foreign models work full-time in the market.

❖ Portfolios:

About 20 % of the market is from direct bookings. Only established models garner these bookings. They must have a strong portfolio with international editorial and campaigns. Clients prefer to see models in person. Shanghai is not a market for brand new faces. The agencies prefer established models with at least 2 years experience.

❖ Agencies Preferences:

The Shanghai market prefers models with super personalities that are open-minded as well as very, very flexible and easy going, because as with any new market, Shanghai comes with the usual beginner client disorganization. Models must maintain a nice disposition as well as be able to emote and move well. For castings, clients prefer models to have clear skin with minimal to no make-up, straight hair that is well kept and wear casual clothing. Agencies prefer models to remain on stay in the market 1 to 2 months, depending on their level of experience.

MARCIA ROTHSCHILD MOELLERS
CHINA SHANGHAI

■ TYPICAL BOOKINGS

❖ Length of Work:
Hourly, full day and multiple days.

❖ Type of Work:
Catalogue, editorial, campaign, lingerie, runway, commercial print, TV commercial, trade show, and store informal.

❖ Busiest Seasons:
The busiest times of the year are from November to March and from June to September. The slowest times are Chinese New Year, March and April, and October during a national holiday.

■ TOP CLIENTS
Top clients include car companies Toyota and Volkswagen, cosmetic companies L'Oreal, P&G, Johnson & Johnson, and Yu-xi, beverage & food companies Pepsi, Wa-Ha-Ha and PEC, China Telecom, and Sony.

■ COMPETITION
Competition is minimal because not many models are willing to travel to Shanghai yet. Casting lines are rare and usually no longer than a half hour.

■ PAY RATES
Print averages (CHINESE YUAN) rmb 800-1,200 per hour. Half day rmb3,200-4,800. Full day rmb6,400-9,600. Advertising/campaign rmb12,000-150,000. Runway rmb2,000-5,000. There are no unions for TV/film in China. TV commercials average rmb15,000-40,000.

❖ Agency Cuts:
For commissions, agencies deduct 20-50% varying with each job. Agencies deduct taxes for all foreign models.

❖ Agency Provides:
Some agencies advance full expenses, including airfare, accommodations, laser copies of books, composites, testing, and pocket money. A few of the agencies will offer guaranteed money contracts covering all expenses. Some clients offer money contracts via direct bookings only.

■ LIVING

❖ Housing:
Agencies provide models' apartments or have arrangements with small hotels. The cost of living in Shanghai is cheap but apartments and hotels can be expensive. Inexpensive accommodations average rmb2,500-3,000 per month. Cheap hotels average rmb100-400 per day and rmb3,000 per month.

❖ Transportation:
The Pu-Dong airport is 1 hour from downtown. Shanghai has inexpensive public transportation including bus, subway, and also trains for traveling out of the city. Many models use bikes for transportation. A short ride in a taxi is rmb10-15. Shanghai is very congested with traffic, especially from 7-9 a.m. and 4-6 p.m.

MODEL MARKETS OF THE WORLD
SHANGHAI CHINA

❖ Food & Entertainment:

Food in China is very cheap. An inexpensive lunch is rmb5-10 and an inexpensive dinner is rmb10. A sit down restaurant averages rmb10-200. Models enjoy the wonderful cuisine of Shanghai, sightseeing and shopping. Entertainment includes discotheques, pubs, KTV, and nightclubs.

REQUISITES

Foreign models do not need a work visa for Shanghai, but they must arrive with a tourist visa.

WEATHER

Shanghai enjoys all 4 seasons. Winters can go to -5 Celsius and the summer can go up to 37 Celsius.

CURRENCY

As of January 2005:
US$10 = rmb82.87
C$10 = rmb67.16

MARCIA'S TIPS

Shanghai is a great market to experience a totally different culture while it is catching up with the 21st century. Models with desire for no-frills travel and new adventures will love it. Living in Shanghai makes you part of its fast-paced growth into becoming an international city. Everything is mixed in this city – the poor, the elderly, the modern, the hip and the ultra trendy. Models will need to learn some basic Chinese as it is not easy to navigate Shanghai without it. Less than 5% of the city speaks even basic English.

SINGAPORE

Singapore is a medium size market in Asia with a metropolitan area population of 4,500,000 and has approximately 5 fashion agencies. Singapore is known for its great tearsheets, primarily all in English. The market is also known for its strong sense of style. Clothing, hair and make-up stylists rein more power in this market than perhaps any other, making almost all of the final decisions on models booked. Asian clients like to cast in Singapore and book models on beautiful location trips throughout Asia Pacific. Models from all over the world are interested in coming to Singapore to improve their portfolios. The market is very inexpensive in comparison to most international markets. Singapore is a powerful Asian banking hub, and is very clean and safe. Combine all of these facts and this makes Singapore a strong destination point for all models with the right look for the market.

MARKET PREFERENCES

❖ Models:

The market uses mainly adults. Women are preferably looking the ages of 18-21, relatable/lifestyle minimum of 5'7", editorial/fashion 5'9"-5'11.5", Italian 38 (American 2-4), no more than a small B-cup, no larger than a 35" hip; for runway 5'9"-5'11.5", Italian 38 (American 2-4). Men are preferably looking the ages of 22-28, 5'11"-6'2", Continental suit 48-52 (American 38-42); for runway 6'1"-6'2", Continental suit 48-52 (American 38-42). Singapore prefers darker hair and brown eyes due to its demographics. Models that can pass as Eurasian, or are truly Eurasian, will work very well in the market. Otherwise, the market uses mainly Caucasian, Hispanic and Native American. Black models work for runway show season but only with a very good show resume. There is no work in the market for blonde females but blonde males do work. Freckles and moles pose a big problem in Singapore. About 80% of the market works full-time.

❖ Portfolios:

20% of the market is from direct bookings. Mainly, models for beauty, both male and female, get the direct bookings, and are Eurasian. Models with no experience have very little opportunity unless they have an absolutely perfect beauty face for the market. These models will either need polaroids/snapshots or 1 good test to enter. Due to the large influx of models visiting Singapore, clients are getting spoiled and prefer to work with models with strong portfolios that contain no catalogue pictures unless high end, such as Neiman Marcus. Clients prefer tastefully done testing, campaign/advertising and fashion editorial. Often,

MODEL MARKETS OF THE WORLD
SINGAPORE

clients will ask the agencies to e-mail the portfolio links after a casting.

❖ Agencies Preferences:

Agencies prefer models that are cheerful, polite, and ready to work hard. Divas do not fare well in the Singapore market place. For castings, hair and make-up must be light and not messy. Clothing must be casual, fashionable and trendy. Agencies prefer models to remain on stay 4-6 weeks.

■ TYPICAL BOOKINGS

❖ Length of Work:

Hourly, half day and full day. The market is starting to get more multiple days.

❖ Type of Work:

A good amount of editorial, catalogue, commercial print and TV Commercial, as well as campaign, lingerie, runway, trade show and showroom.

❖ Busiest Seasons:

The busiest time is from July to November, which is also the TV commercial season. The market is the slowest in December as well as for the 2 weeks around Chinese New Year (which either falls in January or February).

■ TOP CLIENTS

Top clients include Nivea, Pond's, Robinson's (dept. store), Sony, Pierre Cardin Lingerie, electronics companies Samsung and Osim, Nokia, ad agencies Hakuhodo, DYR, and DMB&B, Procter & Gamble, telecommunication networks Singtel and Starhub, banks, spas, clothing catalogues from all over Asia, and many direct bookings to Malaysia.

■ COMPETITION

Competition is intense because there are many models that remain on stay with good portfolios. Castings are mainly appointment only and lines are usually no more than 10 minutes.

■ PAY RATES

Print averages (SINGAPORE DOLLAR) S$250 the first hour and then S$200 per hour. Half day S$850 (4 hours of work plus an additional hour for hair and make-up). Full day S$1,600 (8 working hours plus an additional hour for hair and make-up). Advertising/Campaign S$10,000-60,000. Runway S$250 per half hour show. All TV commercials are non-union in Singapore. TV commercials average half day S$1,200 and full day S$2,200.

❖ Agency Cuts:

For commissions, all agencies deduct 35% and they do not deduct taxes for foreigners.

❖ Agency Provides:

Most agencies advance airfare, accommodations, composites, website, testing and pocket money, dependent upon the caliber of the model. Neither agencies nor clients offer money contracts.

SINGAPORE

LIVING

❖ Housing:

Most agencies provide models' apartments Inexpensive accommodations average S$680 per month. Moderate S$800. Cheap hotels average S$165 per night. Most hotels are as much as S$350 per night.

❖ Transportation:

The airport is 20 minutes from downtown and is about S$25 in a taxi. Singapore has inexpensive public transportation including subway and bus, averaging between S$.80-1.80 per ride. A short ride in a taxi is S$2.50. Traffic is efficient and usually never jammed, unless an accident occurs.

❖ Food & Entertainment:

An inexpensive lunch is S$3 and an inexpensive dinner is S$4-5.

Drinks average about S$.60. Singapore is surrounded by many islands and the ferry rides to the islands are inexpensive. There is a huge water theme park where models can go to spend the entire day experiencing all the different rides. Singapore is known for having the largest variety of cuisine in Asia and prices are reasonable, depending on the type of establishment.

REQUISITES

Work visas are not necessary for American and Canadians. Models enter as a tourist through customs.

WEATHER

The weather is hot and sunny with occasional showers all year round.

CURRENCY

As of January 2005:
US$10 = S$16.30
C$10 = S$13.24

MARCIA'S TIPS

Models need to be really aware of the weather and they have to be dressed comfortably for the warm climate, but still look stylish and fashion forward. Model bags should include a light sweater as some indoor temperatures can be chilly, as well as a swimsuit and umbrella for castings. Many models take advantage of the bargain priced latest electronic goods available in Singapore, including cameras, ipods, laptops and mobile phones. Short trips to nearby islands are beautiful and inexpensive. Navigating Singapore is very easy as 90% of the population is proficient in English.

TAIWAN
TAIPEI

Taipei is a smaller medium size market in Asia and for its size, this city has an amazing amount of work. The metropolitan area population is 6,850,000 with approximately 10 fashion agencies and clients extending all the way into Grand China. Agents and models alike, are surprised by the level of creativity in Taipei. Some of the magazine editorial is quite beautiful and it is a lucrative market for models with the bulk of work focused in catalogue, advertising and TV commercial. The Taipei market has the capacity to work models 7 days a week, 2 bookings per day, if a model can handle it. The tearsheets and the money make the market very appealing.

■ MARKET PREFERENCES

❖ Models:

The Taipei market uses junior/teen (female only starting at age 14, 1.70-1.74 cm/5'7"-5'8.75"), and adults. Women are preferably looking the ages of 18-24, 1.72-1.78 cm (5'7.75"-5'10"), sizes 2-6, no more than a C-cup, no larger than a 35.5" hip; for runway 1.74-1.78 cm (5'9.5"-5'10"), sizes 2-6. Men are preferably looking the ages of 18-35, 1.78-1.84 cm (5'10"-6'.05"), Continental suit 48-50 (American 38-40); for runway 1.80-1.85 cm (5'11"-6'1") Continental suit 48-50 (American 38-40). The market is strict about sizes as they are the exact sample sizes their clients receive. The market uses primarily Caucasian, Asian and Eurasian models. Skin is mainly white to olive toned. Black models solely work for runway or specific advertising. Smiles are great for catalogue and editorial but not essential to work the market. 100% of foreign models work full-time, and the majority of local models do as well, unless they are students.

❖ Portfolios:

The Taipei market has quite a bit of direct bookings, especially for advertising and TV commercials for clients from Taiwan, Hong Kong and China. Direct bookings are garnered by established models with lots of experience and a full book of tearsheets. For cosmetic and other types of direct bookings, it is more the model's look than the level of the portfolio. Caucasian models garner more direct bookings than Asian or Eurasian. Junior/teen new faces can enter the market with 2 good tests in their portfolios. Older models will need to be established with a portfolio with good testing as well as international experience including catalogue, editorial and advertising/campaign tearsheets.

❖ Agencies Preferences:

Agencies like models that are independent, hard working, cheerful, easy going and those that can communicate their needs well. Personality is a major concern for Taipei agencies. Hair and make-up will be job specific and should be easy to change per casting. Dress can be casual and trendy as long as it is well put together. Healthy, clear skin and a perfect body are paramount to the Taipei market. Agencies prefer catalogue models to remain on stay for contracts from 45-60 days. Editorial models with edgier looks can work as well in this fashion market, but the contract guarantees will usually be the minimum.

TYPICAL BOOKINGS

❖ Length of Work:

Half day and full day. TV commercials are booked in packages of 12-60 hours in multiple days.

❖ Type of Work:

Catalogue, campaign, editorial, lingerie, swimwear, commercial print, TV commercial, infomercial, runway, trade show, store informal, showroom, and industrial.

❖ Busiest Seasons:

Taipei is busy throughout the year. Catalogue season is busiest from May to September and from November to March. The market never slows much.

TOP CLIENTS

Top clients include ad agencies Ogilvy & Mather, J. Walter Thompson and Dentsu, Taiwan magazines Elle, Marie Claire, Vogue, GQ, FHM and Beauty, car companies Toyota, Ford and Mitsubishi, hair/beauty clients Ponds, L'Oreal, Max Factor and Kao, department stores Sunrise, Sincere, Breez Center and Mitsukoshi, designers Shiatz Chen, Elizabeth Wen and Jamie Chen, and electronic companies Benq, Moto, Sony Erricsson, Panasonic, Nokia, Sharp, Sanyo, Asus, Acer, Taiwan Telecom, and Chung Hwa Telecom.

COMPETITION

Competition is fierce. The amount of models competing for jobs is parallel to Milan or Tokyo. Casting lines can be as long as an hour.

PAY RATES

Print averages (NEW TAIWAN DOLLAR) NT$ 13,000-18,000 per half day. Full day NT$ 22,000-32,000. Advertising/campaign NT$ 60,000-1,000,000. Runway NT$ 10,000 – 28,000 per show. Taiwan is all non-union for TV/film TV commercials average NT$ 60,000-1,000,000 per shoot.

❖ Agency Cuts:

For commissions, agencies deduct 40-50%, including taxes, for on stay foreign models. For direct bookings, agencies deduct 10-20% for taxes for foreign models.

❖ Agency Provides:

The agencies offer guaranteed money contracts including advances of airfare, accommodations, composites, weekly

MODEL MARKETS OF THE WORLD
TAIPEI TAIWAN

salary, and transportation. Some agencies will not give weekly salaries until the second week to ensure the model will work. If the model does not work, the contract may be cut short and the model sent home without having to reimburse expenses. For direct bookings, the agencies have the clients cover the expenses and some clients offer money contracts as well.

LIVING

❖ Housing:

Agencies provide models' apartments. Inexpensive accommodations average NT$ 700-800 per day. Moderate NT$ 900-1,000. Inexpensive hotels are often used averaging NT$ 1,000-2,000 per day.

❖ Transportation:

The airport is 45 km from the city and is 45-60 minutes from downtown. Taipei has inexpensive public transportation including MRT (subway/metro system), train and bus costing NT$ 20 for 2-4 subway stops. For castings, the agencies provide private taxis for models. Taxis start at NT$ 70, then each 0.4 km/waiting 2 minutes is NT$ 5, and an additional 20% for 11 p.m. - 6 a.m. Traffic is fine except during rush hour which can be as bad as New York City.

❖ Food & Entertainment:

An inexpensive lunch is NT$ 50-100 (a drink with a sandwich or a meal box) and an inexpensive dinner is NT$ 75-100 (a noodle soup or pasta). The city never sleeps. They have 24 hour convenience stores, internet cafes, coffee shops, book stores, discotheques, restaurants and movie theaters.

REQUISITES

Models must get a visitor's visa before arrival, and they can apply before or after arrival for a work permit which is only available to a limited amount of Taiwan agencies. For the work permit, models must present a passport and an agreement from their parents if they are under the age of 20, photos and related support documents. All models are required by the agencies to have travel insurance.

WEATHER

The weather is humid and warm throughout the year. It is especially hot in the summer.

CURRENCY

As of January 2005:
US$10 = NT$ 317.74
C$10 = NT$ 258.47

MARCIA'S TIPS

Models will not be surprised by Taipei if they remain open-minded and prepared for a different cultural experience than what they are accustomed to. Taipei has some fabulous designers, great photographers, and other wonderful behind the scenes people in its industry. If female models have a shoe size larger than

9, they must bring a good range of basic shoes – neutral and black pumps, sandals and casual shoes along with white keds. The country is progressing quickly and Taiwanese clients expect models to work as hard and rapidly as they do. Most photographers work 2 full day clients into a day. Competition is high and everything in the industry is very efficient so models must be prepared to work, work, work while making good money at the same time.

ISRAEL
TEL AVIV

Tel Aviv is a small market with a city population of 750,000 and a metropolitan area population of 3,000,000. The city has approximately 5 fashion agencies catering to this market with a small amount of fashion, minimal catalogue and loads of TV commercials. Fashion models are primarily booked for local clients geared towards sportswear and casual wear. Tel Aviv's clients are each usually booking for about 100 shops spread across Israel. Clients will shoot national campaigns including advertising, billboards and catalogue. Tel Aviv does have some international clientele, including swimwear giants Gottex and Obersson. Because of the demand, Tel Aviv is one of the best international markets for plus/full-size. There are many TV commercials shot for all sorts of products aired on Israel's 2 TV channels. Models can either direct book into the market or come for Tel Aviv's two fashion seasons during the year. Although politically turbulent, this market has many positives for the strong and willing. Models like the bonus of being paid in US$ currency and the opportunity to book into unique editorial magazines.

■ MARKET PREFERENCES

❖ Models:

The market uses junior/teens. The market is a great market for plus/full-size,1.75-1.80 cm (5'9"-5'11"), Continental sizes 44-50 (American 14-20). The market also uses athletic (booked by regular fashion models that are in great shape), and adults. Women are preferably looking the ages of 18-30, 1.70-1.80 cm (5'7"-5'11"), Continental sizes 36-38 (American 4-6), no larger than a B-cup, no larger than a 92 cm/36.5" hip; for runway 1.75-1.80 cm (5'9"-5'11"), Continental sizes 36-38 (American 4-6). Men are preferably looking the ages of 21-35, 1.80-1.85 cm (5'11"-6'1"), Continental suit 52 (American 42); for runway 1.83-1.85 cm (6'0"-6'1"), Continental suit 52 (American 42). The market mainly uses Caucasian and rarely needs any other ethnicities. Smiles are important for catalogue and editorial. 50% of the market works full-time.

❖ Portfolios:

30% of the market is from direct bookings that mainly go to models with good portfolios and/or from repeat bookings. This is not a market for new faces and established models must enter the market with tearsheets that have a good balance between high fashion editorial and relatable fashion advertising/campaign in their portfolios.

❖ Agencies Preferences:

Agencies prefer models that are professional, open minded, smart, fashion savvy, nice, sweet, and those that speak politely and informatively. For castings, clients prefer to see models with minimal make-up and natural hair. Some castings can be more specific with additional make-up, hair or clothing requests. Dress is casual as long as the model has a great fashion sense. Agencies prefer models to remain on stay for 2 months.

TYPICAL BOOKINGS

❖ Length of Work:

Very rarely half day, mostly full day and multiple days (2-3 days long).

❖ Type of Work:

Catalogue, editorial, campaign, athletic, lingerie, swimwear, runway, commercial print, lots of TV commercial, film, store informal, and showroom.

❖ Busiest Seasons:

The market is busiest during Tel Aviv's two fashion seasons from January to March and from June to September. The market is slowest from the end of September to October and from April to May.

TOP CLIENTS

Top clients include magazines 360 degrees, At, La Isha, Olam Ha'Isha, Time – Out, Layla, and Shamenet, Wella (hair care), Coca-Cola, Careline (hair care & cosmetic), swimwear companies Gottex and Obersson, fashion companies Castro, Fox, TNT Tanmnun and Honigman, advertising agencies BBDO and Grey, and production company Rabel Paradiso.

COMPETITION

Tel Aviv is competitive because the city has quite a few agencies for such a small market. Casting lines can be as long as 2 hours.

PAY RATES

Models are paid in (US DOLLAR) US$. Print averages $200-500 per half day. Full day $1,500-2,000. Advertising/campaign $3,000-50,000. Runway $200-500 per show. Israel has a union for TV/film. Union rates for TV commercials average $750-1,500. 25% of the market is non-union with rates averaging $500-5,000 per TV commercial.

❖ Agency Cuts:

For commissions, agencies deduct 30% for print and TV/film. 20% for runway. Agencies may deduct taxes up to 25%, depending on which country the model is from.

❖ Agency Provides:

At this time, only one Tel Aviv agency has models that remain on stay. Most agencies advance on airfare, accommodations, transportation to castings, gym memberships, haircuts, composites, laser copies of book, tests, and pocket money, dependent upon the caliber of the model. Agencies do not offer money contracts. Some clients will offer money contracts in exchange for exclusivity.

MODEL MARKETS OF THE WORLD
TEL AVIV ISRAEL

■ LIVING

❖ Housing:

The one on stay agency provides models' apartments. Inexpensive accommodations average 1,540-1,760 NIS (NEW ISRAELI SHEKEL) per month including utilities. Moderate 2,400- 2,080 NIS. Cheap hotels average 220-1100 NIS per day. Per week 1540-2,650 NIS. Per month 4,400-8,800 NIS.

❖ Transportation:

The airport is 30 minutes from downtown. Tel Aviv has public transportation in the form of buses. Models mainly use taxis or an agency driver because they are usually very cheap. A short ride in a taxi is 8-13 NIS. Traffic is very busy in the city.

❖ Food & Entertainment:

An inexpensive lunch is 17-25 NIS and an inexpensive dinner is 43-85 NIS. Coffee houses are always packed and busy all day long. The nightlife in Tel Aviv is wonderful and crazy with many bars and nightclubs open all night long. 70's and 80's music, as well as, MTV music is very popular in Tel Aviv. There are 4-5 festivals a year in Tel Aviv that are up to 7 days long.

■ REQUISITES

Work visas are required for foreign models. Models enter the market as tourists through customs and then the agency will arrange for the visa upon arrival.

■ WEATHER

Israel is hot throughout the year. The rainy season is from December to January.

■ CURRENCY

As of January 2005:
US$10 = 43.76 NIS
C$10 = 35.81 NIS

■ MARCIA'S TIPS

Make sure to soak up the culture and history of this region. Go see Jerusalem, the Dead Sea, Nazareth and the Sea of Galiley. The Israeli mentality is very open and friendly – they enjoy topical conversation but when it's time to work, they give 100%. Models must be prepared to work hard – the days are long and clients are tough and expect models to produce their absolute best. Models will find it quite easy to navigate with over 90% of the city speaking English. Israel has been a war torn country since its establishment in 1948. The direct consequence of this has been few models committing to remain on stay. Models that are strong and willing will get 5 star treatment and the best of service because this is how Tel Aviv is luring models to remain on stay. The agencies hope that someday peace will happen and then direct bookings and on stay models will prosper.

JAPAN
TOKYO

Tokyo is the Paris and New York City of Asia, with approximately 25 modeling agencies. The population for the city proper is over 8,000,000 but the city covers a metropolitan population area, including Yokohama and Kawasaki, of over 31,000,000. Tokyo is the largest, most sophisticated and competitive market in Asia. Tokyo is a wonderful, busy city with a culture based on sensitivity and politeness. It has so much to offer from art to history to entertainment to shopping and allows models the opportunity to do catalogue and editorial as well as earn money. Plus, it's one of the only markets in the world that offers guaranteed money contracts.

MARKET PREFERENCES

❖ Models:

The market uses junior/teens (starting at age 15) and adults. Women are preferably looking the ages of 17-25, 5'7"- 5'9.75", sizes 2-4, no more than a B-cup, no larger than a 36" hip; for runway 5'9.5"-5'11", sizes 2-4. Men are preferably looking the ages of 17-35, 5'11"-6'2", suit 40R; for runway 6'0"-6'2", suit 40R-40L. Perfect skin is a must. Smiles and perfect body shape are absolutely essential. The market books mainly Caucasian and sometimes light Native American. Spanish, Italian and South American work well as long as they are not too olive skin toned. Other ethnicities need to be top star models to work in Tokyo. Female Black models are very rarely booked and only if they have top show resumes for the Tokyo Collections. Redheads and freckled models do well for editorial, but not as much for catalogue. Models with lots of moles do not work well. In order to work the catalogue market, models must learn the poses provided by the agencies before arrival. These are very important as many of the clients do not speak English, and it is very difficult for the clients to work with models if they cannot move well for the bookings. These poses are not important for editorial bookings, but good movement is still crucial. 100% of the models work full-time because they come on contract.

❖ Portfolios:

There are direct bookings for top models or via repeat bookings, but they are rare. Clients prefer to see models in person. If a model is the perfect look for Tokyo, they can come with a few good tests in their portfolios. Some perfect-for-the-market models have only worked in Tokyo and have never traveled anywhere else internationally. Established models should come with a good book of tearsheets in editorial and advertising/campaign as well as experience from major international markets.

MODEL MARKETS OF THE WORLD
TOKYO JAPAN

❖ Agencies Preferences:

Agencies prefer models to be nice, polite, outgoing, cheerful, hardworking, and open-minded. For castings, clients want models to have natural hair and make-up. Dress should be casual with a trendy and put together touch. Perfect skin and a great shape are demanded by the clients. Agencies prefer to have models remain on stay with guaranteed money contract for 6-8 weeks; however, top star models can obtain shorter contracts.

■ TYPICAL BOOKINGS

❖ Length of Work:

Hourly, half day, full day and some multiple day bookings.

❖ Type of Work:

Catalogue, athletic, editorial, campaign, lingerie, swimwear, runway, commercial print, TV commercial, very rare film, infomercial, trade show, showroom, store informal, and industrial.

❖ Busiest Seasons:

Since it is the largest market in Asia, it is busy year round. It is even busy in December, with some models contracting straight through the holidays with only a week off. The busiest times are from March to April and from September to November. The Tokyo Collections are from the end of March to the beginning of April and again from the end of October to the beginning of November. It is slower around the Japanese holidays.

■ TOP CLIENTS

Top clients include advertising agencies Dentsu, Hakuhudo and McCann-Erickson, cosmetic companies Shiseido and Kose, Cecile (lingerie), department stores Isetan and Takashimaya, Foxy (designer & wedding), Peach John (lingerie – the Victoria's Secret of Japan), magazines Japan Vogue, Japan Elle, Japan Marie Claire, Japan Harper's Bazaar, and Spur, Honda, Toyota, Sony, and Panasonic.

■ COMPETITION

The competition is very, very fierce as Tokyo is the "New York City of Asia". Casting days can be long and go well into the evening. Some castings can take up to an hour or longer. Models will want to bring a book or headphones for the van on casting days.

■ PAY RATES

The market has hourly (usually only infomercial and fitting jobs) averaging (YEN) ¥7,000-30,000. Half day ¥80,000-200,000. Full day ¥150,000-400,000. Advertising/campaign ¥500,000-10,000,000. Runway – Tokyo Collection ¥50,000-400,000, Foreign Designers Show ¥150,000-500,000, and regular shows ¥100,000-250,000. There is no union for TV/film in Japan. TV commercials average ¥500,000-3,000,000 per booking.

❖ Agency Cuts:

For commissions, agencies deduct 40% for print, runway and TV/film. USA models must submit the IRS Tax Form 8802 to request the IRS Tax Form 6166 and Canadian models must have the Fiscal Attestation upon arrival in order to avoid having 20% deducted for taxes.

❖ Agency Provides:

Models arrive on guaranteed money contracts which advance airfare, accommodations, model composites, laser copies of portfolios, van transportation and a weekly salary. This is all included in the contract and then deducted from the model's guaranteed earnings. New faces usually go on minimum contracts that only cover these expenses. More experienced models have extra wages attached to their contracts for incentive. The contract price only reflects the guarantee and models can make much more if they exceed their contract in bookings. Contracts include a two-week period to see if the model will work. If the model does not work, they can be sent home and will not owe monies back from their expenses covered on the contract, or their contract can be renegotiated. Some clients offer money contracts in exchange for exclusivity.

LIVING

❖ Housing:

Agencies either provide models' apartments or place models in weekly hotels. Apartments average ¥135,000-210,000 per month. Cheap hotels average ¥180,000-300,000 per month.

❖ Transportation:

The airport is approximately 60 km from the city. Most models take the bus into the city. Tokyo has public transportation including train, subway and bus; however, it is expensive in comparison to other cities. A taxi is ¥660 for 2 km. Traffic is heavy.

❖ Food & Entertainment:

An inexpensive lunch is ¥800 and an inexpensive dinner is ¥1500. There is so much to do in Tokyo. Most models like to go to the movies, karaoke and nightclubs. The shopping is incredible and the city has a great sense of eclectic style.

REQUISITES

Models must have a work visa to work in Tokyo which must be worked out with the agency and the Japanese Consulate prior to arrival. It can take up to 3 weeks for the entire process. Americans need to submit the IRS Tax Form 8802 to request the IRS Tax Form 6166 and Canadians must have the Fiscal Attestation in order to avoid having taxes deducted.

WEATHER

Winter is from November to February and is very cold. Summer is June to September and very hot and humid. Models should carry an umbrella during the rainy season – from the end of June to the end of July.

MODEL MARKETS OF THE WORLD
TOKYO JAPAN

CURRENCY

As of January 2005:
US$10 = ¥1027.90
C$10 = ¥835.31

MARCIA'S TIPS

Models should be prepared with basic Japanese words as only 5% of the population speaks English. They should ask their English-speaking Japanese agency to help navigate the city and most models rave about how safe they feel in Tokyo. Models must know their poses for catalogue before arrival because it is essential to garner bookings. Females should bring their own line of products for personal hygiene as the products are different in Japan. Japan is a wonderful country where beauty, respect and culture are paramount. There are amazing places to visit that are only a train ride away including the seaport towns, Mt. Fuji as well as some lovely spa/resorts.

EUROPE

Amsterdam 131
Athens 134
Barcelona 137
Berlin 140
Brussels 144
Copenhagen 147
Dusseldorf 150
Geneva 154
Hamburg 157
Lisbon 160
London 163
Madrid 166
Milan 169
Munich 173
Oslo 177
Paris 180
Stockholm 184
Vienna 187
Zurich 190

NETHERLANDS
AMSTERDAM

Amsterdam is a larger small market with a metropolitan area population of 2,150,000 and approximately 7 fashion agencies. Amsterdam is a small but interesting market because it has great fashion magazines with very nice editorial. Amsterdam also has catalogue and advertising/campaign clients along with some wonderful young designers and quite a few established fashion brands. Models love to go to Amsterdam because the city is so much fun; however, this is mainly a market for the working model that has a modern look and a strong, established resume. It's a great place to beef up a portfolio with editorial while making some money at the same time.

MARKET PREFERENCES

❖ Models:

The market uses experienced junior/teens. Girls can be as young as 14 and boys as young as 15. Amsterdam rarely uses plus/full-size and they are booked through casting agencies – not the fashion agencies. The market mainly books adults. Women are preferably looking the ages of 18-35, 1.72-1.80 cm (5'7.75"-5'11"), Continental size 36-38 (American 4-6), no more than a B-cup, no larger than a 92 cm/36.5" hip; for runway 1.75-1.82 cm (5'9"-5'11.75"), Continental size 36 (American 4). Men are preferably looking the ages of 18-50, 1.83-1.89 cm (6'0"-6'2.5"), Continental suit 50 (American 40); for runway 1.83-1.89 cm (6'0"-6"2.5"), Continental suit 50 (American 40). The market uses Caucasian, Black, Light Black, Asian, Eurasian, and Hispanic models. Smiles are somewhat important but not the first thing that clients look at, as they are more concerned with an overall interesting appeal and the model's ability to move and express well. Models can only work full-time in Amsterdam if they combine the city with other larger markets in Europe.

❖ Portfolios:

Amsterdam has direct bookings which are composed of about 50% of the market. Direct booking clients prefer models that are a combination of editorial and catalogue with portfolios reflecting this. Clients prefer to see models in person, which is not always possible. Therefore, the clients will book directly from a model's portfolio. However, models will obtain work faster if they have seen the clients first. New faces will need experience from other markets to work in Amsterdam. Sometimes a client will book a new face with just testing, but it is rare and the model would have to be exactly what the client wants. Established models must have nice, clean editorial that is updated and modern along with some good testing that shows the face and body well.

❖ Agencies Preferences:

Agencies prefer models that are professional and confident with a nice personality. Clients prefer no make-up or as natural as possible. Hair should be neat. Women need to look ladylike and trendy clothing is optimum. Men can be casual and wear jeans. Agencies prefer that models come for 2-3 days for client appointments. Afterwards, if the response is good, they can direct book while working in other markets in Europe.

TYPICAL BOOKINGS

❖ Length of Work:

Direct bookings – full day and multiple days. In town bookings – hourly, half day, full day and multiple days.

❖ Type of Work:

Catalogue, editorial, campaign, commercial print, runway, and TV Commercial.

❖ Busiest Seasons:

Amsterdam is busy all year long. The busiest times are from April to June and from October to November. The slowest times of the year are from the end of July to the end of August and around the Christmas holidays.

TOP CLIENTS

Top clients include Tommy Hilfiger, Mexx (clothing), Liz Claiborne, Kuyichi (clothing), Keune (hair care), MAC (cosmetics), department stores De Bijenkorf and V&D, G Star (clothing), magazines Elle and Marie Claire, along with many advertising agencies and production companies.

COMPETITION

Amsterdam is competitive because there are many models that find it easy to add it to their resume while working the other markets of Europe. Amsterdam does not have a lot of castings, but when they do they are very well organized and the lines are usually short.

PAY RATES

Print averages (EURO) €110-615 per hour. Half day €300-2,000. Full day €545-3,600. Advertising/campaign €545-50,000. Most of the time, usage for an advertisement or brochure is included in the work fee. Other usage is additional and the rate depends on the product, the amount of markets, the period of time and quantity. Runway averages €200-1,200 per show. Holland does not have a union for TV commercials. There is an additional fee on top of the day rate dependent on where the TV commercial will air and for what period of time. Fees average €1,500-30,000 per booking.

❖ Agency Cuts:

For commissions, agencies deduct 20% for print, runway and TV/film. The agen-

MODEL MARKETS OF THE WORLD
AMSTERDAM NETHERLANDS

cies do not deduct taxes.

❖ Agency Provides:

Most agencies advance composites and laser copies of books. Agencies will sometimes advance accommodations for the 2-3 days of seeing clients. Models must wait for their wages from a job until the client has paid the agency. Agencies do not offer money contracts and it is very rare that a client will.

■ LIVING

❖ Housing:

Agencies do not provide model's apartments. When a model comes in for appointments, most agencies have the model stay at a bed & breakfast which averages €50 per night, including breakfast. Inexpensive apartments average €1,000-1,500 per month. Hotels are expensive, starting at €100 per night.

❖ Transportation:

The airport is approximately 20 minutes via Tram from downtown. Amsterdam's public transportation is called the Tram, which is a type of train. Models can also rent a bicycle. Holland does have other public transportation including train, metro/subway and bus, but it is mainly outside of the city. Taxis are expensive with a short ride averaging €15. Traffic is pretty average and rush hour is a bit more difficult.

❖ Food & Entertainment:

In Amsterdam models can find many types of cuisine. An inexpensive lunch is €7.5 and an inexpensive dinner is €10. There is all kinds of entertainment in the city and Amsterdam has a wonderfully modern and free attitude that many foreigners enjoy. There are cinemas, theaters, and a great night life with many restaurants, nightclubs, and festivals of all sorts.

■ REQUISITES

A work visa is not required for foreign models.

■ WEATHER

Holland normally has 4 seasons. Fall is rainy. Winter is cold and icy, and it can snow and rain in the same day. Spring has more sun and less rain. Summer is nice and sunny with some rainy days.

■ CURRENCY

As of January 2005:
US$10 = €7.69
C$10 = €6.20

■ MARCIA'S TIPS

Models should bring good walking shoes and use them because Amsterdam is a lovely city to walk around and enjoy. Dutch people are very relaxed as long as one behaves nicely and not too crazy. During their free time, models should check out some of the great art galleries throughout the city. About 80% of Holland can speak English so it is very easy to navigate.

GREECE
ATHENS

Athens is a medium size market with approximately 5 fashion agencies in a metropolitan area population of 3,500,000. The market has many types of clients – big advertising agencies, good magazines, fashion designers, catalogue and many production companies for TV commercials. Most models come to the market for the editorial as there are many internationally known magazines and there is less competition in Athens than in other larger markets. The magazines are published quickly so models can have their editorial tearsheets within one month and while waiting, they can do catalogue and TV commercials to earn their living expenses.

MARKET PREFERENCES

❖ Models:

The market uses juniors/teens (at least 16 years of age), athletic, and adults. Women are preferably looking the ages of 17-26, 1.72-1.80 cm (5'7.75"-5'11", Continental size 36-38 (American 4-6), preferably a B-cup but no more than a C-cup, no larger than a 91 cm/36" hip; for runway 1.75-1.80 cm (5'9"-5'11"), Continental size 36-38 (American 4-6), no larger than a B-cup. Men are preferably looking the ages of 22-30, 1.83-1.88 cm (6'0"-6'2") Continental suit 50 (American 40); for runway 1.85-1.88 cm (6'1"-6'2"), Continental suit 50 (American 40). If models have a lot of freckles, it can be a problem unless they are redheads. Clients book mainly Caucasian models; however, Latin models work well. All the other ethnicities do not garner as much work – maybe 1 or 2 editorials or a commercial – so it is best for these models not to remain on stay in Athens. Smiles are important for catalogue and editorial. Foreign models are working full-time. Some of the Greek models combine modeling with school. This puts the market at about 80% working full-time.

❖ Portfolios:

20% of the market is from direct bookings. For catalogue and editorial direct bookings, the models must have a strong book with at least 4 or 5 good editorials and proof of positive experience in other markets. For TV commercial direct bookings, models must send their agency an audition tape and they must have a very relatable, lifestyle fashion look. Clients definitely prefer to see models in person. New faces can come from other markets with 3 or 4 good fashion tests and begin working. The market frowns on new faces that only have 1 test in their portfolios. Pictures must show good expression and movement. To begin working, established models should come with 4 or 5 editorials and a good resume of proven work from other larger markets.

MODEL MARKETS OF THE WORLD
ATHENS GREECE

❖ Agencies Preferences:

Agencies prefer models that communicate well with the clients making it clear they are professional. For castings, hair and make-up should be very natural. Models may wear what they like as long as they definitely present themselves as models and not just tourists passing through the city. This is very important in Athens because Clients tend to prefer to know they are booking models by seeing it for themselves. Agencies prefer for models to remain on stay in the market for at least 4-6 weeks.

TYPICAL BOOKINGS

❖ Length of Work:

Some half day, full day bookings are predominant, and lots of multiple days in the summer as clients book models for trips.

❖ Type of Work:

Catalogue, athletic, editorial, campaign, lingerie, swimwear, runway, commercial print, TV commercial (lots), film (not as much for models), trade show, store informal, showroom, and industrial.

❖ Busiest Seasons:

Athens is busy all year long. The busiest times are from the middle of January to the beginning of April, May to July, and September to the beginning of December. The slowest time is in August when everyone goes on holiday. Traditional holidays are very slow as well.

TOP CLIENTS

Top clients are all international magazines including Greek Vogue, Greek Marie Claire, Greek Elle, Greek Men's Health, as well as large advertising agencies Spot Thomson, Euro RFCG and BBDO, and production companies that shoot for multinational brands, such as Coca-Cola and Toyota.

COMPETITION

The competition is fierce because each agency has so many models, but it is not as tough as it is in the other larger markets. Sometimes models have to deal with long casting lines but they are usually no more than 10-15 minutes.

PAY RATES

Print averages (EURO) €300-500 per half day. Full day €650-1,000. Advertising/campaign €800-3,000. Runway €450 per show. All of Greece's TV commercials are non-union. Rates average €600-3,000 for a main role.

❖ Agency Cuts:

For commissions, agencies deduct 35% for print, runway and TV. They deduct 20% for taxes for foreigners.

❖ Agency Provides:

Agencies usually advance accommodations, composites, laser copies of books and tests. Dependent upon the caliber of the model, they will advance airfare and pocket money. Agencies do not offer money contracts; however, some clients do.

LIVING

❖ Housing:

Most agencies in Athens provide models' apartments. Inexpensive accommodations average €450 per month. Moderate averages €630 per month. Cheap hotels average €14-21 per night.

❖ Transportation:

The airport is 15-20 minutes from downtown. Athens has inexpensive public transportation including the metro/subway, train and tram/bus. A short ride in a taxi is €5. Traffic is bad in Athens.

❖ Food & Entertainment:

An inexpensive lunch is €5-8 and an inexpensive dinner is €10. Entertainment is very good around the Acropolis, which is the old city and is very nice. Athens has a lot of nightclubs to go to as long as models don't have early castings the next day.

REQUISITES

A work visa is not required for foreigners. Models enter through customs as tourists.

WEATHER

The weather is great. Most of the time it is warm and it rains quite often. Even in the winter the temperature is mild.

CURRENCY

As of January 2005:
US$10 = €7.69
C$10 = €6.20

MARCIA'S TIPS

Models should bring good facial products because the pollution is bad in Athens. Models should also bring sunscreen and a good hat because the sun is strong. About 70-75% of the Greek people speak English; however, it always helps when arriving models have learned some basic Greek phrases in advance. Models will need to be very patient with taxi drivers because they are hard to find. If models give a good amount of time to the Greek market, it can definitely contribute to their success in the other larger markets.

SPAIN
BARCELONA

Barcelona is a medium size market with a population of over 1,500,000 and a metropolitan area population of 2,800,000 and there are approximately 4 fashion agencies. It is smaller when compared to London, Paris or New York, but the quality of work is on the same scale as the larger markets, with strongholds in fashion design, lingerie/swimwear and commercial work. Barcelona's fashion market is rising because some of Spain's best designers are becoming internationally known. Barcelona is the center of the fashion business for Spain as most clothing companies and top advertising agencies are based there. Models love Barcelona because it is a welcoming city with a wonderful, relaxed attitude. Models want to stay and drink up the city's atmosphere and find it hard to leave as they don't want to deal with some of the more intense markets of Europe.

■ MARKET PREFERENCES

❖ **Models:**

The market uses junior/teens, and adults. Women are preferably looking the ages of 18-25, 1.75-180 cm (5'9"-5'11"), Spanish sizes 36-38 (American 4-6), no more than a C-cup, no larger than a 36" hip; for runway 1.77-1.80 cm (5'9.5"-5'11"), Spanish sizes 34-36 (American 2-4). Men are preferably looking ages 24-27 and around 35, 1.83-1.88 cm (6'0"-6'2"), Continental suit 50-52 (American 40-42); for runway 1.85-1.88 cm (6'1"-6'2), Continental suit 50-52 (American 40-42). Great bodies are a must, especially for athletic, lingerie and swimwear clients. Smiles are important for catalogue, but not as much for designer/editorial clients. Clients do not prefer the American stereotype of Hispanic, which is Mexican, but prefer ethnicities with an international, European look. Depending on the look, Native American is possible. It's a good market for redheads, as well as all other hair colors. Black models usually enter the market via runway with a top show resume, and then print work may follow. Asian/Eurasian females can do well with show and lingerie. About 90% of the market works full-time, unless they are attending school.

❖ **Portfolios:**

40% of the market is from direct bookings. These bookings are garnered by models that have strong portfolios with editorial and advertising/campaign or models with the perfect look for a specific job. To enter the market, new faces need to have some fashion tests in their books and a strong desire to be developed with parental support and/or their own means of support. Established models must have good tearsheets with an international flair, not just the typical catalogue pages.

❖ Agencies Preferences:

Agencies prefer models that are confident, self-aware, fresh, spontaneous and uninhibited. Clients like to see natural beauty and a sense of style, but not straight off the runway in clothing, make-up and hair. Agencies prefer models to remain on stay 2 months so they have time to be developed as well as for the agency and model to profit. Top models can come in for a short stay and do appointments, but must be available for direct bookings afterward.

TYPICAL BOOKINGS

❖ Length of Work:

Half day (called a "session") and full day (8 hours). There are not many multiple day bookings.

❖ Type of Work:

Catalogue, editorial, campaign, lingerie, swimwear, runway, commercial print, showroom, and editorial. Non-European citizens cannot do TV commercial or film in Spain, except under very specific circumstances.

❖ Busiest Seasons:

The market is busiest from the end of February to the end of July and again from the end of September to the beginning of December. The two main show seasons are in February and September. There are smaller show seasons in June for bridal and swimwear. The market closes down for vacation in August and slows down again around the holidays.

TOP CLIENTS

Top clients include clothing companies Mango, Zara, and Massimo Dutti, El Corté Inglés (dept. Store), magazines Spanish Vogue, Spanish Elle, Spanish Marie Claire, Woman, and Telva, major ad agencies J. Walter Thompson, McCann-Erickson and Grey Advertising, as well many bridal and swimwear companies.

COMPETITION

The Barcelona market is very competitive. There is not as much work as in the larger markets; however, aggressive models come to garner the upscale work, which helps them launch into even larger markets.

PAY RATES

Print averages (EURO) €400-800 per half day. Full day averages €1,000-3,000. Advertising/campaign average €2,000-20,000. Runway averages €600-1,500 per show. TV/film is non-union only in Spain. The TV/film (see note in Type of Work) day rate, depending on the model, can average €2,000-6,000 with additional usage fees.

❖ Agency Cuts:

For commissions, agencies deduct 20% for print and runway. Agencies deduct 25% for taxes from foreign models.

MODEL MARKETS OF THE WORLD
BARCELONA SPAIN

❖ Agency Provides:

Most agencies advance accommodations, composites, website, and laser copies of books. Dependent upon the caliber of the model, they may advance testing and airfare. Agencies do not offer money contracts; however some clients may, but usually only for product clients.

LIVING

❖ Housing:

Most agencies have models' apartments. Inexpensive accommodations average €500 per month. Moderate average €1,500 per month. Cheap hotels average 80 € per night.

❖ Transportation:

The airport is 7 km from the city. Public transportation is very good with train, subway, and bus. Public transportation is efficient, clean and inexpensive. A short ride in a taxi is €3-4. Traffic is light.

❖ Food & Entertainment:

<<<<<Missing>>>>

REQUISITES

Work visas are not necessary for foreign models and they may enter as tourists through customs. Spanish law defines the model as self-employed, yet the present immigration legislation does not accept a foreign self-employed request for a working visa. Non-EU (European) citizens cannot work TV/film.

WEATHER

Warm, welcoming climate with pleasant temperatures year round.

CURRENCY

As of January 2005:
US$10 = €7.69
C$10 = €6.20

MARCIA'S TIPS

Barcelona is a wonderful city – especially for type-A personalities. This city is a solid stepping stone for models gently setting them into the groove of Europe while not being as busy or frenetic as most of the larger European markets. The market has good quality work and the city makes sure no one takes themselves too seriously but still demands that models focus on their craft. Spaniards love the art of the craft and models will learn to see their career that way, as everywhere they go there are examples of how this is exemplified from architecture to museums to small little boutiques on the cobble stoned side streets with beaches close by. Spanish people like good vibration people! It is important for models to have a language translation book because only about 20% of the city's population speaks English; however, most fashion industry people speak a good amount of English.

GERMANY
BERLIN

Berlin is a rather small market that is growing and developing. There are approximately 9 fashion agencies in this city with a metropolitan area population of 4,150,000. Now that the city is united as one, with both east and west sides together, Berlin is again the capitol of Germany. The market generally direct books models into whatever city the clients are based in. Berlin itself is mainly a TV commercial market and fashion is rapidly returning with young, upcoming designers and a group of good quality photographers. The city is gaining a reputation for being a cool, happening spot in Germany. Many magazines and campaigns are shot there by top photographers using the hip locations of Berlin.

MARKET PREFERENCES

❖ Models:

The Berlin market uses very little junior/teens or big & tall, some athletic that are fashion types, and mainly adults. Women are preferably looking the ages of 18-40, 1.73-1.80 cm (5'8"-5'11), Continental sizes 36-38 (American 4-6), no more than a C-cup and sometimes D-cup is okay, no larger than a 93 cm/37" hip; for runway 1.76-1.80 cm (5'9.5"-5'11"), Continental size 36 (American 4). Men are preferably looking the ages of 18-40, 1.85-1.90 cm (6'1"-6'3"), Continental suit 50 (American 40); for runway 1.85-1.90 cm (6'1"-6'3"), Continental suit 50 (American 40). Lighter eyes sell better than darker. The market loves freckles as they make the model more interesting. The majority of models have European looks – 80% Caucasian and 20% a mix of Asian and Black descent. Smiles are very important for catalogue but not often needed for editorial as it tends to be more serious. About 50% of the market works full-time with these models having lots of experience and being exactly what the market wants.

❖ Portfolios:

60% of the market is from direct bookings. Portfolios need to be high profile. The better the book, the better the chance of selling the model for direct bookings. The portfolio must be a good mixture of high-end editorial and relatable advertising and catalogue. If the book is just filled with French Vogue, it will not be enough to get a money booking from a catalogue client. Tearsheets are essential as clients look for these as the stamp of approval of a good quality model. Just make sure there is a diverse mixture of looks. Clients prefer to see a model in person, if possible. When perfect for the market, agencies will take on new faces by reviewing good quality polaroids/snapshots. Otherwise, if already represented by another market, new faces will need to

MODEL MARKETS OF THE WORLD
BERLIN GERMANY

enter with very good testing with photography at the level seen in top magazines. Established models should enter with a well developed book with good tests and tearsheets.

❖ Agencies Preferences:

Agencies prefer models that are open-minded, not boring or shy, polite but not uptight, a balanced personality with a good sense of humor, interesting, energetic but not too American – a bit more subtle. They prefer light make-up – no eyeliner, just pretty and natural with freshly washed hair. The market is more or less casual in dress. Jeans are good but not grungy or punk. Trendy is good but not too designer. Keep it cool, using vintage pieces mixed with designer pieces. No high heels or short skirts. Agencies prefer new faces to remain on stay 4-8 weeks and experienced models 3-4 weeks.

TYPICAL BOOKINGS

❖ Length of Work:

Hourly (very few), half day, full day and some multiple days.

❖ Type of Work:

Catalogue, editorial, campaign, some athletic, lingerie, swimwear, runway, commercial print, TV commercial, store informal, very little showroom, and industrial.

❖ Busiest Seasons:

Berlin is busy all year long. January to February is very busy as well as August. March is slow with April being a bit slower.

TOP CLIENTS

Top clients include designers Jil Sander and Hugo Boss, Beiersdorf (skincare), Johnson & Johnson (baby & skincare), Henkel (cosmetic), magazines Deutsch and Hommes Uomo, Jung Von Matt (ad agency), Spengler (catalogue), L'Oreal, and department stores C&A and Karstadt.

COMPETITION

Berlin is a relatively easy market to enter and to get the ball rolling. It is not as tough as the larger markets. Casting lines do not happen often with print clients. For TV commercials, models sometimes have to wait up to an hour.

PAY RATES

Print averages (EURO) €600-2,000 per half day. Full day €1,000-4,000. Advertising/campaign €800-25,000. Buyouts are normally 300% the day rate. Runway €500-2,500 per show. Germany does not have a union for TV/film. Berlin rates for TV commercials can vary depending on what character a model portrays. A main character averages €1,500-2,000 per day rate. A side character averages €800-1,000, and an extra averages €400-500. On top of day rates there can be additional percentages depending on what countries the TV commercial will be aired and the amount of time it runs.

MARCIA ROTHSCHILD MOELLERS
GERMANY BERLIN

❖ Agency Cuts:

For commissions, agencies deduct 25% for print, runway and TV. Taxes are deducted for foreign models depending on laws that change frequently. Germany is now in flux with this. At the moment, models are responsible for their own taxes. Models should make sure to check with the agency before arrival. A "foreigner tax" is now deducted for TV commercials and can be up to 25%. The model can take the receipt home for proof of having already paid taxes. At this time, for print and catalogue, agencies tax the model on commissions only. For example, the agencies deduct 25% for commissions on a €1,000 booking, and the model will be taxed 16% on the €250 commissioned.

❖ Agency Provides:

Most agencies will advance accommodations, airfare (dependent upon the caliber of the model), composites, laser copies of books, and testing (only if necessary). It is very rare for agencies to advance a weekly salary as they do not want to be perceived as a bank. Agencies do not offer money contracts and it is rare for a client to do so.

LIVING

❖ Housing:

Most agencies have models' apartments. Inexpensive accommodations average €450 per month. Moderate accommodations average €700 per month. Cheap hotels average €30-150 per night.

❖ Transportation:

Berlin has 3 airports. The main airport, Berlin Tegel, is located in the city and is 30 minutes from downtown. The second one is Schoenefeld and is 45 minutes from downtown. The third one is a very small airport, Tempelhof, and is 20 minutes from downtown. Berlin has public transportation including train, tram/subway and bus. Berlin's public transportation system is one of the best in the world but is expensive. A short ride in a taxi is €7-10. Traffic is not heavy and most often is pretty calm.

❖ Food & Entertainment:

An inexpensive lunch is €10 and an inexpensive dinner is €15-20. Berlin is very young and quite energetic. There are a lot of hot urban clubs – punk, reggae, hard core rock & roll, techno, house music, to name a few. It's a very cool scene and is one of the best places in the world for DJs. There are lots of museums and very good restaurants. The art scene is vibrant with young artists, galleries and exhibitions. There is a lot to do in Berlin.

REQUISITES

The work visa situation seems to either be simple or complicated, depending on the mood of government to government relationships between Germany and each individual country.

MODEL MARKETS OF THE WORLD
BERLIN GERMANY

Models should request information from their agency before arrival.

WEATHER

Berlin has typical 4 season weather. Winters are very, very cold with temperatures as low as minus 15 C.

CURRENCY

As of January 2005:
US$10 = €7.69
C$10 = €6.20

MARCIA'S TIPS

Models must have patience in this market, as Berliners tend to do things a bit slower - be prepared to go with the flow. Berlin is much more laid back compared to other fashion cities in Germany. Some foreigners think that Berliners are a bit rude as they talk fast and come back with sarcastic answers, but it's really nothing more than just the attitude of the city. Berliners always have a quick answer with a note of sarcasm, especially when they feel that someone is talking strangely to them, and they volley it back. It may feel offensive but really is just typical behavior and is a reminder for models to be open minded.

BELGIUM
BRUSSELS

Brussels is very similar to the Dutch market of Amsterdam, just slightly smaller. Brussels has approximately 6 fashion agencies in a city with a population of around 1,000,000 and although petite in size, it is full of very talented people from the Academy of Antwerp (notably Dries Van Noten and Ann Demeulemeester who have put Brussels on the map). Thanks to these designers, many local models have been launched into international fame, and there seems to be no end to Belgium producing top models. Brussels also has many French catalogue clients. It's a great market to start your career and learn about the industry.

MARKET PREFERENCES

❖ Models:

The Brussels market uses junior/teens (from ages 13 up), some big & tall (only used for relatable commercial print work and not fashion), some petite (under 1.70 cm/5'7"), and a lot of adults. Women are preferably looking the ages of 18-28, 1.72-1.80 cm (5'7.75"-5'11"), Continental sizes 34-38 (American 2-6), no larger than a B-cup, no larger than a 92 cm/36.5" hip; for runway/showroom 1.75-1.80 cm (5'9"-5'11"), Continental |sizes 34-38 (American 2-6). Men are preferably looking the ages of 18-50, 1.82-1.88 cm (5'11.75"-6'2"), Continental suit 50-52 (American 40-42); for runway/showroom 1.85-1.88 (6'1"-6'2"), Continental suit 50-52 (American 40-42). Brussels uses mainly Caucasian models with very little use of other ethnicities due to the client demographics. Smiles are important for catalogue but not for editorial. Models cannot work full-time in the market, so it's a great market to visit on the way to Paris, Amsterdam or the larger markets in Germany.

❖ Portfolios:

About 50% of the market is from direct bookings. Models must be based in Europe and be stellar with strong portfolios to garner direct bookings. Clients prefer to see models in person and no experience is necessary for new faces. Agencies prefer to see good polaroids/snapshots first. If already represented in another market, it is not an option to come to Brussels until the model is established with a strong portfolio and resume of experience.

❖ Agencies Preferences:

Agencies prefer models that are self-confident and spontaneous with great smiles. For castings, clients prefer natural hair and make-up. Models should look nice but not overly done. Dress for females can be a skirt or jeans, high heels and a body-conscious white shirt. Men can wear jeans and a t-shirt. Agencies

MODEL MARKETS OF THE WORLD
BRUSSELS BELGIUM

prefer models to remain on stay for 2-3 days to see clients and then be available for direct bookings from another market in Europe.

TYPICAL BOOKINGS

❖ Length of Work:
Clients mainly book full day and multiple days and rarely hourly or half day.

❖ Type of Work:
Catalogue, commercial print, editorial, campaign, and runway/showroom.

❖ Busiest Seasons:
The market is busiest from February to April, then from September to November, and it is usually slowest in the summer.

TOP CLIENTS

Top clients include Belgian magazines Knack, Feeling and Flair, catalogues La Redoute, 3 Suisses, la Fuma, La Camif, Quelle, Blance Porte and Damart, as well as Marie Jo (lingerie).

COMPETITION

The competition is fierce because the market is so close to the French and Dutch marketplaces. Many castings are appointment specific and when there are general castings, the lines can be as long as 2 hours.

PAY RATES

Print rates average (EURO) €40 per hour. Half day €592-1,480. Full day €800-2,000. Advertising/campaign €5,000-25,000. Runway/showroom €460 per day.

❖ Agency Cuts:
For commissions, agencies deduct as much as 40%, depending on the booking. Agencies do not deduct taxes for foreign models.

❖ Agency Provides:
Dependent upon the caliber of the model, agencies will advance accommodations, airfare, laser copies of books, composites, tests and weekly salaries. Some clients offer money contracts; however, agencies do not.

LIVING

❖ Housing:
Agencies do not provide models' apartments due to the small nature of the market and models do not remain on stay. Most agencies accommodate models in inexpensive hotels which average €50 per night.

❖ Transportation:
The airport is 30 minutes from downtown. Brussels has inexpensive public transportation. The train is good; however, the metro is very bad. A short ride in a taxi is €6-7. Traffic in Brussels is quite busy.

❖ Food & Entertainment:
An inexpensive lunch is €10 and an inexpensive dinner is €20. Going out in Brussels is fun because there is a lot of culture – art, concerts and expositions. As it is a small country, the streets are not crowded

and the attitude is laid back.

REQUISITES

A work visa is not required for foreign models to work in Brussels.

WEATHER

It rains a lot in Belgium.

CURRENCY

As of January 2005:
US$10 = €7.69
C$10 = €6.20

MARCIA'S TIPS

Belgians are very modest, down to earth people, and sometimes quite reserved. Belgian clients rarely demonstrate affection and more often than not, remain conservative. Models should never respond meanly or rudely. The Belgian clients like models with upbeat personalities and smiling faces. About 90% of the Belgian industry speaks English and approximately 70% of the city does as well. Models should have few problems navigating Brussels and they should never leave Belgium without trying their world famous chocolate.

DENMARK
COPENHAGEN

Copenhagen is a small market with a metropolitan area population of over 1,500,000. Denmark has approximately 5 fashion agencies located in Copenhagen and another 3 agencies that are located in the northern part of Denmark in Aarhus. Denmark is well known for development and specializes in developing high-end fashion types. The region is also known for its native beautiful people that have the perfect features and height for modeling. Models are discovered, portfolios are built and then once a resume has been developed, most Danish models travel to other markets. Amsterdam does not have models remain on stay but rather flies them in and out via the market's many direct bookings.

■ MARKET PREFERENCES

❖ Models:

The market uses junior/teens (beginning at age 17) and adults. Women are preferably looking the ages of 18-30, 1.74-1.80 cm (5'8.5"-5'11"), Continental sizes 36-38 (American 4-6), no more than a B-cup although C-cup can work for lingerie/swimwear, no larger than a 36" hip; for runway, 1.74-1.80 cm (5'8.5"-5'11"), Continental sizes 36-38 (American 4-6), no more than a B-cup. Men are preferably looking the ages of 18-35, 1.83-1.88 cm (6'0"-6'2"), Continental suit 48-50 (American 38-40); for runway, 1.83-1.88 cm (6'0"-6'2"), Continental suit 48-50 (American 38-40). The market uses all ethnicities as Denmark is becoming quite multi-ethnic. Smiles are important for catalogue but not as much for editorial. About 15% of the market works full-time with most models based in Copenhagen combining modeling with attending school.

❖ Portfolios:

About 50% of the market is from direct bookings. The models that garner direct bookings have very strong portfolios as clients do not want to invest in less developed models that have not been seen in person. Portfolios need to represent a variety of fashion looks. Generally, it is not essential for the clients to see the models in person unless for a show casting. Clients will book the models directly from portfolios or by the suggestions from the agencies. New faces do not need experience depending on the type of booking. For editorial, clients are open to booking new faces, but catalogue clients want to see good testing first. Established models must enter with a strong portfolio reflecting their image. For catalogue models, a strong book is essential reflecting lifestyle and high fashion commercial print/advertising as well as some editorial tearsheets. A high fashion, couture model must be recognizable and present in current magazines.

❖ Agencies Preferences:

For agencies, personality is very important and they prefer models that are nice, open-minded, professional and easy to work with. Natural hair and make-up is the look in Copenhagen and cannot be overly done. Dress for castings is casual and "come as you are." Foreign models are flown in and out for direct bookings only. If models are seeking representation in the market, they will need to send their portfolios in advance.

TYPICAL BOOKINGS

❖ Length of Work:

Full day and multiple days. Editorial will usually book full day. Campaign or catalogue can be from 1 day to multiple days.

❖ Type of Work:

Catalogue, lingerie, swimwear, runway, commercial print, TV commercial, editorial and campaign.

❖ Busiest Seasons:

The Copenhagen market is consistent throughout the year. The busiest times of the year are from January to February and from August to September. The slowest times of the year are around national holidays and from Christmas to New Year's.

TOP CLIENTS

Top clients include clothing companies Sand, Vero Moda, Only, and Selected, L'Oreal, Pilgrim (jewelry), and magazines Vogue UK, German Vogue, Cover, Eurowoman and Dansk.

COMPETITION

The competition is light in Copenhagen, especially in comparison to the larger European markets. Casting lines are consistently obsolete.

PAY RATES

Print averages 5.000-150.000 DKK (DANISH KRONE) per full day. Advertising/campaign 10.000-1.000.000 DKK. Runway 2.500-150.000 DKK per show. Denmark does not have a union for TV/film. TV commercials are booked at the same rates as print bookings.

❖ Agency Cuts:

By law, the agencies are not allowed to deduct any commissions from model wages. The agencies do not deduct taxes for foreign models either.

❖ Agency Provides:

Agencies only advance on the models that they act as mother agency to. For direct bookings, clients pay for models' airfare and accommodations. Neither agencies nor clients offer money contracts.

MODEL MARKETS OF THE WORLD
COPENHAGEN DENMARK

■ LIVING

❖ Housing:

Agencies do not provide model's apartments. It is not necessary because most models based in the market already have housing with family or due to school. Cheap hotels average 1.000-1.800 DKK per night.

❖ Transportation:

The airport is 15-20 minutes from downtown. Copenhagen does have public transportation including metro/subway and bus. The prices are reasonable. Copenhagen is very small so models can easily walk to most castings. A short ride in a taxi costs 80 DKK. Traffic is mild.

❖ Food & Entertainment:

An inexpensive lunch is 150 DKK and an inexpensive dinner is 600 DKK. Copenhagen has a variety of cuisine, with Thai, Japanese and Italian being far more popular than those found in a traditional Danish kitchen. There are many things to do in the evening. The café life is very popular, and there are many bars, lounges, and nightclubs. Copenhagen is full of museums – small ones with exhibits of new, upcoming Danish artists and the more well known ones are at the Louisiana (30 minutes outside of Copenhagen), as well as the National Museum.

■ REQUISITES

A work visa is usually not necessary for foreign models, depending on the model's originating country and passport. Models should check with their agency before arrival.

■ WEATHER

Copenhagen has all 4 seasons.

■ CURRENCY

As of January 2005:
US$ = 57.22 DKK
C$10 = 46.15 DKK

■ MARCIA'S TIPS

Denmark is a very open-minded country which makes it very easy for models to feel at home while working there. For the Danish, it's always important to be professional no matter what one does for a living. This is especially important when working with other people in the fashion industry of Copenhagen. The majority of Denmark is easy to navigate because most Danish start learning English in school from the age of 10 up. Interesting places of note include the Funa Fair Tivoli, Denmark's internationally renowned interior design district, and the northern part of the country including Aarhus and Skagen. Many models have noted these two cities are definitely worth the trip!

GERMANY
DÜSSELDORF

Düsseldorf is a small to medium size market with a population of 600,000 and a metropolitan area population nearing 1,500,000 with approximately 6 fashion agencies located in the city. Düsseldorf is a very relatable catalogue, commercial print and TV market. Established models with strong portfolios fare best in Düsseldorf. The market scouts for new faces but only does a slight amount of development, and then moves those models into a larger market. Düsseldorf is a very compact, clean and rather elegant city. The city's fashion street, Königsallee, includes shops for all the top designers. Experienced models on their way to Hamburg and Munich should make sure to stop by this little gem of a city if they want to maximize work opportunities in the German marketplace.

MARKET PREFERENCES

❖ Models:

Düsseldorf uses junior/teens (starting at age 15), only a few petite, plus/full-size (1.75-1.80 cm/5'9"-5'11", Continental sizes 44-46/American 12-14), a lot of athletic (using fashion models that play certain sports), and adults. Women are preferably looking the ages of 18-35, 1.74-1.81 cm (5'8.5"-5'11.5"), Continental sizes 36-38 (American 4-6), no more than a C-cup, no larger than a 93 cm/37" hip although if at the taller end, a slightly larger hip might do; for runway 1.75-1.80 cm (5'9"-5'11"), Continental size 36 (American 4). Men are preferably looking the ages of 18-45, 1.82-1.90 cm (5'11.75"-6'3"), Continental suit 48-52 (American 38-42) but the majority wearing a Continental suit 50 (American 40); for runway 1.83-1.90 cm (6'0"-6'3"), Continental suit 48-52 (American 38-42). Düsseldorf has a difficult time booking exotic models as the market is very conservative. The clients prefer very Dutch or German looks. Black and Light Black models mainly work for show and sports catalogue. Smiles are absolutely essential for catalogue and for the very limited editorial in the market. 95% of the market works full-time.

❖ Portfolios:

70% of the market is from direct bookings. The majority of models who garner these bookings are either very good at sports or do lingerie. The market only direct books established models with portfolios that have a good mixture of campaign and editorial. The clients like to see high fashion pictures but they also need to see some natural ones along with proven experience, good movement and catalogue. Clients prefer to see the models in person. Dusseldorf is not the market for new faces and established

MODEL MARKETS OF THE WORLD
DUSSELDORF GERMANY

models will definitely need to have some tearsheets with pictures that reflect experience along with a good mixture of sporty, natural beauty and smile shots.

❖ Agencies Preferences:

Agencies prefer models that are cheerful, polite, positively confident, open minded, modern, professional, natural, motivated, on time, and disciplined. For castings, the look is natural and clean with freshly washed hair, no make-up if the model has good skin and light make-up for those that don't. Dress for castings must be figure emphasizing and casual – tight jeans and a t-shirt are okay. Dusseldorf does nor pursue on stay models. Usually agencies bring in established models for 2-3 days to see clients. If models have a really good portfolio and are right for the market, they can remain on stay up to 2 weeks.

TYPICAL BOOKINGS

❖ Length of Work:

Hourly, half day, full day and multiple days. The very few client trips are usually multiple day bookings.

❖ Type of Work:

Catalogue, commercial print, editorial (very little), swimwear, lingerie, athletic, runway, campaign, TV commercial, film, showroom, and industrial.

❖ Busiest Seasons:

The market is pretty consistent year round. The summer is usually busy from April to August and slower from Christmas to New Year's.

TOP CLIENTS

Top clients include catalogue companies Karstadt, Metro and Quelle, department stores Kaufhof and C&A, advertising agencies Grey and Euro RSCG, designers Hugo Boss and Van Laack, L'Oreal, and Style (magazine).

COMPETITION

The competition in Düsseldorf is light. Models never deal with casting lines.

PAY RATES

Print averages (EURO) €150-200 per hour. Half day €400-1,000. Full day €1,000-3,000.

Advertising/campaign €2,000-25,000. Runway €600-1,500 per show. TV/film is all non-union in Germany. Rates average €1,000-2,500 per day. Düsseldorf has many TV commercial buy-outs including residuals. Buy-outs are calculated by percentages per country. For example, agencies will calculate 300% of the day rate for all of Germany.

❖ Agency Cuts:

For commissions, agencies deduct 25% for print, runway and TV/film. If models want their wages before the agency is paid by the client, the agencies deduct 30%. Taxes are deducted for foreign models depending on laws that change frequently. Germany is now in a flux with this and

GERMANY DUSSELDORF

at the moment, models are responsible for their own taxes. Models should make sure to check with the agency before arrival. A "foreigner tax" is now deducted for TV commercials and can be up to 25%. The model can take the receipt home to prove they have already paid taxes. At this time, for print and catalogue, agencies tax the model on commissions only. For example, the agencies take 25% for commissions on a €1,000 booking, and the model will be taxed 16% on the €250 commissioned.

❖ Agency Provides:

Agencies advance accommodations, airfare, composites, laser copies of books, and tests, dependent upon the potential for work. Agencies do not offer money contracts in Germany as it is illegal. Clients sometimes offer money contracts, however, it is seldom.

LIVING

❖ Housing:

A few agencies provide models' apartments. Inexpensive accommodations average €300-500 per month. Moderate €600-800 per month. Cheap hotels average €35-80 per night.

❖ Transportation:

The city's airport is 10-15 minutes from downtown. Düsseldorf has inexpensive public transportation including train, metro/subway and bus. A short ride in a taxi is €10-15. Traffic is very light in the city.

❖ Food & Entertainment:

An inexpensive lunch is €4-5 and an inexpensive dinner is €8-12. Düsseldorf has lots of galleries and museums. The city's restaurants offer a good range of cuisine. Düsseldorf has a larger Asian population than the rest of Europe; therefore, the market offers a lot of fantastic Asian cuisine. For nightlife, there are cinemas, coffee shops, bars and nightclubs.

REQUISITES

The work visa situation seems to either be simple or complicated, depending on the mood of government to government relationships between Germany and the other individual countries. Models should request information from their agency before arrival.

WEATHER

Düsseldorf is cold in the winters and warm in the summers.

CURRENCY

As of January 2005:
US$10 = €7.69
C$10 = €6.20

MARCIA'S TIPS

Düsseldorf is a very good market for models coming from abroad with strong books. Models should not underestimate Düsseldorf. Some models are motivated to go only to Hamburg and Munich and they miss this very busy market. Clients prefer

MODEL MARKETS OF THE WORLD
DUSSELDORF GERMANY

models to have skin colored lingerie and hosiery in their model bag. Models should try to see the famous building designed by architect Frank O. Gehry in Düsseldorf Harbor, as well as take a short trip to the very beautiful city of Cologne. 50% of the market speaks English so it is beneficial for models to learn some simple German to navigate this wonderful little city.

SWITZERLAND
GENEVA

Geneva is a very small market with a population of nearly 500,000 and approximately 3 fashion agencies. Geneva is dependent on international clients outside of the city's borders for survival. There are very few fashion photographers based in Geneva, but on the upside, the market does have a lot of advertising agencies. Geneva has a relaxed atmosphere and at the same time is quite a chic city. It is not an ideal market for new faces. If a model has a good book, a beautiful smile, wants a market that garners top international commercial print and advertising clients, and wants extra work from direct bookings, Geneva may be the right market to pursue.

MARKET PREFERENCES

❖ Models:

Geneva uses plus/full-size (1.75-1.80 cm/5'9"-5'11", Continental sizes 42-44/American 10-12), plus models must have a round face), and adults. Women are preferably looking the ages of 20-28, 1.72-1.80 cm (5'7.75"-5'11") -- preferably 1.74 (5'8.5"), Continental sizes 36-38 (American 4-6), no more than a C-cup, no larger than a 93 cm/36.5" hip; for runway 1.75-1.80 (5'9"-5'11"), Continental sizes 36-38 (American 4-6). Men are preferably looking the ages of 20-40, 1.84-1.88 cm (6'.05"-6'2"), Continental suit 50-52 (American 40-42); for runway 1.84-1.88 cm (6'.05"-6'2"), Continental suit 50-52 (American 40-42). Clients mainly use Caucasian models along with some Black and Hispanic and will rarely use Asian or Eurasian. Some of the bigger international companies want a variety of nationalities, but the Geneva market is pretty much Caucasian with a bit of Black. A lot of freckles or moles may cause a bit of a disadvantage. Smiles are absolutely indispensable for catalogue and are important for editorial as well. 20% of the market works full time.

❖ Portfolios:

About 85% of the market is from direct bookings. Direct booking portfolios must be very strong with tearsheets and advertising/campaigns that are elegantly styled, clean and sporty with an essence of chic. Clients would appreciate seeing models in person but usually are not given the opportunity. Thus, they book models from portfolios and resume of work. To enter the market, established models must have at least one or two years of experience. Portfolios will need to have a variety of pictures from serious to smiles to sporty to bathing suit to lingerie with catalogue pictures and editorial tearsheets. Smiling pictures are paramount – no smiles, no bookings.

MODEL MARKETS OF THE WORLD
GENEVA SWITZERLAND

❖ Agencies Preferences:

Agencies prefer models that are pleasant, down-to-earth types with a penchant for fashion. Models that have a nice, happy personality will work the most. If models are difficult, Geneva clients aren't interested. Clients want to see natural make-up that enhances a model's features. Hair needs to look put together and not messy. The look for the Geneva marketplace is different than those for Paris or New York City castings. Models should be nicely dressed and preferably not in jeans. Models should be a little upscale and look as if they are going out on a nice lunch date. Models will need to schedule one or two days in Switzerland to see clients in advance. Models do not remain on stay in Geneva.

TYPICAL BOOKINGS

❖ Length of Work:

Half day, full day, and many multiple days. The catalogues normally book anywhere from a minimum of 4 days up to 2 weeks at a time.

❖ Type of Work:

Catalogue, athletic, campaign, very little editorial, lingerie, swimwear, runway, commercial print, a little TV commercial and film, showroom and very little trade show.

❖ Busiest Seasons:

Geneva is busiest from March to June, then September to October, and again in December. The slowest months are August and November.

TOP CLIENTS

Top clients include catalogues Gus, G.D. Williams, Ackermann, Daxon, Damart, Camis, Witt Weiden, Veillon, as well as Nike and L'Oreal.

COMPETITION

The market is very competitive as the agencies are extremely selective with whom they work with. There are never long casting lines.

PAY RATES

Print averages (Swiss Franc) CHF 600,00-1200,00 per half day. Full day CHF 1200,00-2500,00. Advertising / campaign CHF 5000,00-50000,00. Runway CHF 300,00-800,00 per show. Switzerland does not have a union for TV/film so all rates vary.

❖ Agency Cuts:

For commissions, agencies deduct 20% for print, runway and TV/film. Agencies may deduct taxes for non-European citizens depending on the home country of the model. Switzerland does agree to the double taxation law, so models do not have to pay taxes in Switzerland as well as their home country. USA models must request the IRS Tax Form 8802 in order to bring the IRS Tax Form 6166 and Canadian models must bring the Fiscal Attestation in order to avoid having taxes deducted.

❖ Agency Provides:

Dependent upon the caliber of the model, agencies will advance accommodations, airfare, laser copies of books and tests. They do not advance weekly salaries. Neither agencies nor clients offer money contracts.

LIVING

❖ Housing:

Agencies do not provide models' apartments. Inexpensive accommodations average CHF 500,00-1000,00 per month. Moderate CHF 1500,00. Cheap hotels average CHF 100,00-300,00 per night.

❖ Transportation:

The airport is 15-20 minutes from downtown. Geneva does have public transportation, including tram, metro/subway, and bus. Public transportation is approximately CHF 2.60 per day. A short ride in a taxi is CHF 15,00. Traffic in the market is fair.

❖ Food & Entertainment:

An inexpensive lunch is CHF 15,00 and an inexpensive dinner is CHF 25,00. The city is very nice with good restaurants, night clubs, lots of museums, tours that are given on the lakes, and mountains everywhere.

REQUISITES

A work visa is not required for non-citizens. Models can work for up to 3 months before having to apply for one.

WEATHER

Winters are beautiful with a covering of snow and summers are filled with lots of blue sky. Geneva has all 4 seasons.

CURRENCY

As of January 2005:
US$10 = CHF11.86
C$10 = CHF 9.60

MARCIA'S TIPS

Models must be able to speak French in Geneva; however, English is okay but the city is mainly French-speaking. The clients and photographers in the business speak English but only 30% of the city can. Models will want to smile a lot at castings because clients find it important. The city is very relaxed with a healthy financial structure. Geneva is a good city for models to visit to meet clients while on their way to another major market.

GERMANY
HAMBURG

Hamburg is the largest market in Germany with a city population of approximately 2,250,000. The Hamburg market has approximately 15 fashion agencies and has the most bookings for magazines out of all of the German markets. The city is also a top notch catalogue market. For editorial models, Germany can truly be a great source of income as Hamburg pays better for magazine work than many of the other international markets. American editorial rates average $150 per day whereas German rates average (EURO) €200-400 per day. One of the greatest assets of the Hamburg market is how precise the German agencies are – no messing around. They tell models what they can and can't do along with how long to stay in the market and they are usually right.

■ MARKET PREFERENCES

❖ Models:

The market uses junior/teens. Some catalogues will look for very young junior/teens but they must be very professional and the opportunity is seldom. Plus/full-size is becoming more and more in demand, models are 1.75-1.80 cm (5'9"-5'11"), Continental size 42 (American 10). Clients use fashion models in great shape for athletic. Hamburg mainly uses adults. Women are preferably looking the ages of 18-40, 1.76-1.79 cm (5'9.5"-5'10.5"), Continental sizes 36-38 (American 4-6), no more than a C-cup, no larger than a 95 cm/37.5" hip; for runway 1.77-1.81 cm (5'9.75"-5'11.5"), Continental size 36 (American 4). Men are preferably looking the ages of 25-40, height is very important for men in Germany, 1.85-1.88 cm (6'1"-6'2"), must be a perfect Continental suit 50 (American 40); for runway 1.86-1.88 cm (6'1.5"-6'2"), Continental suit 50 (American 40). Models who have lots of freckles or moles will have limited opportunity for work in the market. The German market does have a few catalogues that like to book natural redheads with freckles. Most agencies in Hamburg only bring redheads in for 1 week to see clients. The market uses mainly Caucasian models with very little work for Black or light Black. Eastern looks are most preferable due to the population demographics of the city, but it must be a very, very light Eastern look. There is nothing more important than a great smile in Germany. About 95% of the market works full-time, unless attending school, parenting or holding a full-time job.

❖ Portfolios:

About 45% of the market is from direct bookings. Models that garner direct bookings are established with

MARCIA ROTHSCHILD MOELLERS — GERMANY / HAMBURG

a good amount of experience in different markets and their portfolios must reflect this. Models must have good, clean editorial and advertising/campaign. Direct bookings are strong; however, clients prefer to see models in person and the competition is fierce. Hamburg is a good market for new faces and they do not have to have a book filled with tearsheets, but they must have a good test book as well as be prepared to test while in the market. More importantly, new faces must be financially prepared to stay in the market in order to be developed. Established models must enter with experience from other top markets in catalogue and advertising. Clients consider four things paramount — perfect height and shape, a good smile, effortless movement in an array of poses, and the ability to sell what is being worn.

❖ Agencies Preferences:

Agencies like models that are smart, communicative, fun-loving, enjoy life and are positive. Make-up should be very, very light, extremely natural, and hair should be freshly washed with a good cut. Dress should be clean, fresh and modern. Jeans are okay; however, clothes should show off the body tastefully. New faces should plan on staying at least 4-6 weeks. Established models can remain on stay anywhere from 1-3 weeks and if the response is good, they can stay longer if they like.

TYPICAL BOOKINGS

❖ Length of Work:
Hourly, half day, full day and lots of multiple days.

❖ Type of Work:
Catalogue, editorial, campaign, very little athletic, lingerie, swimwear, small amount of runway and showroom, commercial print, TV commercial, and industrial.

❖ Busiest Seasons:
Hamburg is busy all year long - from February to November. December to January is the slowest time in the market.

TOP CLIENTS

Germany is the #1 producer of catalogues in the world. Hamburg's top clients include catalogues Otto Versand, Baur, Klingel, Wit Weiden, Veillion, Karstadt, Quelle and Neckermann, magazines, *Brigitte*, *Fur Sie*, as well as many top internationally recognized names, Triumph (lingerie/swimwear), Kaufhof (dept. store), and Joop! (designer).

COMPETITION

The competition is fierce due to the large amount of agencies. There are usually no casting lines as clients usually set appointments. At the longest, models wait 20 minutes.

PAY RATES

Print averages €100-350 per hour. Half

day €200-2,000. Full day €1,000-5,000. Advertising/campaign €1,500-15,000. Runway €100-500 per show. Hamburg produces many TV commercials. They are all non-union. Rates average €1,000-2,500 per day. Most TV commercials are package deals with residuals. These are calculated by percentages per country. For example, agencies will calculate 300% of the day rate for all of Germany.

❖ Agency Cuts:

For commissions, agencies deduct 25% for print, runway and TV. Taxes are deducted for foreign models dependent upon laws that change frequently. Germany is now in a flux with this. At the moment, models are responsible for their own taxes. Models should make sure to check with the agency before arrival. A "foreigner tax" is now deducted for TV commercials and can be up to 25%. The model can take the receipt of home and prove they have already paid taxes. At this time, for print and catalogue, agencies tax the model on commissions only. For example, the agencies deduct 25% for commissions on a €1,000 booking, and the model will be taxed 16% on the €250 commissioned.

❖ Agency Provides:

Most agencies advance accommodations for the first two weeks. If the model is working well, a longer accommodation advance will be considered. Dependent upon the model's situation, agencies may advance on composites and tests. Neither agencies nor clients offer money contracts.

LIVING

❖ Housing:

Agencies provide models' apartments via deals made with private owners of apartments or homes. Inexpensive accommodations are €90 per week. Moderate €120 per week. Cheap hotels average €100-300 per night.

❖ Transportation:

The airport is 20 minutes from downtown. Hamburg has inexpensive public transportation including train, metro/subway and bus. A lot of models walk the city as it is easy to navigate. A short ride in a taxi is €10. Traffic is not as bad as it is in New York City or Los Angeles, but it has its moments. Friday after work can be tough.

❖ Food & Entertainment:

An inexpensive lunch is €5 and an inexpensive dinner is €8-10. Being one of the bigger cities in Germany, Hamburg has it all, including cinema, theater, bars, nightclubs, music venues, museums, discotheques and great restaurants.

REQUISITES

The work visa situation seems to either be simple or complicated, dependent upon the mood of government to government relationships between Germany and each individual country. Models should request information from their agency before arrival.

WEATHER

The weather from November to February can be cold and quite rainy with some snow. The weather is very unpredictable into May. Summer through early fall is beautiful.

CURRENCY

As of January 2005:
US$10 = €7.69
C$10 = €6.20

MARCIA'S TIPS

Models must be open-minded, patient and cannot expect fast results even if agencies only bring them in for a little while to see clients. Models have to stick it out in Hamburg and keep persevering, especially for the first week or two. Hamburg is an old harbor city with beautiful surroundings – lots of parks, trees, rivers and lakes. Many models walk or bike around the city and find it easy to navigate. 100% of the Hamburg fashion market speaks English and the younger people of Hamburg do as well. Communication is a little more difficult with the older citizens. No model should come to Hamburg without touring the fabulous castles and festivals in Germany! They are equally amazing.

PORTUGAL
LISBON

Lisbon is one of the smallest markets in Europe. It is also one of the newer hotspots in the European fashion scene. Lisbon has a metropolitan area population of nearly 3,000,000. There are approximately 6 fashion agencies located in the city. The Lisbon fashion industry has only been around about 25 years and already touts 15 fashion designers. Lisbon has its runway Fashion Week twice a year, and the market also has several very good Portuguese magazines. There are not many money clients in Portugal. The best thing about Lisbon is the good, inexpensive testing that allows models to build their portfolios the easiest way possible before stepping into the larger markets of Europe.

MARKET PREFERENCES

❖ Models:

The market uses junior/teens (only local models), athletic (using regular fashion models in good shape), and primarily adults. Women are preferably looking the ages of 18-26, 1.75-1.80 cm (5'9"-5'11"), Continental sizes 34-36 (American 2-4), no more than a B-cup, no more than a 89 cm/35" hip; for runway 1.76-1.81 cm (5'9.5"-5'11.5"), Continental size 34 (American 2). Men are preferably looking the ages of 20-30, 1.82-1.86 cm (America 5'11.75""-6'1.5"), Continental suit 50 (American 40); for runway 1.88-1.92 cm (6'2"-6'3.5"), Continental suits 48-50 (American 38-40). The market uses all ethnicities. Smiles are important for catalogue and depend on the editorial story. The Portuguese fashion market likes working with foreign models. 75% of foreign models work full-time. Many local models combine modeling with school. 30% of the entire market works full-time.

❖ Portfolios:

Less than 5% of the market is from direct bookings. Most of these bookings are garnered by Eastern European looks with very solid top level editorial. Clients prefer to see models in person and new faces can start in the market with very good polaroids/snapshots if they have the right look and test thereafter. Established models should enter with a balanced book between fashion and relatable advertising tearsheets.

❖ Agencies Preferences:

Agencies like models that are very friendly, cooperative and willing to work. Clients do not like models that complain and want them to be polite, professional and not at all stiff, but instead very expressive with their body language. For castings, hair should be clean and natural. Make-up should be composed of a little mascara and lip gloss, foundation to cover blemishes and all should be undetectable. Dress should be casual yet fashionable. Agencies prefer models to remain on stay for 6-8 weeks.

TYPICAL BOOKINGS

❖ Length of Work:

Full day and multiple days. There are lots of multiple days for Fashion Week and as well as for advertising.

❖ Type of Work:

Catalogue, editorial, athletic, lingerie, swimwear, runway, commercial print, lots of TV commercial, not as strong for film, trade show, store informal, showroom and industrial.

❖ Busiest Seasons:

The busiest times are from March to July and from mid-September to Christmas. The slowest times are January and August.

TOP CLIENTS

Top clients include communication companies Vodafone, TMN and Optimus, Ympala (major magazine publisher), L'Oreal, Sonae (dept. store conglomerate), Fatima Lopes (designer), Moda Lisboa (fashion week for designers), Euro RSCG (ad agency), Ford (automotive), Marques & Soares (catalogue), and Portugal Fashion (fashion week for the industry).

COMPETITION

The competition is light in the market but some castings can be as long as 3-4 hours.

PAY RATES

Print averages (EURO) €175-2,000 per full day. Advertising/campaign €350-3,500. Runway €175-2,000 per day per show. TV/film is all non-union in Portugal. TV commercial rates can run from a small part for €300-350 to a big part for €2,000-2,500.

❖ Agency Cuts:

For commissions, agencies deduct 20% for print and TV/film, and 10% for runway. Agencies do not deduct taxes for USA models who have submitted the IRS Tax Form 8802 to request the IRS Tax Form 6166 and Canadian models with the Fiscal Attestation. Otherwise, they must deduct 20% for taxes.

❖ Agency Provides:

Agencies will usually advance accommodations, composites, laser copies of books, testing and pocket money, depending on the situation. They do not advance airfare. Agencies do not offer money contracts; however, some clients will.

LIVING

❖ Housing:

Most agencies have models' apartments. Inexpensive accommodations average €400-600 per month. Moderate average €700-800 per month. Cheap hotels average €80-150 per day.

MODEL MARKETS OF THE WORLD
LISBON PORTUGAL

❖ Transportation:

Lisbon's airport is inside the city and it takes no more than 20 minutes to get anywhere downtown. The city has inexpensive public transportation including train, subway and bus. A short ride in a taxi is €4-5. Traffic is light.

❖ Food & Entertainment:

An inexpensive lunch is €4-5 and an inexpensive dinner is €10. The city is filled with things to see – tons of amazing churches, lots of monuments dating back to the 15th century, art galleries and museums. The nightlife is filled with cinemas, discotheques, nightclubs and interesting restaurants.

REQUISITES

A work visa is not required for foreigners. Models enter as a tourist and can remain on stay for up to 3 months without a work visa.

WEATHER

The temperatures can be very hot and rarely ever too cold. It never snows in the city, only North in the mountains.

CURRENCY

As of January 2005:
US$10 = €7.69
C$10 = €6.20

MARCIA'S TIPS

Portuguese people are very friendly and it is easy to make acquaintances. Models should take advantage of how much there is to see historically. Lisbon is a nocturnal city and there are things to do around the clock. Models should never comment negatively on jobs. It's a small market and everyone talks to each other. If it gets around Lisbon that someone is a complainer, work for that model could come to a dead halt. Portuguese clients feel very strongly that models are there to do a job and that job is not as a commentator. It is not hard to navigate Lisbon because the young population usually learns English in school or from the movies.

ENGLAND
LONDON

London is a large market and is considered one of the most prestigious in the world along with Paris and New York City. With a metropolitan area population of over 12,000,000, there are approximately 25 fashion agencies in the city. London is a highly creative market with amazing editorial opportunities from internationally renowned Vogue and Elle to young, cutting edge magazines. The town is full of artistic, hip photographers and amazing behind the scenes creative people. Books are not only developed in London, they are superbly orchestrated. Most new faces that put the time and energy into this fabulous market can practically launch into any other market with success.

MARKET PREFERENCES

❖ Models:

The market uses junior/teens (starting at age 15), some plus/full-size, athletic (fashion models only), and adults. Women are preferably looking the ages of 18-45, 5'8"-5'11.5", UK Sizes 8-12 (American 2-6), no more than a C-cup; no larger than a 36" hip; for runway, 5'9"-5'11.5", UK sizes 8-10 (American 2-4). Men are preferably looking the ages of 18-45, 5'11"-6'2", UK Suit 38-40 (American 38-40); for runway, 6'0"-6'2", UK Suit 38-40 (American 38-40). The market uses all ethnicities. Smiles are important for catalogue and editorial. The majority of the market works full-time with the exception being those models that are students or parents.

❖ Portfolios:

30% of the market is from direct bookings. Established models garner these bookings with strong portfolios filled with editorial and advertising/campaign or they are from repeat bookings. Clients prefer to see models and experience is not necessary for new faces; however, they must have either very good polaroids/snapshots or testing. Established models must have portfolios that have editorial and advertising/campaign specified to marketability.

❖ Agencies Preferences:

Agencies prefer models that are independent, confident, polite, modern, friendly, open-minded and patient. For castings, hair and make-up should be simple and fresh. Dress should be urban/street, young and fresh. Agencies prefer models to remain on stay a minimum of 1 month or longer, dependent upon the level of development.

TYPICAL BOOKINGS

❖ Length of Work:

Hourly, full day and some multiple days.

MODEL MARKETS OF THE WORLD
LONDON ENGLAND

❖ Type of Work:

Catalogue, editorial, campaign, athletic, lingerie, swimwear, runway, commercial print, TV commercial, film, infomercial, showroom and industrial.

❖ Busiest Seasons:

The market is busy all year long. Heavier times are during the runway show seasons in January/February and September. Slower times are national holidays and Christmas to New Year's.

TOP CLIENTS

Top clients include magazines Vogue, I-D, Arena, Marie Claire and Elle, advertising agencies Saatchi & Saatchi and J. Walter Thompson, department stores Marks & Spencer and Next, and catalogues Freeman's and Gus.

COMPETITION

The competition is very fierce in London. Casting lines can be hours long because models are competing to work with some of London's top clients.

PAY RATES

Print averages £75-100 per hour. Full day averages £350-2,500 and up per day. Advertising/Campaign £2,000-1,500,000. Runway £305-5,000 per show. England has a TV/film actor's union called Equity. Models become part of this union if they have a speaking part. London does not have separate commercial agencies from fashion agencies, as sometimes seen in North America. TV commercials are negotiated on a basic studio day rate guided by the United Kingdom Repeat Fees and average £350-500 per day rate plus residuals.

❖ Agency Cuts:

Commissions are called an "agency supplement" in England. Agencies deduct 20% for print, runway and TV/film and they are required to deduct taxes for foreign models.

❖ Agency Provides:

Dependent upon the situation, most agencies advance accommodations, airfare, composites, website, laser copies of books, tests and very rarely pocket money. Agencies do offer money contracts; however, some clients will for exclusivity.

LIVING

❖ Housing:

Most agencies provide models' apartments. Inexpensive accommodations average £400-500 per month. Moderate average £600-800 per month. Cheap hotels average £80 per night.

❖ Transportation:

The airport is 45 minutes from downtown. London has inexpensive public transportation including metro/subway and bus. A travel card is £22 per week. A short ride in a taxi is £8. Traffic is busy most of the time.

ENGLAND LONDON

❖ Food & Entertainment:

An inexpensive lunch is £8 and an inexpensive dinner is £15-20. The restaurants are multi-cultural in cuisine. There really is not much traditional English food, unless one wants to eat fish & chips, which the agencies do not recommend. There is a lot of sightseeing in the London area, from amazing castles to incredible music festivals to prestigious art galleries and museums. The nightlife is unique in that bars close at 11:00 p.m., nightclubs close between 2-4 a.m. London has a big music scene as well as a big, expensive high end bar/lounge scene which most of the industry frequents.

REQUISITES

A work visa is necessary for foreign models and London agencies arrange this for their models beforehand.

WEATHER

London has a good amount of rain and grey skies. The summers are quite beautiful with more sunshine.

CURRENCY

As of January 2005:
US$ = £5.35
C$10 = £4.33

MARCIA'S TIPS

North American models really love London. It may be because it is easier to navigate the city in English, but most likely it is because of the level of culture in Britain. It is unique, very intelligent and verbose. Brits are very friendly and helpful, and they love humor. Models should be prepared to take it and to dish it out, but only in the most appropriate of situations. Agencies and clients alike enjoy models that are smart, fashion savvy and like working in the industry. London has some laid back factors but will not tolerate a lack of class or professionalism. London is a very cool city with a highly creative, success-oriented work ethic and models should be prepared to be the same.

SPAIN
MADRID

Madrid is a smaller medium size market with a metropolitan population area of 5,250,000 and there are approximately 5 fashion agencies. Madrid is known as the center for top magazine publishers in Spain, including magazines Vanidad, Alter Ego, Down Town, and Vogue. Consequently, this manifests Madrid as a very good market for editorial. The Madrid market has catalogue and TV commercial even though they are not at the same level as Barcelona. Cibeles Fashion Week takes place every February and September and is the big runway event of Spain with lots of shows and parties. Madrid is an excellent place for new faces to build their portfolios as editorial is the mainstay of the market. Madrid is the celebration city of Spain. Not only is it Spain's capital, but it is also a city that is truly alive and festive with a lot of charm.

■ MARKET PREFERENCES

❖ Models:

The market uses junior/teens (ages 15 and up), athletic (using only fashion models that are in super shape), and adults. Women are preferably looking the ages of 18-30, 1.74-1.80 cm (5'8.5"-5'11"), Continental sizes 36-38 (American 4-6), no more than a C-cup (B-cup is preferred); no larger than 89 cm/35" hip; for runway 1.75-1.80 cm (5'9"-5'11"), Continental sizes 36-38 (American 4-6). Men are preferably looking the ages of 18-35, 1.83-1.90 cm (6'0"-6'3"), Continental suit 50-52 (American 40-42); for runway 1.85-1.90 (6'1"-6'3"), Continental suit 50-52 (American 40-42). The Madrid market prefers blonde models with blue eyes but it's a good market for brown and red hair as well. Freckles and well placed beauty marks can be seen as an advantage by individualizing the model. The market mainly books Caucasian models with European looks. Madrid is a difficult market for all other ethnicities. Smiles are important for catalogue but not as much for editorial. 25% of the market works full-time.

❖ Portfolios:

50% of the market is from direct bookings. Direct bookings are either repeat bookings or garnered by models with strong portfolios including editorial and advertising/campaign. Clients prefer to see a model in person; however, if a model has a strong portfolio, it is not necessary. Experience is not required for new faces. If a model is perfect for the market, polaroids/snapshots will suffice to see clients. Otherwise, new faces will need to have good testing in their portfolios. Established models should arrive in Madrid with nice editorial from well known photographers in order to work for higher level editorial and advertising/campaign clients.

❖ Agencies Preferences:

Agencies prefer models to have a nice attitude about life, people and the business. For castings, models should have natural hair and wear minimal to no make-up. Some castings are job specific. The market requires classic as well as edgy and trendy models. Dress should be casual and clean, unless otherwise specified. Agencies prefer models to remain on stay for at least 1 month. This allows enough time for the models to see the clients and start to work. The first week is composed of castings to meet all the clients and by the second week, usually the model is working.

TYPICAL BOOKINGS

❖ Length of Work:

Half day and full day. Direct bookings are a full day or more.

❖ Type of Work:

Editorial, runway, catalogue, commercial print, TV commercial and in very rare cases of showroom and industrial. Non-European citizens cannot do TV commercial or film in Spain, except under very specific circumstances.

❖ Busiest Seasons:

The market is consistent year round. The busiest times are February, September and from November to just before Christmas. The slowest time is the month of August when everyone goes on holiday.

TOP CLIENTS

Top clients include magazines Vanidad, Vogue, Alter Ego and Down Town, department stores El Corté Inglés, Zara Mango and Lowe, Sybilla (designer), Zindara Producciones, and Cibeles Fashion Week catering to all of Spain's designers.

COMPETITION

The competition is strong but not as difficult as it is in the larger markets. There are usually no casting lines but occasionally they can last as long as a couple of hours.

PAY RATES

Print averages (EURO) €400-1,000 per half day. Full day €600-3,000. Advertising/campaign €2,000-20,000. Runway €350-3,000. TV/film is non-union only. The TV/film (see note in Type of Work) day rate, depending on the model, can average €2,000-6,000 with additional usage fees.

❖ Agency Cuts:

For commissions, agencies deduct 20% for print, runway and TV/film. Agencies deduct 25% for taxes from foreign models.

❖ Agency Provides:

Dependent upon the caliber of the model, agencies will advance airfare and pocket money. Agencies usually advance

MODEL MARKETS OF THE WORLD
MADRID SPAIN

accommodations, composites and laser copies of books. Neither agencies nor clients offer money contracts.

LIVING

❖ Housing:

Most agencies provide models' apartments. Inexpensive accommodations average €17 per night. Moderate €20 per night. Cheap hotels average €100.

❖ Transportation:

The airport is 15 minutes from downtown. Madrid has public transportation including metro/subway and bus. Agencies say the metro is fast, fabulous and cheap at €6 for 10 tickets (that can also be used on the bus). A short ride in a taxi is €4. Traffic in Madrid is heavy and noisy.

❖ Food & Entertainment:

An inexpensive lunch including drinks and dessert is €10 and an inexpensive dinner is €25. Madrid offers so much – everything from museums and cinemas to wonderful restaurants and nightclubs. The city is well known as "the place where nobody sleeps". Sports fans will love the city for its "futbol" (soccer) lead by legendary Real Madrid, which is one of Europe's top teams.

REQUISITES

Work visas are not necessary for the majority of foreign models. Models enter as tourists through customs. Spanish law defines the model as self-employed, yet the present immigration legislation does not accept a foreign self-employed request for a working visa. Non-EU (European) citizens cannot work any TV.

WEATHER

Madrid is 650 meters above sea level, which makes the city dry and very hot during the summer and very cold during the Winter. During the cold season there are rare possibilities of snow.

CURRENCY

As of January 2005:
US$ = £5.35
C$10 = £4.33

MARCIA'S TIPS

Madrid is a very intimate market and models really enjoy remaining on stay. The only problem that most agents claim is that the clients sometimes pay late, due in part, to a typical Spanish mentality of "mañana" – everything can be done tomorrow instead of today. Madrid is renowned for its architecture and its museums. The Prado Museum is considered one of the best in the world hosting artists such as Rubens, Goya, Velásquez, Picasso, Bosco, and "El Greco", just to name a few. About 30% of the city speaks English. It is wise for models to learn some basic Spanish to navigate the city. The "Madrileños" (people from Madrid) welcome foreigners warmly, and there is a popular saying about the city's impact on visitors, "From Madrid to heaven".

ITALY
MILAN

Milan is a larger medium size market in Europe and has a population of 2.5 million with approximately 25 fashion agencies. The market itself is actually larger than New York City and Paris, but is considered secondary due to the fact that the elite clients of Italy take most of their business to Paris, New York City, London and Hollywood. Italy is the leader of the textile industry with Milan as its fashion capital. The market has many magazines, fashion shows and campaigns comparable to Paris and New York City. Milan is well-known for its large, high paying hosiery, lingerie & swimwear industry. The market is particularly known for the creative development of new faces.

MARKET PREFERENCES

❖ Models:

The market uses junior/teens, but Italian legislation has strict laws regarding minors under the age of 16 working in Italy. The market is primarily focused on adult fashion models. Women are preferably looking the ages of 18-25, 1.70-1.83 cm (5'7"-6'0"), Italian sizes 40-42 (American 4-6), no larger than a C-cup, no larger than a 91 cm/36" hip; for runway 1.75-1.83 cm (5'9"-6'0"), Italian 38-40 (American 2-4). Men are preferably looking the ages of 18-30, 1.83-1.88 cm (6'0"-6'2"), Italian suit 58 (American 40); for runway 1.83-1.88 cm (6'0"-6'2"), Italian suit 58 (American 40). The market likes natural looks. Hair color must look natural, all body parts must look natural, and everything must be as natural as possible. Too many freckles or moles can be a problem with lingerie and swimwear. The market uses very few ethnicities due to the demographics of buyers and they can use Black female models but not too dark. They can use Asian models but not too Asian. Ethnics should have some features that are closer to European. White or olive skin is fine. Smiles are important for catalogue and editorial. 90% of models in the market are focused full-time on the development of their careers and the only models that work part-time are usually students or residents.

❖ Portfolios:

40% of the market is from direct bookings. Direct booking portfolios that work best are big with lots of editorial and campaigns, or portfolios that specialize in hosiery, lingerie and swimwear showing a really beautiful body via good testing and tearsheets that signify experience from other markets. Clients prefer to see models, especially for shows and TV commercials as well as new faces. Very often new faces arrive with no portfolios and clients want to book them from polaroids/snapshots since they are fresh and

MODEL MARKETS OF THE WORLD
MILAN TALY

new. If new faces come back to the market, the response may not be as favorable since clients have already seen them. To remain on stay, established models will need good editorial throughout their portfolio to ensure work.

❖ Agencies Preferences:

Agencies prefer models with a strong personality, lots of energy, independent and very social. For castings, they prefer absolutely no make-up. The most natural are the most welcome. Clothing should be casual with a touch of style. Models should show some fashion flair with a nice pair of shoes or a nice belt – something that differentiates them from a student and makes them a model. Agencies prefer models to remain on stay in the market for three months.

TYPICAL BOOKINGS

❖ Length of Work:

Very few half day with the majority being full day. Milan has a good amount of multiple day bookings.

❖ Type of Work:

Catalogue (a good amount), athletic (not as much), editorial, campaign, commercial/advertising print, TV commercial, film (not much for models), trade show, informal, showroom (a good amount), and industrial. Milan has many bookings for hosiery, lingerie and swimwear. There is lots of runway with Milan hosting the prêt-a-porter shows and Rome hosting the haute couture shows twice a year.

❖ Busiest Seasons:

Milan is very busy year round. The busiest times are during the shows from the end of January until the middle of February and in September. Milan is also very busy from June to July and December. The slowest times are March, April, November, and holidays.

TOP CLIENTS

Top clients include swimwear and lingerie clients Calzedonia and La Perla, designers Armani, Versace, Dolce Gabbana, Fendi, Missoni, magazines Grazia and Amica, Wella (hair care), as well as many catalogues and brochures of bridal, leather, furs, jewelry, hosiery, lingerie, swimwear and accessories.

COMPETITION

The competition is very, very fierce in Milan. In Paris and New York City castings are organized in a more individual way. In Milan, models must be prepared for huge castings where hundreds of models may show up, even those who don't fit the clients' criteria. Sometimes models can wait as long as 1-2 hours. The competition is deemed worthy due to the opportunity to meet Italy's great clients.

PAY RATES

Print averages (EURO) €100-300 per hour. Half day averages €400-800. Full day averages €1,000-3,000. Advertising/cam-

MARCIA ROTHSCHILD MOELLERS
ITALY MILAN

paign average €2,000-20,000. Runway averages €1,000-15,000 per show. TV/film is non-union only in Italy. TV commercials, dependent upon the model, average €8,000-10,000 per day plus additional usage for the amount of countries it airs in and how long it runs.

❖ Agency Cuts:

For commissions, agencies deduct 30% for print, runway and TV/film. Non-European residents are responsible for their own taxes. USA models must submit the IRS Tax Form 8802 to request the IRS Tax Form 6166 form and Canadian models must bring the Fiscal Attestation in order to avoid an additional 20% in taxes being deducted.

❖ Agency Provides:

Dependent upon the potential of the model, agencies will advance accommodations, airfare, composites, laser copies, tests and weekly expenses. Agencies do not offer money contracts; however, sometimes clients will.

LIVING

❖ Housing:

Most agencies provide models' apartments. Inexpensive accommodations average €750-1,000 per month. Moderate accommodations average €2,500. Cheap hotels average €120-200 per night.

❖ Transportation:

There are two airports near Milan. Linate is approximately 30 minutes from downtown. Malpensa is about 40-45 minutes. Milan has very easy, inexpensive public transportation including subway, bus and tram. A short ride in a taxi is €12-15. Traffic in the market is moderately busy.

❖ Food & Entertainment:

An inexpensive lunch is €10 and an inexpensive dinner is €15. The city is full of museums, jazz and discotheques, lots of good food. The nights are very nice and full of things to do.

REQUISITES

No work visa is required as long as the model is at least 16-years-old. If the model is under 16 years, a visa is required which is very, very difficult to get, and most agencies will not bother. For U.S. citizens, the IRS Tax Form 8802 to request the IRS Tax Form 6166 is required, and for Canadians the Fiscal Attestation from the Canada Customs and Revenue is required to avoid having taxes deducted.

WEATHER

It never gets very cold in Milan; however, it is very hot in the summer and rainy between February and April – models should carry an umbrella.

CURRENCY

As of January 2005:
US$ = £5.35
C$10 = £4.33

MODEL MARKETS OF THE WORLD
MILAN, ITALY

MARCIA'S TIPS

Milan is a discovery day by day. The people are very engaging and will provide models with anything they need as they open up to the beauty of Milan and Italy. There is a lot of great food, entertainment and tourism to discover. The majority of the fashion business speaks English but not the average Italian, with only about 30% of the population speaking English. Models should bring a translation book. Many agents think models arrive afraid and worried they will have problems with people on the street. Milan is a very civilized town but it is a big city and can have the same problems that any major metropolis has. In truth, it's a wondrous city, with beautiful parks and expressive people.

GERMANY
MUNICH

Munich is a smaller medium size market with a metropolitan area population of 1,925,000 and approximately 10 fashion agencies. German fashion agencies view the entire country as its client base. Germany is the largest catalogue market in the world. Munich is known for having a larger amount of junior/teen work than the other markets in Germany. Models enjoy working in Munich because it is the most southern geographic market in Germany closest to Italy, which makes it very easy for models to go back and forth from the larger market of Milan. Outside of its organized business manner, Munich is very relaxed with a good attitude and there is a larger young population because it is a university city.

MARKET PREFERENCES

❖ Models:

The market uses junior/teens (preferably girls ages 15-18, boys 18-20), plus/full-size (1.76-1.80 cm/5'9.25"-5'11", Continental sizes 40-44/American 10-14), athletic (only fashion models), and adults. Women are preferably looking the ages of 18-25, 1.73-1.80 cm (5'8"-5'11"), Continental sizes 36 (American 4) no larger than a C-cup (B-cup is perfect), no larger than a 86 cm/34" hip; for runway 1.78-1.83 cm (5'10"-6'0"), Continental sizes 34-36 (American 2-4). Men are preferably looking the ages of 20-40, 1.83-1.88 cm (6'0"-6'2"), Continental suit 50 (American 40, Long is good), Continental suit 52/American 42 is too difficult; for runway 1.83-1.88 cm (6'0"-6'2", Continental suit 50 (American 40). The market uses primarily Caucasian models and very rarely Black, Light Black or Eastern. Smiles are absolutely essential for catalogue but not as important for editorial. Clients prefer models with really good bodies. 80% of the models in the market work full-time.

❖ Portfolios:

60% of the market is from direct bookings. Portfolios must be very well built for direct bookings. Adults must have editorial, international work from Paris, Milan, London or New York City, with some international campaigns and it cannot just be a test book. Juniors are different and can have a small portfolio with good testing in order to direct book the junior magazines. Clients prefer to see models in person unless they are already a top model. New faces can come into the market if super perfect with just polaroids/snapshots alone. Otherwise, some testing is needed to enter. Established models must have a strong portfolio and catalogue work will not help their portfolio in Munich unless it is high end from clients such as Neiman Marcus. Established models must have a good range

MODEL MARKETS OF THE WORLD
MUNICH GERMANY

of editorial, advertising and campaign to start working.

❖ Agencies Preferences:

Agencies prefer models that are outgoing, very friendly and have the ability to sell themselves at castings and bookings. Clients like models that are open, fresh and smiling. Clients prefer to see clean, washed hair and very light make-up that looks like none. Dress should be clean and nice but not over-dressed. Agencies prefer new face junior/teens to remain on stay in the market for 2-3 months for development. For established models, they can come for as little as a week to see the clients and then move onto another market.

■ TYPICAL BOOKINGS

❖ Length of Work:

Hourly, half day, full day and lots of multiple days.

❖ Type of Work:

Catalogue, athletic, editorial, campaign, lingerie, swimwear, runway, commercial print, TV commercial, trade show, store informal, showroom, and industrial.

❖ Busiest Seasons:

Munich is busy all year long. It is busiest from February to April and from August to October. The slowest time is January.

■ TOP CLIENTS

Top clients include catalogues Otto Versand, Neckermann, and Quella, department stores Karstadt and Kaufhof, designers Hugo Boss, Strenesse and Jil Sander, and magazines German Vogue and German Elle.

■ COMPETITION

Competition is very fierce because so many models compete for these top catalogue clients and editorial. Models do not deal with long casting lines and most castings are by appointment only.

■ PAY RATES

Print averages (EURO) €150-350 per hour. Half day €400-1,000. Full day €800-5,000. Advertising/campaign €300-50,000. Runway €300-10,000 per show. TV is all non-union. Agencies calculate a day rate, dependent upon the caliber of the model, with the average for a new model at €1,000 to a top, top model at €20,000. Most TV commercials are package deals with residuals. These are calculated by percentages per country. For example, agencies will calculate 300% of the day rate for all of Germany.

❖ Agency Cuts:

For commissions, agencies deduct 25% for print, runway and TV. Taxes are deducted for foreign models based on laws that change frequently. Germany is now in flux with this. At the moment, models are responsible for their own taxes. Models should make sure to check with the agency before arrival. A "foreigner tax" is now deducted for TV commercials and can be up to 25%. The model can take the receipt home to prove they have already paid taxes. Currently for print and catalogue, agencies tax the model on commissions only. For example, the agencies deduct 25% for commissions on a €1,000 booking, and the model will be taxed 16% on the €250 commissioned.

❖ Agency Provides:

Agencies usually advance accommodations and they will advance on airfare; however, it is very rare for them to do so. They usually advance composites, laser copies of books and tests. Depending on the level and potential of the model, they will sometimes advance pocket money. Agencies do not offer money contracts; however, some clients will.

LIVING

❖ Housing:

Most agencies provide models' apartments. Inexpensive accommodations average €80-120 per week. Moderate €100-150 per week. Cheap hotels average €35-200 per day.

❖ Transportation:

The airport is about 30 minutes by train from downtown. Munich's public transportation system is well established including train, metro/subway and bus. A weekly pass for all transportation is about €12. A short ride in a taxi is €15. Traffic is crazy in Munich. It is not quite as crazy as New York City traffic – just busy, but safe.

❖ Food & Entertainment:

An inexpensive lunch is €3-5 and an inexpensive dinner is €10-20. Munich is very nice and entertaining. The university life of the city leads to a lot of exhibitions, museums, art galleries, cinemas in different languages, sightseeing tours including Bavarian castles, and a great night life including bars, clubs and restaurants. There are lots of things to do.

REQUISITES

The work visa situation seems to either be simple or complicated, dependent upon the mood of government to |government relationships between Germany and other individual countries. Models should request information from their agency before arrival.

WEATHER

Cold winters. Nice summers.

CURRENCY

As of January 2005:
US$ = £5.35
C$10 = £4.33

MARCIA'S TIPS

Clients do not like models that are not on time. If the client says 9:00 a.m., the model must be there by 9:00 a.m. Everything is very organized in Munich and models should follow the rules. The Germans like hard working people, and to succeed in Munich models have to be just that. Munich is really safe. People are very

MODEL MARKETS OF THE WORLD
MUNICH GERMANY

friendly and helpful so models should not hesitate to ask for help. 100% of the fashion business speaks English, and about 70-80% of the city does because there are so many young people learning to speak English in school.

NORWAY
OSLO

The market in Norway is rather small, and Oslo itself is a tiny city. With a metropolitan area population of just over 500,000, there are approximately 2 fashion agencies catering to the city. Most of Norway's bigger clients travel to South Africa for seasonal shoots because they love the beautiful locations. The Norwegian market mainly books local models and foreign models may only find working there worthwhile if they have family ties or personal relationships in Norway. Oslo is working on building up its own fashion market by establishing Oslo Fashion Week. The market books editorial and relatable looks. Oslo was included in the book because the European and NY agents recommend this little gem of a market that continually produces top models. Hopefully, the market will continue to grow due to this.

MARKET PREFERENCES

❖ Models:

The Oslo market uses petite (1.65-1.70 cm/5'5"-5'7", Continental sizes 32-34/American 0-2), plus/full-size 1.75-1.80 cm/5'9"-5'11", Continental size 40/American size 8), and adults. Women are preferably looking the ages of 18-24, 1.75-180 cm (5'9"-5'11"), Continental sizes 36-38 (American 4-6), no larger than a B-cup, no more than a 96 cm/38" hip; for runway 1.75-1.80 cm (5'9"-5'11"), Continental sizes 36-38 (American 4-6). Men are preferably looking the ages of 18-28, 1.80-1.88 cm (5'11"-6'2"), Continental suit 50 (American 40); for runway 1.84-1.88 cm (6'.05"-6'2"), Continental suit 50 (American 40). The market uses mainly Caucasians due to its demographics, and very little Blacks. Smiles are important for catalogue but not for editorial. Established models cannot work full-time in the market and must combine it with other larger markets.

❖ Portfolios:

The Oslo market direct books less than 5%. These bookings are usually garnered by a top model that has caught the client's eye or are from repeat bookings. Clients prefer to see models in person. If models come to see clients while visiting family and then leave to base elsewhere in Europe, it is important to note that clients may book them direct from where they are based, but will not pay for airfare or accommodations Norway is known for developing great new faces. If new faces are not already represented, they can send good polaroids/snapshots to agencies. Established models must have an excellent portfolio with a resume of experience.

MODEL MARKETS OF THE WORLD
OSLO, NORWAY

❖ Agencies Preferences:

Agencies like models that are modern, well-educated, a little laid back and easy to get along with. For castings, hair and make-up need to be natural. Dress can be trendy with a natural look. Models do not have to dress up to see clients but they must look clean and fresh with a working knowledge of fashion. The clients like models that are cool and relaxed like the nature of the city. Models do not come to remain on stay, but if in Oslo for other reasons, agencies can make appointments for them to see clients.

■ TYPICAL BOOKINGS

❖ Length of Work:
Half day and full day.

❖ Type of Work:
Very little catalogue, some runway, lots of commercial print, TV commercial, lots of film (Norwegians only), and a little bit of trade show, store informal and showroom.

❖ Busiest Seasons:
The market is busiest from April to June. It is slowest in July.

■ TOP CLIENTS
Top clients include You (clothing), Varner (men's store), Vik Vok (dept. store), Cubus (women's clothing), magazines Norwegian Elle, Tique and Fjords, ad agencies Kitchen and Virtual Garden, and Nina Lisbeth (designer).

■ COMPETITION
The competition is not easy because there are a lot of models to choose from locally in Norway. The clients would like to use new models but they will not want to pay to bring them in. Casting lines are never long.

■ PAY RATES
Print averages (NORWEGIAN KRONE) NOK 7,000-15,000 per half day. Full day NOK 10,000-20,000. Advertising/campaign NOK 5,000-30,000. Runway NOK 2,000-4,000. TV commercials are all non-union in Norway, averaging NOK 10,000-60,000.

❖ Agency Cuts:
For commissions, agencies deduct 33%. For taxes, foreign models apply for a card from the Tax Authority where they must earn a certain amount before having to pay taxes. After the amount is reached, agencies must deduct 15% for taxes.

❖ Agency Provides:
Due to the small client base and size of the market, agencies do not advance anything. Neither agencies nor clients offer money contracts.

■ LIVING

❖ Housing:
Agencies do not have models' apartments as models do not remain on stay. Inexpensive accommodations average NOK 2,000 per month. Moderate NOK

5,000 per month. Cheap hotels average NOK 700 per month.

❖ Transportation:

The airport is 30 minutes from downtown. Oslo has expensive public transportation including, train, subway/metro and bus. A short ride in a taxi is NOK 80. Traffic is not as bad as New York City, but can be very heavy.

❖ Food & Entertainment:

An inexpensive lunch is NOK 80 and an inexpensive dinner is NOK 160. Entertainment is very Norwegian, especially in the city. Oslo has cinema, cabaret, the music is very good, and Norway has some of the best festivals in the world. There are lots of restaurants and cafes, as well as many nightclubs. The Norwegians likes to party.

REQUISITES

Work visas are not necessary to enter, but models must get a work permit upon arrival or send an invoice listing all their work in Norway.

WEATHER

The weather is very similar to upstate New York or Minnesota.

CURRENCY

As of January 2005:
US$10 = NOK 63.22
C$10 = NOK 51.26

MARCIA'S TIPS

If models choose to live in Oslo, they will need to have another flexible job to make ends meet. The market is very light and laid back. Norwegians are notorious for making jokes in the middle of a serious business meeting. Models should not get angry if people make fun of them as Norwegians are just joking around and it is ingrained in their culture. Norwegians don't take themselves too seriously and they don't want anyone else to either. Models must be open-minded and prepared to experience a different culture. Many Norwegians speak English as there are a lot of English programs on TV. About 75% of Oslo speaks English very well, so models shouldn't have a problem navigating the city.

FRANCE
PARIS

Paris is the "New York City" of Europe. This large market has a population of over 2,500,000 and covers a metropolitan area of over 11,000,000 with approximately 20 fashion agencies in the city. In certain ways, Paris surpasses New York City with its cutting edge on creativity and fashion. Paris is actually a conglomerate of everything. The market uses all types of models from high end couture to more relatable, next door types. It's not just about the cover of Vogue in Paris. There are huge advertising dollars to be made in Paris. It is an amazing city, alive well into the night, and it's sometimes difficult to keep focused and professional because entering an agency is opening the door to the entire Parisian fashion world with its promotional parties and other evening events. There isn't a model that can make it to the top without having worked the fabulous market of Paris.

■ MARKET PREFERENCES

❖ Models:

The market use junior/teens, but France also has a law that models under the age of 16 are not allowed to work without a full-time chaperone, severely limited hours, and very difficult to obtain paperwork. The market has work for athletic and adult models, but does not have enough work for petite, plus/full-size, or big & tall. Women are preferably looking the ages of 18-25, 170-183 cm (5'7"-6'0"), Continental sizes 34-38 (American 2-6), no more than a C-cup, no larger than a 92 cm/36.5" hip; for runway 176-181 cm (5'9.5"-5'11.5"), Continental sizes 34-38 (American 2-6), no more than a B-cup, no larger than a 90 cm/35.5" hip. Men are preferably looking the ages of 17-40, 180-188 cm (5'11"-6'2"), Continental suit 50 (American 40), for runway 180-188 cm (5'11"-6'2"), continental suit 50 (American 40). The market uses all ethnicities, but the work can be limited, compared to the amount of work for Caucasians. Smiles are very important for catalogue but not as much for editorial. 90% of the models work full-time.

❖ Portfolios:

20% of the market is from direct bookings and these are garnered by models with portfolios full of tearsheets that are indicative of who the model really is - some clean beauty shots, good body shots, some smiles, different angles and attitudes. Clients like to see some visually artistic shots as well. Direct bookings are not as predominant due to the high number of top models in Paris. Experience is not necessary if models are perfect for the market with amazing personalities. Established models must have strong tearsheets that are clear depictions of actual appearance. Clients don't like to see extravagant hair and make-up and they prefer seeing clean, artistic pictures. Tearsheets that work best are from top markets, such as Milan, London and New York City.

❖ Agencies Preferences:

Agencies prefer models who don't crumble from the first hint of criticism – those that calmly persevere day by day while staying focused. Models need to be professional, polite, work with the agency and not against it, communicate well, stay positive and be self-sufficient. It is very important for models to stay focused and be well rested for castings. Clients prefer literally no make-up or just a hint of mascara and lip gloss. Hair coloring should never be noticeable. Models must keep the style simple – nice pair of jeans, a body conscious t-shirt and a cool pair of shoes or boots. Agencies like to help the models find inexpensive Paris fashion for castings.

TYPICAL BOOKINGS

❖ Length of Work:

Hourly, half day, full day and quite a few multiple days.

❖ Type of Work:

Many types of work are available in Paris – catalogue, editorial, campaign, athletic, lots of lingerie & swimwear, runway, commercial print, many TV commercials, film, trade show, showroom, and industrial.

❖ Busiest Seasons:

Paris is consistent all year long. The market is busiest from February to March and from September to October. May, August and December are the slowest times due to national holidays.

TOP CLIENTS

Paris has many top clients including French Vogue, French Elle, French Men's Health as well as many internationally recognized magazines, Chanel, Dior, Jean Paul Gaultier, L'Oreal, Wella (hair care), Galleries Lafayette (dept. store), and Nivea (skincare). The market is flooded with top designers, photographers, international clients, couture and boutique catalogues and advertising agencies.

COMPETITION

The competition is fierce - there are so many great models and agencies vying for the large number of clients working in Paris. Big castings are common with lines being as long as two hours.

PAY RATES

It is a bit difficult to explain pay rates in Paris in comparison to other cities; however, the rate charts are really as simple as multiplication charts. Paris agencies must be licensed by the government. UNAM (Union Nationale Agences de Mannequins) and SAM (Sydndicat des Agences de Mannequins) suggest rates but they are not regulated by the government because

MODEL MARKETS OF THE WORLD
PARIS FRANCE

France is a free market. Models are employees of the agencies and agencies must pay models that remain on stay a minimum salary of €400 per month (usually covered by agency advances). Suggested rates are at http://unam.org/fra/prestadultes.htm and the first chart displays rates for runway, advertising and catalogue/commercial print. The chart suggests 2 hour bookings from €457-4,320. Half day averages €861-8,350. Full day €1,063-10,356. Agencies negotiate much higher, than rates listed, for top models. The second chart has suggested rates for editorial with 2 hour bookings averaging €180-457. Half day €310-861. Full day €375-1,063. Most magazines pay the minimum of €375 per day with powerhouse publisher Conde Nast having rates around €100 per day. Advertising/campaign average €2,000-1,500,000. TV commercials pay very well with higher residuals than anywhere else in Europe or the U.S.A. The French government oversees payment, giving the models a good percentage of the residuals, as well as insurance of payment even if the agency defaults.

❖ Agency Cuts:

French law requires agencies to have an employment contract with the model. Agencies deduct 20% for commissions and 33% for taxes, French social security, retirement and unemployment.

❖ Agency Provides:

Agencies will advance accommodations, airfare, testing, composites, laser copies, website, and pocket money, dependent upon the caliber of the model. Some agencies offer money contracts through contests and clients will offer money contracts for exclusivity.

LIVING

❖ Housing:

Most of the agencies provide models' apartments. Inexpensive accommodations average €400-500 per month. Moderate averages at least €600 per month. Cheap hotels average €50-120 per night.

❖ Transportation:

Paris has two airports, Charles de Gaulle which is 45 minutes from downtown, and Orly which is 30 minutes from downtown. Paris has excellent, inexpensive public transportation including train, metro/subway, and bus and it covers an extensive amount of the metropolitan area. A monthly pass is €50. A short ride in a taxi is €7. Traffic is very bad and parking is very expensive.

❖ Food & Entertainment:

Parisians are known for their culinary delights. An inexpensive lunch is €7 and an inexpensive dinner is €10. Paris is culturally one of the richest cities in the world. Le Pariscope is a weekly magazine with a small section in English that reports everything there is to see and do. The Fusac, is the English equivalent, and is available every other Wednesday. Models can visit the Louvre for €7.50 a day.

REQUISITES

Work visas are not required for Americans or Canadians. Models who are 16-17 years of age must come with an original birth certificate with a notarized translation in French, copies of their parents' passports or drivers' licenses, along with a signed parental authorization form that can be obtained from their Paris agency. Paris agencies are subject to pay social tax and income tax if the model is not a French resident. These taxes are withheld from all jobs, with the exception of tax on residuals the model receives. In this case, USA models must submit the IRS Tax Form 8802 to request the IRS Tax Form 6166 and Canadian models must bring the Fiscal Attestation to reduce income tax withheld; however, this procedure does not apply to taxes withheld for regular day rates.

WEATHER

Paris is temperate with all the seasons, but the weather can change from rain to sun or from hot to cold on any given day.

CURRENCY

As of January 2005:
US$10 = €7.69
C$10 = €6.20

MARCIA'S TIPS

Models should purchase a good Paris guide book before arrival because there is so much amazing culture to take advantage of during their free time. It is important for models to remain open-minded. Parisians, depending on the way a model perceives it, are either rushing around or seem too reserved in social interaction. This can be typical of any large city in the world. In Paris, looking a stranger directly in the eye and smiling as is done on the streets in the USA and Canada, is considered somewhat rude, and at the very least, confusing. Sometimes that is hard for anyone from North America to understand. Every culture is different. Parisians are amazing, intellectual, artistic, and perhaps just more realistic. When they let someone in, they're in for life. Models will have the opportunity to make some interesting and loyal friends in France.

SWEDEN
STOCKHOLM

Stockholm is a small market. The city has approximately 6 fashion agencies in a metropolitan area population over 1,800,000. Stockholm is a very editorial market with some good magazines shot by some top notch photographers and a few very strong advertising agencies as well. Sweden is cold most of the year with lots of snow. This leads clients to direct book models to locations outside of the country. The market is very efficient and everything is done on time. The city itself is very beautiful and clean, but only a handful of clients, particularly the editorial magazines, shoot around the city. With so many direct bookings, it is easy for strongly established models to come to Stockholm, meet the clients, base elsewhere, and then hopefully direct book.

MARKET PREFERENCES

❖ Models:

The market uses a very small amount of junior/teens, a small portion of plus/full-size (local models only), athletic (fashion models that are in great shape), and mainly adults. Women are preferably looking the ages of 18-25, 1.75-1.80 cm (5'9"-5'11"), Continental sizes 36-38 (American 4-6), preferably B-cup but C-cup is okay for lingerie, no larger than a 91 cm/36" hip. Men are preferably looking the ages of 18-40, 1.84-1.88 cm (6'.05"-6'2"), Continental suit 48-50 (American 38-40). For runway, only local models are used as there is very little work in the market. The market prefers Caucasian European and Nordic looks. The market very seldom uses Black, and will sometimes use Hispanic. Smiles are absolutely important for catalogue but not for editorial. Models do not work full-time in the market and must supplement their income with other markets.

❖ Portfolios:

About 90% of the market is direct bookings. Clients direct book models for catalogue that have very relatable, lifestyle fashion books with lots of smile shots. For editorial, they choose models with lots of editorial and edgy pictures in their portfolios. Clients do not need to see models in person, unless it is a TV commercial casting. New faces will need to have some good testing along with some editorial to enter Stockholm and start earning money jobs. Established models must enter either with a strong catalogue/commercial print portfolio and resume, or a very strong editorial portfolio.

❖ Agencies Preferences:

Agencies prefer models that are professional, easy going and down to earth. This is especially important for clients who are booking multiple day trips as they don't want to be stuck with someone who is a pain in the neck the entire time. For castings, models should wear no make-up and hair should be natural. Clothing can be individualized with a fashion sense. Agencies prefer models stay for 3-4 days to see the clients and then be available for direct bookings from whatever market they choose.

TYPICAL BOOKINGS

❖ Length of Work:

Hourly, half day, and full day. Clients book multiple days the majority of the time.

❖ Type of Work:

Catalogue, athletic, lingerie, swimwear, very little runway, commercial print, TV commercial, infomercial, and industrial.

❖ Busiest Seasons:

The market is busiest from January to March and then from September to October. The slowest times of the year are April to May and June to July.

TOP CLIENTS

Top clients include H&M (dept. store), designers Johan Lindberg and Filipa K., magazines Elle and Cosmopolitan, Bon Plaza, Café, H&M Rowells (catalogue), and advertising agencies McCann Erickson and ANR BBDO.

COMPETITION

Competition is tough in the market. Even so, casting lines are very seldom. For TV commercials, it can be as long as 1 hour but it is rare.

PAY RATES

Print averages 0-1000 SEK (SWEDISH KRONA) per hour. Half day 0-500 SEK. Full Day 0-30,000 SEK. Advertising/campaign 5,000-40,000 SEK. Only a very few local models earn money in runway. Sweden does not have a union for TV/film. TV commercials average 20,000-100,000 SEK per booking.

❖ Agency Cuts:

For commissions, agencies deduct 20-25% for print, runway and TV/film. Agencies deduct taxes and social security from foreign models if the job is in Sweden. If the booking is out of the country, agencies do not have to deduct anything from the model's pay.

❖ Agency Provides:

Some agencies will advance accommodations and composites. Depending on the situation, they may advance airfare and pocket money. Neither agencies nor clients offer money contracts.

LIVING

❖ Housing:

Agencies do not have models' apartments. Inexpensive accommodations average 5,000 SEK per month (outside the borders of the city). Stockholm is very expensive in the city, up to 25,000 SEK and higher per month. Most agencies have

MODEL MARKETS OF THE WORLD
STOCKHOLM SWEDEN

models stay in hotels. Cheap hotels average 500-800 SEK per night.

❖ Transportation:

The airport is 45 km to downtown. Stockholm has public transportation including train, metro/subway, and bus. They are expensive in comparison to other cities' transportation costs. A short ride in a taxi costs 100 SEK. Traffic is okay in Stockholm.

❖ Food & Entertainment:

An inexpensive lunch is 40 SEK. An inexpensive dinner is 80-90 SEK. Stockholm has all kinds of entertainment options. Swedish food can be pretty good, especially the seafood and the salmon is excellent. The city has a range of international cuisine. Nightlife is busy from Wednesday to Saturday night with many nightclubs and bars open late. The summers in Stockholm are beautiful..

■ REQUISITES

A work visa is necessary if models are not from the European community known as the EU. Models should ask their agency in advance, as the visa is difficult to apply for and they must have it upon arrival.

■ WEATHER

The weather is snowy, rainy and cold most of the year.

■ CURRENCY

As of January 2005:
US$10 = 69.34 SEK
C$10 = 56.29 SEK

■ MARCIA'S TIPS

Sweden is not a good weather country. Models should be prepared with a warm coat and even an umbrella. Swedish clients are tough but they are very nice to work with. Photographers are rather picky about time and models definitely do not want to show up late. Client pet peeves include sleeping on the job, talking on a mobile phone, complaining about not feeling good or lack of sleep. Everyone in Stockholm speaks English so it is easy to navigate the city. Swedes are very friendly and helpful to tourists. By nature the Swedes are pretty shy and usually foreigners don't understand when joking with them doesn't go over well. Models will have to know Swedes for a long time before they can be that free in conversation with them. Models should take heed and be very polite and conservative, but still remain friendly and nice.

AUSTRIA
VIENNA

Vienna is a small market and is based in Austria and has a population of 1,875,000. Approximately 7 fashion agencies in Vienna cater to Austria's entire population of over 7,000,000. The market does mainly editorial and advertising/campaign. The magazines lean toward a very clean, modern style and the editorial is very good quality and quite useable for most markets worldwide. Vienna is a beautiful, historical city well situated in the European market. It is an easy stop for models traveling from Paris, Germany or Milan.

MARKET PREFERENCES

❖ Models:

The market needs junior/teens (beginning at age 15) and adults. Women are preferably looking the ages of 16-40, 1.74-1.80 cm (5'8.5"-5'11"), Continental sizes 36-38 (American 4-6), no more than a B-cup, no larger than a 91 cm/36" hip; for runway 1.76-1.80 cm (5'9.5"-5'11"), Continental size 36 (American 4). Men are preferably looking the ages of 20-50, 1.80-1.88 cm (5'11"-6'2"), Continental suit 48-50 (American 38-40); for runway 1.84-1.88 cm (6'.05"-6'2"), Continental suit 48-50 (American 38-40). All ethnicities work in Vienna except Black models due to the demographics of the market. Smiles are important for catalogue and editorial. 30% of the agency boards work full-time in the market.

❖ Portfolios:

Vienna has a good amount of direct bookings at 35% of the total market. Clients prefer to see models in person, but it is not necessary. New faces will need to have some experience with at least 2 very good tests and 1 editorial spread before entering Vienna. Established models will need full books with a variance of jobs and looks with good editorial being an absolute. Models' portfolios will need to show some clean, fresh looks so the clients can see a true depiction of the model.

❖ Agencies Preferences:

Agencies prefer models that are cheerful, polite, confident, open-minded, modern, and sweet. For castings, hair and make-up needs to be very natural and never messy. Dress should be casual but fashion forward. Agencies prefer models to remain on stay 3-4 weeks to give the market a good try and to ensure that all the clients have been seen.

TYPICAL BOOKINGS

❖ Length of Work:

Half day and full day. Clients very rarely book models for multiple days.

MODEL MARKETS OF THE WORLD
VIENNA AUSTRIA

❖ Type of Work:
Advertising, campaign, TV commercial, editorial and runway.

❖ Busiest Seasons:
Vienna is busy all year long. The busiest time of the year is hard to gauge in this market as it actually changes year to year. Typically, the slowest time of the year is from mid-July to mid-August.

TOP CLIENTS
Top clients include Palmers (lingerie), Silhouette (glasses), mobile phone companies A1, 3, T-mobile, Telering and One, Schöps (textile), Weinper & Co. (photographer agency), advertising agencies GGK and Demner, Merlicek & Bergmann, as well as Austrian banks.

COMPETITION
The market is small but has enough work and the competition is light. Casting lines are usually short unless for a TV commercial and then lines can be as long as 2 hours.

PAY RATES
Print averages (EURO) €400-700 per half day. Full day €700-1,200 or more, depending on the model. Advertising/campaign €1,000-30,000 depending on the usage or buy-out. Runway €200-400 per show. Austria does not have unions for TV commercials. Generally, TV commercials are booked for 1 year at the day rate plus usage fees.

❖ Agency Cuts:
For commissions, agencies deduct 30% for non-residents because they are usually paid before the agencies receive payment from the clients. For local models, 20% is deducted for commissions.

❖ Agency Provides:
As with most small markets in Europe, Vienna agencies advance accommodations. They sometimes advance pocket money, dependent upon the situation and caliber of the model.

LIVING

❖ Housing:
Most agencies provide models' apartments. Inexpensive accommodations average €15-20 per day. Moderate €25-30 per day. Inexpensive hotels average €35-90 per day.

❖ Transportation:
The airport is 25 minutes from downtown. Vienna does have very good public transportation including train, subway/metro (called the U-Bahn) and bus. The "wochenkarte" card is good for all transportation for 1 week and costs €12. A short ride in a taxi is €6-9. Traffic is light in Vienna.

❖ Food & Entertainment:
An inexpensive lunch is €5-7 and an inexpensive dinner is €7-10. Vienna is a very trendy city and has a lot of culture, history, and a wonderful music scene. In their

free time, models can visit the museums as well as try some of the city's restaurants. Vienna is famous for wiener schnitzel, sacher torte, tafelspitz, and strudels.

REQUISITES

Work visas are not required for foreigners in Austria.

WEATHER

Winters can be quite cold.

CURRENCY

As of January 2005:
US$10 = €7.69
C$10 = €6.20

MARCIA'S TIPS

Clients really enjoy meeting foreign models and models will love meeting clients as well because they will take the time to ask about the models' countries, the photographers they have worked with and the style of their books. Models comment on what a nice surprise this is compared to other countries they visit. Models should try to stop by the Albertina Museum. The museum has great expositions and a wonderful restaurant to boot. Models should carry an umbrella along as rain can happen quite suddenly in Vienna. Everyone speaks English in Vienna so it is easy to navigate. Models will find it easy to ask for help as well as enjoy this beautiful city and its people.

SWITZERLAND
ZURICH

Zurich is considered a very small market with a metropolitan area population of 1,125,000. There are approximately 5 fashion agencies with government licenses in Zurich. The market consists mainly of young designers, some editorial magazines, and several big runway shows (Extravaganza, Gwand, Blickfang and Barclay). Most of the better paying jobs are TV commercials and advertising. Like most of the European markets, Zurich direct books with the larger international clientele of the European community. This small market is sometimes overlooked by established models, but it can be a surprising asset to those who stop by Zurich while traveling onto larger European markets, especially those who love to ski.

■ MARKET PREFERENCES

❖ Models:

The market uses some junior/teen (girls starting at age 15, and boys looking age 18) and mainly adults. Women are preferably looking the ages of 18-26, 1.74-1.80 cm (5'8.5"-5'11"), Continental sizes 34-38 (American 2-6), no more than a B-cup, no larger than a 92 cm/36.5" hip; for runway 1.75-1.80 cm (5'9"-5'11"), Continental sizes 34-36 (American 2-4). Men are preferably looking the ages of 20-30, okay at 1.80 cm (5'11"), but mainly 1.83-1.88 cm (American 6'0"-6'2"), Continental suit 48-52 (American 38-42); for runway 1.83-1.88 cm (6'0"-6'2"), Continental suit 48-52 (American 38-42). Men work better if their hair is a bit longer and not super short. Clear skin is very important in the market. The market uses mainly Caucasian and Hispanic, and some Asian and Eurasian. Smiles are important for catalogue and not so much for editorial. Since Zurich is so small, it is almost impossible to work full-time unless a model is combining the market with other European markets as well.

❖ Portfolios:

About 10% of the market is from direct bookings. To garner these bookings, models must have a strong portfolio with editorial and some lifestyle fashion. Clients prefer to see models in person. The market is quite difficult for foreign new faces. Established models must have a strong resume of experience and be balanced between editorial and lifestyle fashion in commercial print and catalogue. Even junior/teen models will need to have a roster of experience to make the market work.

❖ Agencies Preferences:

Agencies like models that are cheerful, confident, definitely not arrogant, and open-minded. For castings, minimal to no make-up is preferred with hair that is well groomed. Clients prefer to see models dress casual and a bit trendy. Agencies prefer that models come for about a week for client appointments and then direct book afterward. The market does not have models that remain on stay.

TYPICAL BOOKINGS

❖ Length of Work:

Half day, full day and multiple days. Bookings are usually 1-2 days.

❖ Type of Work:

Catalogue, editorial, campaign, rarely athletic, lingerie, swimwear, runway, a good amount commercial print and TV commercial, rarely film, very rarely infomercial, showroom and a little bit of industrial.

❖ Busiest Seasons:

Zurich is busiest from September to early December and then again from late March through May. The slowest times are January and July to August.

TOP CLIENTS

Top clients include magazines Annabelle, Bolero, Bolero Men, Edelweis and Elle Germany, Smart (car company), Nivea, grocery stores Coop and Migros, L`Oreal, department stores Jelmoli, Grieder, Globus, and Trois Pommes, media publishers Ringier, NZZ and TA Media, as well as advertising agencies Publicis and Publicitas.

COMPETITION

The market is very competitive, which sometimes leads to pricing wars among the agencies and some agents complain that rates are coming down. Casting lines are usually not a problem.

PAY RATES

Print averages (SWISS FRANC) CHF 0-1,000,00 per half day. Full day CHF 0-2,000,00. Advertising/campaign CHF 2,000,00-200,000,00. Runway CHF 800,00-1,200,00 per show. Switzerland does not have unions for TV/film. All rates vary depending on the job.

❖ Agency Cuts:

For commissions, agencies deduct 10-20% for print, runway and TV/film. Agencies may deduct taxes for non-European citizens, depending on the home country. Switzerland does agree to the double taxation law, which states that models do not have to pay taxes in Switzerland and at home. Models should have this clarified prior to their arrival by their agency.

❖ Agency Provides:

Agencies may advance accommodations and airfare in conjunction with an advanced booking. Agencies might advance composites, laser copies of books, testing and pocket money, but it would have to be a model extremely perfect for their clients. Neither agencies nor clients offer money contracts.

MODEL MARKETS OF THE WORLD
ZURICH SWITZERLAND

■ LIVING

❖ Housing:

Agencies do not have models' apartments. Inexpensive accommodations average CHF 500,00-1,000,00 per month. Moderate CHF 1,500,00-2,500,00 per month. Cheap hotels average CHF 90,00-150,00 per night.

❖ Transportation:

The airport is 10-20 minutes to downtown, depending on traffic, and the train is about 15 minutes. Zurich has excellent public transportation including train, tram and bus. It is the best and fastest way to get around town. An inexpensive day card is CHF 20,00. A short ride in a taxi is CHF 20,00. Traffic in Zurich is okay.

❖ Food & Entertainment:

An inexpensive lunch is CHF 15,00. An inexpensive dinner is CHF 20,00. The food is excellent but pretty pricey compared to American standards. The city is filled with many nightclubs, bars and lounges. Zurich has a little bit of everything, especially the beautiful mountains for outdoor sports.

■ REQUISITES

A work visa is required for USA and Canadian models. Agencies will help models obtain their visa in advance. If models are from some European-designated countries, they can work for up to 3 months before having to apply for a work visa.

■ WEATHER

Winters are cold, especially in the mountains. Summers tend to be warmer. Still, there can always be rain and cooler temperatures.

■ CURRENCY

As of January 2005:
US$10 = CHF 11.86
C$10 = CHF 9.60

■ MARCIA'S TIPS

Zurich is a nice place to obtain good money jobs and some editorial while staying in a beautiful place. Switzerland is economically stable and has a very high standard of security. Models feel very safe while in the city. There are many beautiful towns, lake and mountains nearby. Models should not have a problem navigating the city at all as 75% of Zurich speaks English because they are taught the language in school. The Swiss are known to be shy by other countries' standard, but are really quite friendly.

OCEANIA

Auckland 194
Melbourne 197
Sydney. 201

NEW ZEALAND
AUCKLAND

Auckland is the main fashion center of New Zealand. It's a smaller medium size market with a metropolitan area population of over 1,250,000 and approximately 8 fashion agencies. Models enjoy going to this market as they can combine it in one trip with other markets in Australia or Asia. The New Zealand market is surprisingly current. Auckland is a smaller market than Sydney but has more magazines per capita, with a myriad of really progressive editorial magazines and is growing strong in lifestyle fashion as well as commercial print.

MARKET PREFERENCES

❖ Models:

The Auckland market uses junior/teens on the older end as there are only a few teen magazines in the market (preferably 16 and older), plus/full-size (5'7"-5'11", sizes 14 and up), athletic (must have a swimwear body unless a professional athlete), and adults. Women are preferably looking the ages of 18-35, 5'7"-5'11" (5'10" is ideal), NZ sizes 8-12 (American 4-8), no more than a C-cup, no larger than a 36" hip; for runway 5'8.5"-5'11", NZ sizes 8-10 (American 4-6). Men are preferably looking the ages of 18-35, 5'11"-6'1", NZ suit 38-42 (American 40-43); for runway 5'11-6'1", NZ suit 38-42 (American 40-43). The Auckland market uses all ethnicities. Clients are open to booking someone interesting, so pretty much anything goes. Freckles and moles are fine, although a very distinctive mole could be problematic. Smiles are important for catalogue and can be for editorial, depending on the magazine story. Foreign models work full-time as they are more focused on the work. Residents of New Zealand usually combine modeling with school or other work. This brings the total for full-time models in the market to 20%.

❖ Portfolios:

Direct bookings are growing and right now garner about 20% of the market. In order to be direct booked, portfolios must be full of tearsheets and they must be appropriate for the prerequisites of the job. Clients do not need to see models in person as they have to obtain work visas to get the models into the country. Most agencies can start a new face with polaroids/snap shots; however the model must be exceptional. The majority of new faces must have good testing as it is difficult to get a work visa without advanced bookings, which are hard to come by without tearsheets. Established models must have good tearsheets and a great composite. The tearsheets should be a mixture from anywhere around the world

MARCIA ROTHSCHILD MOELLERS
NEW ZEALAND AUCKLAND

As long as the tearsheets are good, it will not matter from which market they come.

❖ Agencies Preferences:

Agencies prefer models that are friendly, as the Auckland market is small, close-knit and everyone knows each other. If a model has an attitude, it will get around, and that model might work once and never again. Models have to be very communicative and upfront in Auckland. Clients prefer to see models that look pretty, natural and clean. Models can wear a pair of jeans and sandals to castings. Even though it is a casual clothing market, models still need to look put together. Agencies prefer for models to remain on stay for 2-4 weeks. It is best to combine it with Sydney or other markets in Asia to make the time worthwhile.

TYPICAL BOOKINGS

❖ Length of Work:

Hourly, half and full day with multiple day bookings happening frequently.

❖ Type of Work:

Catalogue, athletic, editorial, campaign, lingerie, swimwear, runway, commercial print, TV commercial, film, very little infomercial, trade show, store informal, showroom, and industrial.

❖ Busiest Seasons:

Auckland is fairly busy most of the year. The busiest times are from January to February, May to June, and September to October. The slowest periods are the beginning of January and April.

TOP CLIENTS

Top clients include Bendon (underwear), Ezibuy (catalogue), Farmers (department store), magazines Pavement, Fashion Quarterly and Style, advertising agencies Saatchi & Saatchi, DDB Needham, and Clemenger, Canterbury (clothing), and designers Karen Walker, Trelise Cooper and Zambesi.

COMPETITION

Competition is light and models never deal with long lines at castings.

PAY RATES

Print averages (NEW ZEALAND DOLLAR) NZ$100-200 per hour. Half day NZ$400-800. Full day NZ$1,200-2,000. Advertising/campaign NZ$1,500-15,000. Runway NZ$150 per hour. New Zealand does not have a union for TV/film. TV/film is primarily offered in 6-12 month contracts with 100% automatic renewal/repayment of the contract built in. A 12-month contract can be anywhere from NZ$1,500-25,000.

❖ Agency Cuts:

For commissions, agencies deduct 20% for print, runway and TV/film. 15-20% in taxes is deducted for foreign models.

❖ Agency Provides:

Most agencies advance accommodations, airfare, composites, laser copies of

MODEL MARKETS OF THE WORLD
AUCKLAND NEW ZEALAND

books (if working), but rarely for tests. Agencies will not advance a weekly salary unless there are advanced confirmed bookings. Neither agencies nor clients offer money contracts.

LIVING

❖ Housing:

Most agencies provide models' apartments with inexpensive accommodations averaging NZ$600 per month. Moderate accommodations average NZ$800 per month. Cheap hotels average NZ$280 per week.

❖ Transportation:

The airport is 20 minutes from downtown and models may take a shuttle for about NZ$15. Auckland has inexpensive public transportation including train, metro/subway and bus that is not considered great. Models usually walk or take the bus. A short ride in a taxi is NZ$5. Traffic is good by international standards; however locals still get irritated.

❖ Food & Entertainment:

An inexpensive lunch is NZ$3 and an inexpensive dinner is NZ$10. Auckland is quite groovy – the nightlife is fun and the tourism is interesting making for a unique experience.

REQUISITES

Models must have a work visa prior to arrival. The visa can either be applied for in a model's own country or the agency will apply for it if they feel the model is strong enough and will garner enough confirmed bookings in advance. In the worst case scenario, it can take up to 3 months to get a work visa. It is recommended models apply for the visa in their own country; however, agencies can get the visa much quicker – in as little as 10 days.

WEATHER

The 4 season weather in New Zealand can be good and bad in one day and models should carry a raincoat. New Zealand's seasons are reverse from the seasons in the Northern hemisphere. If it is winter in North America, it is summer in New Zealand.

CURRENCY

As of January 2005:
US$10 = NZ$14.23
C$10 = NZ$11.33

MARCIA'S TIPS

People tend to be surprised by the quality of editorial coming out of New Zealand. Auckland editorial can definitely bolster a model's ambitions to be successful in larger international markets. Good walking shoes and sunscreen are a must! The country's language is 100% English so navigating is easy. Most models love to work in Auckland, wanting to stay longer. Models should make sure to have a return flight that has leeway in case they decide to extend their stay.

AUSTRALIA
MELBOURNE

Melbourne is the second largest market in Australia. The city has a population of over 4,000,000 with approximately 5 fashion agencies that cater to Australia's 20,000,000 consumers. In Australia's fashion market, Melbourne is equally as large, if not larger, than Sydney, but Sydney carries the weight of the major international magazines which makes the international fashion industry deem Melbourne as the secondary market; however, Melbourne models earn more and work more than models in Sydney. The market in Melbourne is more relatable lifestyle as it is home to a large number of production companies and advertising agencies. The bulk of the Melbourne market's work is TV commercials and recently, the market's catalogues have become more sophisticated so quality editorial models can come and earn a fortune as well. The market has models that have worked in Melbourne for over 10 years and are still continually pulling down over $100,000 a year.

MARKET PREFERENCES

❖ Models:

The market uses junior/teens (girls starting at 15), athletic (fashion models in super fit shape), and adults. Women are preferably looking the ages of 18-35, 5'8"-5'11" which is strictly enforced, Australian sizes 8-10 (American 4-6), no more than a B-cup, no larger than a 93 cm/37" hip; for runway 5'9.5"-5'11", Australian sizes 8-10 (American 4-6). Men are preferably looking the ages of 18-38, 6'0"-6'3", suit 38-42; for runway 6'2"-6'3", suit 38-42. The market uses all ethnicities, but only Caucasian models work consistently. Agencies do not recommend other ethnicities to remain on stay. Smiles are very important in this strong catalogue/TV commercial market. 80% of the market works full-time. The work is strong and the money is substantial.

❖ Portfolios:

The market rarely every direct books. The clients do not like paying the expense to fly someone in for a booking since it's a 24-hour flight from most parts of the world. Clients prefer to see models in person as they do not trust portfolios exclusively. Experience is not needed for new faces but they should enter with at least 2 very good tests. Established models should arrive with a mix of editorial and advertising from relatable to high end fashion along with classic, top end department store styled photographs.

MODEL MARKETS OF THE WORLD
MELBOURNE AUSTRALIA

❖ Agencies Preferences:

Agencies prefer models that communicate well and are very nice to work with. Clients shoot so regularly that they cannot be bothered with models with any kind of an attitude. The agencies are able to charge a premium rate but this can only be given to models that are completely professional on all levels. Hair and make-up can vary casting to casting but generally, clients prefer to see a light and natural look. Clothing can be dress specific per casting but overall it is fairly casual. Agencies prefer models to remain on stay for 6-8 weeks.

TYPICAL BOOKINGS

❖ Length of Work:

The bulk of shoots in the Melbourne market are only a couple of hours. Most models will usually do 2 completely different jobs in a day. There are day bookings but they are not common.

❖ Type of Work:

Catalogue, editorial, campaign, athletic, swimwear, lingerie, runway, commercial print, TV commercial, film, showroom, and industrial.

❖ Busiest Seasons:

The market is very busy all year long. The busiest times are from February to March and from September to October. The slowest times are around December May.

TOP CLIENTS

Top clients include department stores Myer, David Jones, Target and Kmart, Just Jeans, Levi's, advertising agencies, Clemenger, DDBO, Singleton Ogilvy Mather and Campaign Palace, as well as fashion retailers Sportsgirl and Portmans.

COMPETITION

The competition in Melbourne is strong – especially during castings for runway Fashion Week in March when clients want to see multiple models and lines can be as long as 4 hours. Otherwise, castings are on request and with as few as 10 models.

PAY RATES

Print averages (AUSTRALIAN DOLLAR) AUD $205-300 per hour. They do not book jobs by half day or full day and only by the hour. Advertising/campaign AUD $2000-75000. Runway AUD $100 per hour. Australia has the MEAA (Media Entertainment and Arts Alliance) as a union for TV/film, but most agencies will not accept union rates and negotiate on everything. TV commercials average from AUD $2000 for 1 month on air, and up to AUD $6000-8000 for 12 months on air.

❖ Agency Cuts:

For commissions, agencies deduct 20% for print, runway and TV/film. Agencies must deduct taxes for all models. Models cannot work without a tax file number. The actual tax rate for most jobs is 20%. If a model does not obtain the tax file number, the agencies deduct 48.95% per job.

❖ Agency Provides:

Agencies rarely advance airfare or accommodations. They usually advance on composites, laser copies of books and sometimes testing, if necessary. Agencies do not offer and some clients offer money contracts for exclusivity.

▪ LIVING

❖ Housing:

Agencies do not have models' apartments but they are helpful locating sources for rentals. Inexpensive accommodations average AUD $400-600 per month. Moderate AUD $500-800 per month. Cheap hotels (3-star) average AUD $120 per day. Hotels go up to AUD $600 per night for higher quality.

❖ Transportation:

The Melbourne Airport is about 25 km from downtown and takes about 20 minutes in a taxi for AUD $35-40. Melbourne has public transportation that runs from 5 a.m. to 1 a.m. including train, tram and bus. A daily ticket for all modes of transport is around AUD $5. A short ride in a taxi is AUD $7. Traffic runs fairly well as the roads are good but it can be tough at rush hour.

❖ Food & Entertainment:

An inexpensive lunch is AUD $4-6 and an inexpensive dinner is AUD $6-10. There are literally hundreds of bars, cafes, clubs, pubs, cinemas, live music venues, museums, galleries, shops, parks, beaches, as well as walk and bike paths to keep everyone entertained. Australia, as a whole, is very lifestyle oriented so it caters to many different tastes and personal styles. Melbourne is very multicultural with massive Italian and Greek populations as well as southeast Asian immigrants so there is a little something for everyone.

▪ REQUISITES

Foreign models must arrive with a work visa or a holiday work visa. A holiday work visa allows models to work and then be tourists as well; therefore, most models apply for this. The work visa can either be easy or difficult to obtain, depending on the relations between the model's home country and Australia at the time of application.

▪ WEATHER

The dry/hot season is from the end of December through March. Temperatures can soar as high as 40 Celsius. Winters are grey and wet with temperatures averaging 10-15 Celsius. The seasons are reverse from those of North America.

▪ CURRENCY

As of January 2005:
US$10 = AUD $13.16
C$10 = AUD $10.46

▪ MARCIA'S TIPS

While Sydney is very much like an

MODEL MARKETS OF THE WORLD
MELBOURNE AUSTRALIA

American city, visitors to Australia are often surprised at how "European" Melbourne is with its classic architecture, monuments and plentiful English-style parks and gardens. Melbourne is built on a grid system which makes the city easy to navigate. If models feel like escaping, an hour's trip will take them to either the mountains, vineyards or to the ocean. Melbourne is very lifestyle-oriented and the cost of living is about 30% cheaper than it is in Sydney. English is the country's language, but Aussies will say it will do one good to learn some "Australian" while down under.

AUSTRALIA
SYDNEY

Sydney is the largest market in Australia with a metropolitan area population of 5,000,000 and approximately 5 fashion agencies. It is a wonderful, beautiful, captivating city in architecture, style and people. The great thing about the city is that it's both busy and laid back at the same time. Sydney has a powerful business district and is just minutes away from beautiful Bondi Beach. Possibly some of the friendliest people in the world are from Sydney and it's a wonderful place for models to work on their portfolios with plenty of highly reputable magazines, including Vogue, Harper's Bazaar, Marie Claire, Cleo and Oyster. The magazines are so beautiful and relatable in style that they are useable for practically every market in the world.

MARKET PREFERENCES

❖ Models:

The market uses junior/teens (girls starting at age 16), plus/full-size (local models only), athletic (fashion models in super fit shape), and adults. Women are preferably looking the ages of 18-35, 5'8.5"-5'11", Australian 8-10 (American 4-6), preferably a B-cup and no more than a C-cup, no larger than a 90 cm/35.5" hip (if very tall, 92 cm/36.5" could work); for runway 5'9.5"-5'11", Australian 8-10 (American 4-6). Men are preferably looking the ages of 18-38, 6'0"-6'3", suit 38-42; for runway 6'2"-6'3", suit 38-42. The market uses all ethnicities, but only Caucasian models work consistently. There is a very small black population in Sydney; therefore, there is basically no demand for black models. If a client were to take a chance on other ethnicities, it would most likely be Asian or Eurasian. Smiles are very important for editorial and catalogue. About 25% of the market works full-time.

❖ Portfolios:

3% of the market is from direct bookings. It is very rare for a model to be booked directly because Australia has a large base and influx of top models and it is too expensive and time-consuming for models to be flown in from out of the country. For new faces, there are certain times of the year where it is a little bit less competitive and entering with 2-3 very good tests is permissible. Ideally, established models have better opportunities and should enter with a book full of a variety of relatable and high end fashion editorial.

❖ Agencies Preferences:

Agencies prefer models that are professional, nice to work with, easy going and individual. Agencies encourage models to wear as little make-up as possible. Clothing depends on the appointment;

MODEL MARKETS OF THE WORLD
SYDNEY AUSTRALIA

however, Sydney is really not a dressy place. Jeans and t-shirts are fine most of the time as long as it's well put together. Agencies prefer models remain on stay for 7-8 weeks. It gives the model enough time to see all the clients but not get "stale".

TYPICAL BOOKINGS

❖ Length of Work:

Hourly, half day, full day and not so many multiple days.

❖ Type of Work:

Catalogue, editorial, campaign, athletic, swimwear, lingerie, runway, commercial print, TV commercial, film, showroom, and industrial.

❖ Busiest Seasons:

The market is busiest from April to May with runway's Australian Fashion Week. November to December is also busy, thanks to the fabulous weather. The beginning of July, which is Australia's middle of the winter, can be somewhat slower as it is the beginning of the financial year. The Sydney market doesn't have any real dead times.

TOP CLIENTS

Top clients include Australian magazines Vogue, Harper's Bazaar, Oyster, Cleo, Cosmopolitan, Shop and Marie Claire, Ezibuy (catalogue), department stores David Jones and Myer, and Clemenger. DDBO (ad agency).

COMPETITION

Competition is strong but agencies tend to be careful and bring models in for the correct amount of time so there are less unforeseeable delays. Show season can lead to some casting lines as long as 30 minutes or more.

PAY RATES

Print averages (AUSTRALIAN DOLLAR) AUD $205-275 per hour. Half day AUD $820-1250. Full day AUD $1640-2500. Advertising/Campaign AUD $3000-35000. Runway AUD $150 per hour. For some of the shows, designers barter with clothes. Australia has the MEAA (Media Entertainment and Arts Alliance) as a union for TV/film, but most agencies will not accept union rates and negotiate everything.

❖ Agency Cuts:

For commissions, agencies deduct 20% for print, runway and TV/film. Agencies must deduct taxes for models and they cannot work without a tax file number. The actual tax rate for most jobs is 20%; however, if a model does not obtain a tax file number, the agencies deduct 48.95% per job.

❖ Agency Provides:

Agencies do not like to advance flights or much of anything else. The market feels they offer so much in development and tearsheets that the model should be prepared to make the investment for what the market gives them in return. Also, Sydney agents note they are quite particular about the models they bring in and are assured these models can work if their attitude is good. Agencies usually advance accommodations for several weeks or longer, dependent upon the caliber of the model. Neither agencies nor clients offer money contracts.

LIVING

❖ Housing:

Some agencies provide models' apartments. Other agencies work out accommodations through private owners. Inexpensive accommodations average AUD $200-250 per week. Moderate AUD $250-350 per week. Cheap hotels average AUD $90-300 per night.

❖ Transportation:

The airport is 20 minutes from downtown. Sydney has inexpensive public transportation including train, metro/subway and bus and it is easy to navigate. A short ride in a taxi is less than AUD $5. Traffic is typical for a larger city and rush hours are difficult.

❖ Food & Entertainment:

An inexpensive lunch is AUD $7 and an inexpensive dinner is AUD $15. There is something to do every night of the week – parties and nightclubs, a huge scene at Bondi Beach with a plenty of food and nightclubs/bars. Models can also hit Bronte Beach, Taronga Zoo, and Palm Beach. Sydney has all types of cuisine – plenty of amazing Asian restaurants as well as Mexican and Italian.

REQUISITES

Foreign models must arrive with a work visa or a holiday work visa. Many models apply for a holiday work visa which allows models to work and be tourists as well. The work visa can either be easy or more difficult to obtain, dependent upon the relations between the model's home country and Australia at the time.

WEATHER

The seasons in Sydney are opposite from those in the Northern Hemisphere. When it's Summer in the USA, it's Winter in Australia with 4 seasons like North America, just in reverse.

CURRENCY

As of January 2005:
US$10 = AUD $13.16
C$10 = AUD $10.46

MARCIA'S TIPS

Models should remain on stay 7-8 weeks in order to make Sydney worthwhile. By all means, models should not forget to apply for their work visa and it must be done prior to arrival. Great tourist sites include the Sydney Opera House and the Aquarium. The Blue Mountains are a nice day trip. Models are sure to enjoy the city and the country as well as their work. Australian humor is unique, and models

MODEL MARKETS OF THE WORLD
SYDNEY AUSTRALIA

should try to be open-minded and partake in the fun. It takes a bit of time to get used to the locals who speak "Australian" and it takes a bit longer to get used to the jokes. But once models do, they will enjoy the charm of Australia that much more.

SOUTH AMERICA

Rio de Janiero. 206
Santiago. 209
Sao Paulo. 212

BRAZIL
RIO DE JANEIRO

Rio de Janeiro is the second most important fashion market in Brazil with a metropolitan area population of 14,391,282. There are 4 fashion agencies based in this larger medium size market and it is renowned for its beautiful locations for editorial and commercial bookings, including the infamous Ipanema Beach. This beach has put Rio de Janeiro on the map as the discovery point for many top new faces. Rio de Janeiro is also known as a great market for TV commercials. The market has some powerful clients including quite a few powerhouse advertising agencies as well as Rede Globo, the largest TV channel in Latin America.

■ MARKET PREFERENCES

❖ Models:

The market uses junior/teens (girls start at 14, boys at 16), petite (5'5"-5'6"), plus/full-size (not represented by fashion agencies but instead talent or real people agencies), athletic, and adults. Women are preferably looking the ages of 18-26, 1.70-1.79 cm (5'7"-5'10.5"), Continental sizes 36-38 (American 4-6), no more than a C-cup, no more than a 91 cm/36" hip; for runway 1.75-1.79 cm (5'9"-5'10.5"), Continental size 36 (American 4). Men are preferably looking the ages of 18-30, 1.80-1.90 cm (5'11"-6'3"), Continental suit 50-52 (American 40-42); for runway 1.83-1.90 cm (6'0"-6'3"), Continental suit 50 (American 40). Blue or green eyes are preferred because the market has so many brown-eyed models from their own population. All ethnicities are used. Smiles are important for catalogue as well as editorial. Models need to be athletic and healthy looking to work in Rio de Janeiro. About 50% of the market works full-time.

❖ Portfolios:

30% of the market is from direct bookings. Rio de Janeiro mainly direct books models from São Paulo who are established with strong portfolios. No experience is necessary for new faces as the market is known for its strong model development. After the models are developed, they are sent into other larger markets. Established models will need to have portfolios filled with fresh, healthy, active looks in editorial and commercial print in order to enter the market.

❖ Agencies Preferences:

Agencies prefer models that are easy going, fun, focused on their careers and professional. For castings, natural is best. Clients like to see models looking fresh, beautiful and healthy with absolutely no make-up. Casual clothes are preferred for castings. Agencies prefer models to remain on stay for 2 months which is enough time to see all the clients

MARCIA ROTHSCHILD MOELLERS
BRAZIL — RIO DE JANEIRO

and begin working.

TYPICAL BOOKINGS

❖ **Length of Work:**

The Rio de Janeiro market is different from other markets in that it does not charge on an hourly or daily rate. | Bookings are charged by the level of client, usage and the number of days needed and are a determined by a set package price.

❖ **Type of Work:**

Catalogue, editorial, campaign, lingerie, swimwear, runway, commercial print, TV commercial, film, theater, store informal, and showroom.

❖ **Busiest Seasons:**

The market is busiest from January to July for high end fashion clients, from March to April for commercial print, and all year long for TV commercials. The slowest times of the year are December and February.

TOP CLIENTS

Top clients include advertising agencies Conspiracão Films, Zohar, Script, McCann Ericsson, DPZ, Thompson, Giovanni FCB and Salles Norton, lingerie companies Du Loren and Triumph, swimwear companies Blue Man, Lenny Riggy, and Salinas, magazines V, Vogue, Marie Claire, Citizen K., Vizoo, O Globo, and Jornal do Brasil, and international photographers Mario Testino and Patrick Demarchelier as well as Pedro Garrido, Vicente de Paulo, Murillo Meirelles, Ernesto Balban and Aderi Costa.

COMPETITION

The competition is lighter than the São Paulo market, but can still be heavy because of the great deal of clients in the market.

PAY RATES

Print averages (REAL) R$3.000,00-100.000,00 for advertising/campaign. Runway R$400,00-4.000,00 per show. Brazil is all non-union but may not be for long as the producers and directors are trying to form a union. TV/film averages R$1.00,00-50.000,000 per job, depending on the usage and what level of role the model books in the production.

❖ **Agency Cuts:**

For commissions, agencies deduct 28% for print, runway, and TV/film. Models are required to pay taxes for each job. Models must request to be reimbursed by the tax authorities before leaving Brazil.

❖ **Agency Provides:**

Agencies do not give advances. Neither agencies nor clients offer money contracts.

LIVING

❖ **Housing:**

Agencies do not provide models' apartments. Inexpensive accommodations average R$700,00 for a small apartment and

MODEL MARKETS OF THE WORLD
RIO DE JANEIRO BRAZIL

slightly higher for moderate accommodations. Cheap hotels average R$70,00 - 300,00 per night.

❖ Transportation:

The Galeão Airport is 20 minutes from downtown, and the Santos Dumont is 5 minutes from downtown. Rio de Janeiro uses buses for public transportation. They are inexpensive and average R$2,00. A short ride in a taxi is R$30,00. Traffic can be difficult during rush hour.

❖ Food & Entertainment:

An inexpensive lunch is R$5,00 and an inexpensive dinner is R$10,00. Rio has lots of good restaurants where models can eat excellent seafood or barbeque. There are many theaters, museums, shopping malls, cafes and nightclubs.

REQUISITES

Models should inquire with the Brazilian consulate if they need a visa to enter Rio de Janeiro. Most models will need to apply for a work visa and a tourist visa if they plan to see more of Brazil beyond work.

WEATHER

The weather is hot and humid.

CURRENCY

As of January 2005:
US$10 = AUD $13.16
C$10 = AUD $10.46

MARCIA'S TIPS

Foreign models need to be discretely dressed in Rio de Janeiro. Agencies recommend that models not wear jewelry. It is best for models to ask their agency or local people to help show them how to navigate the city. The city is very much alive, which is best exemplified by some of the city's culture and its wild and boisterous events, depicted best by the most popular show in the world, Carnival, with a huge parade, the Samba school, days of parties, happening every year in February. Wonderful places to see outside of the city limits are the Great Forest of Jijuca, the Botanical Garden and the beautiful beaches of Ipanema, Barra and Prainha. Buzios and Angra dos Reis are only 2 hours from Rio where some of the greatest vacation resorts and beaches in the world can be found.

CHILE
SANTIAGO

Santiago is a medium size market and is one of the larger fashion markets in South America. The city has a metropolitan area population of over 6,000,000 with approximately 5 fashion agencies. Santiago is enjoying a strong economic upward swing and is considered a very safe and clean city in South America. The fashion industry is quite new in this market establishing in the 1990's when international trade allowed for international franchise stores to open and advertising campaigns began in the country. The strongest clients are department stores and jeans companies. Models love Santiago because it is an excellent market with easy access to top international magazines such as Elle. Plus, there are money jobs to book while waiting for tearsheets to be published and models can leave the market with cash in hand.

MARKET PREFERENCES

❖ Models:

The market uses junior/teens (starting at age 14 for girls and age 17 for boys), and adults. Women are preferably looking the ages of 18-27, 1.70-1.78 cm (5'7"-5'11"), Continental sizes 36-38 (American 4-6), no more than a B-cup, no more than a 36" hip; for runway 1.75-1.78 cm (5'9"-5'11"), Continental sizes 36-38 (American 4-6). Men are preferably looking the ages of 18-30, 1.80-1.86 cm (5'11"-6'1.25"), Continental suit 50 (American 40); for runway 1.82-1.88 cm (5'11.75"-6'2"), Continental suit 50 (American 40). Clients prefer a very relatable European look, usually blonde or brunette hair with blue or green eyes. Nordic looks work very well in Santiago. The market only uses Caucasian models. Smiles are important for catalogue and editorial. 100% of the foreign models are working full-time, which consists mainly of models from Brazil, Uruguay and Argentina. Only 30% of the local models work full-time balancing it with school, parenting or another job.

❖ Portfolios:

60% of the market is from direct bookings. Models must have a very relatable fashion portfolio with good testing and tearsheets in order to garner these bookings. Many top clients will offer money contracts for up to a year for a model they want to represent their line. Once a client has exclusively contracted a model, they do not want them to remain on stay unless it is for their bookings. Models in Santiago work well for editorial and TV commercials and clients prefer to see them in person first. New faces need at least 2 good tests to enter the market or polaroids/snapshots will do, if absolutely perfect for the market.

MODEL MARKETS OF THE WORLD
SANTIAGO CHILE

Established models need a strongly established book with very good tests and relatable fashion tearsheets. If a model has more of an edgy, editorial look, a strong book full of high end tearsheets is paramount.

❖ Agencies Preferences:

Agencies prefer models that are very polite and well educated. For castings, hair needs to be long and straight for females, and well-groomed and not super short for males. Make-up must look very natural. The market is very conservative and does not deal well with any extreme or edgy looks in make-up or dress and it is preferred models look upscale, nice and casual. Agencies prefer for models to remain on stay 2-3 months.

TYPICAL BOOKINGS

❖ Length of Work:

The majority of bookings are full day. For catalogues, they are mostly multiple days.

❖ Type of Work:

Editorial, lots of catalogue, campaign, lingerie, swimwear, runway, commercial print, lots of TV commercial, and showroom.

❖ Busiest Seasons:

The busiest times are January to February (winter campaigns), mid-April to August (catalogue, runway and TV commercial), September to October (spring-summer campaigns), and November to December (Christmas & sales catalogues). January is quite slow for strong editorial looks. Other slow times are March to the beginning of April and from June to July.

TOP CLIENTS

Top clients include department stores Riple, Falabella, Almacenes Paris, jean companies FES and Barbados, cosmetic giants Revlon and L'Oreal, telecommunication companies Smartcom, Telefonica and Entel PSC, Alto Las Condes (shopping mall,) and magazines Blank, Paparazzi, Elle, YA and Caras.

COMPETITION

For foreign models with strong books, the competition is light. Casting lines can last up to 40 minutes for TV commercials.

PAY RATES

Models are paid in (US DOLLAR) US$. Print averages US$100-300 per half day. Full day US$250-1,000. Advertising/campaign US$2,000-5,000. Runway US$200 per show. Chile is all non-union for TV commercials. TV commercials average US$1,500 per day, including 1 year usage in Chile.

❖ Agency Cuts:

For commissions, agencies deduct 30% for print and TV commercial. 20% for runway. Agencies deduct 10% for taxes for foreign models with work visas.

MARCIA ROTHSCHILD MOELLERS
CHILE SANTIAGO

❖ Agency Provides:

Dependent upon the caliber of the model, most agencies will advance accommodations, airfare, laser copies of books, tests and pocket money. Agencies do not offer money contracts. A good number of clients offer money contracts for exclusivity.

LIVING

❖ Housing:

Most agencies provide models' apartments. Inexpensive accommodations average $100-250 per month. Moderate $300-400 per month. Cheap hotels average $40 per night or $800 per month.

❖ Transportation:

The airport is 15-20 minutes from downtown, depending on traffic. Santiago has inexpensive public transportation including metro and bus. They are less than $1 per ride. The metro is considered the best because it's quite safe and very clean. A short ride in a taxi is $1.50. Traffic can be awful depending on the time and area of the city.

❖ Food & Entertainment:

An inexpensive lunch is $2.50 and an inexpensive dinner is the same. There are many different types of restaurants. Generally, people do not tend to go out for drinks only because they prefer to go out for dinners. The beaches and the mountains are an hour from the city and many people disappear there for the weekends. There are specific areas in the city for expensive cuisine, discotheques and nightclubs, as well as areas for the more down-to-earth bohemian.

REQUISITES

A work visa is not necessary for foreigners to enter Chile. Models go through customs as tourists and then their work visas are handled by their agency after arrival.

WEATHER

The weather is quite middle range – never too hot, never too cold and it rarely ever rains.

CURRENCY

As of January 2005:
US$10 = 5658 Chile Pesos

MARCIA'S TIPS

Clients detest models that come to castings with too much make-up and models must be steadfast in keeping their look very natural and clean. Santiago clients want models to look elegant and sporty at the same time – think Tommy Hilfiger but in a more refined sense. Foreign models do very well in Santiago because clients love booking models that come to visit their beautiful country. Most of the clients and about 20% of the city can communicate in English. It's a good idea for models to ask their agency beforehand for some basic Chilean words to learn in order to make communication easier.

BRAZIL
SAO PAULO

São Paulo is the most important fashion market in Brazil and has a metropolitan population area of over 10,000,000 with approximately 12 fashion agencies. São Paulo is a larger medium size market in comparison to New York City and Paris. São Paulo has many of the biggest advertising agencies in the world based right in the city with lots of international magazines including Vogue and Elle, as well as one of the best ethnically mixed populations in the world primarily made up of Asian, European and African descent. The ethnic mixtures of Brazil are what make the models so unique and also one of the most famous exports of the country of Brazil – many well known top models.

MARKET PREFERENCES

❖ Models:

The market uses junior/teens (starting at age 14 for girls and age 17 for boys), petite (5'5"-5'6"), plus/full-size (not represented by fashion agencies but by talent or real people agencies), some athletic, and adults. Women are preferably looking the ages of 18-26, 1.70-1.79 cm (5'7"-5'10.5"), Continental sizes 36-38 (American 4-6), no more than a C-cup, no more than a 91 cm/36" hip; for runway 1.75-1.79 cm (5'9"-5'10.5"), Continental size 36 (American 4). Men are preferably looking the ages of 18-30, 1.80-1.90 cm (5'11"-6'3"), Continental suit 50-52 (American 40-42); for runway 1.83-1.90 cm (6'0"-6'3"), Continental suit 50 (American 40). Blue or green eyes are preferred because the market has so many brown-eyed models from their own population. All ethnicities are used. Beautiful smiles are always welcome for catalogue and editorial. 60% of the market works full-time.

❖ Portfolios:

The Sao Paulo market does not direct book, unless a client has either seen a model in person and is using the model on a direct booking outside of the city, or the client is repeat booking a model. The market is good for both relatable and high fashion models. Experience is desired but not necessary because the agencies will develop models. Established models need to enter with really good recent editorials and important campaigns from fashion and advertising clients.

❖ Agencies Preferences:

Agencies prefer models that are cheerful, confident, modern and open-minded. For castings, hair and make-up must be clean and natural. Clothing should be casual in this warm weather market. Agencies prefer models remain on stay 3-4 months.

TYPICAL BOOKINGS

❖ Length of Work:

The Sao Paulo market is unusual in that it does not charge on an hourly or daily rate. Bookings fees are determined by the level of client, usage and the number of days needed and set into one package price.

❖ Type of Work:

São Paulo has it all. Catalogue, editorial, campaign, athletic, lingerie, swimwear, runway, commercial print, TV commercial, film, infomercial, trade show, store informal, showroom, and industrial.

❖ Busiest Seasons:

The market is busy all year long for catalogue, commercial print and TV commercials. It is busiest for high end fashion clients from January to February and from June to early July. The slowest times are the end of July and December.

TOP CLIENTS

Top clients include ad agencies Young & Rubicam, McCann Ericsson, J. Walter Thompson, Africa and DPZ, magazines Vogue, Elle, Marie Claire and Cosmopolitan, car companies GM, Ford, Fiat, Volkswagen and Audi, department stores C&A and Renner, Unilever (skincare/cosmetic), Gillette, as well as designers Forum, Triton, Zoomp, M and Officer.

COMPETITION

The competition is fierce compared to other cities in Brazil and light compared to top markets in Europe and the USA.

PAY RATES

Print averages (REAL) R$3.000,00-100.000,00 for advertising/campaign. Runway R$300,00-5.000,00 per show. Brazil is all non-union for TV/film, but this may not be the case for long because the producers and directors are trying to form a union. TV/film averages R$1.200,00-70.000,000 per job, depending on the usage and the role level the model books in the production.

❖ Agency Cuts:

For commissions across the board, agencies deduct 30% for new faces and 20% for established models. Clients sometimes deduct taxes for foreigners. Models will have to request to be reimbursed by the tax authorities before leaving Brazil.

❖ Agency Provides:

Dependent upon the caliber of the model, agencies will advance on practically anything including airfare, accommodations, composite, laser copy of books, tests, and pocket money. Neither agencies nor clients offer money contracts.

LIVING

❖ Housing:

Most agencies provide models' apartments. Inexpensive accommodations average R$300,00 per month. Moderate R$400,00-500,00 per month. Cheap hotels

MODEL MARKETS OF THE WORLD
SAO PAULO BRAZIL

average R$90,00-200,00 per night. Hotels can be up to R$800,00 per night. For flat monthly rates, hotels average R$950,00-1.500,00.

❖ Transportation:

Guarulhos, the international airport, is 30 minutes from downtown in the best of traffic. Conhonghas, the national airport is 10 minutes from downtown. The city has inexpensive public transportation including train, subway and bus. Prices average R$1,70-3,00 per trip. A short ride in a taxi is R$10,00. Traffic is very heavy.

❖ Food & Entertainment:

An inexpensive lunch is R$5,00-10,00 and an inexpensive dinner is R$10,00-20,00. Food prices range from R$5,00-150,00. Brazil has some wonderful cuisine such as Pão de Queijo, Pastel de Feira and Feijoada. São Paulo has the best entertainment in Brazil with lots of theaters, museums, shopping malls, restaurants, discotheques, nightclubs, national parks and gardens, and many fun things to do for free.

REQUISITES

Models from the USA and Canada must apply for work visas and possibly tourist visas. If models plan on traveling throughout Brazil before or after modeling in São Paulo, they will need both.

WEATHER

The market is always hot and humid.

CURRENCY

As of January 2005:
US$10 = R$27.21
C$10 = R$21.61

MARCIA'S TIPS

Brazilians are very friendly, especially to foreigners. Even if Brazilians don't understand the language spoken, they will always try their best to help. About 40% of the city speaks English and in surrounding areas it is down to about 10%. Models should bring summer clothes, bikinis, high heels for females, and light coats for winter as the coldest it ever gets is 6 Celsius. Like their counterparts in New York City, the clients like hip fashion. During any free time, models should try to visit the Parque do Ibirapuera, Guarujá, Ubatuba, MASP (Museum of Modern Art), Campos do Jordão and Maresias, and outside of the city the Amazônia Rain Forest and Florianópolis. Brazil is amazing.

PHRASES & TERMS
GLOSSARY

Preface Note: There are many other terms that are used within the glossary terms and can be found alphabetically within the glossary.

❖ Advance

A term used when an agency advances anything to a model – from airfare to composites to pocket money to testing. Advancing does not mean agencies are giving it free to the model, but rather they are loaning it to the model and it must be paid back by the model, usually via future bookings. Also, "advances" can be part of a guaranteed money contract.

❖ Advertising

Commercial print jobs and advertisements one sees in a magazine, at the point of sale in a store, or on a billboard, for example. For the sake of less confusion, advertising is photographs done to advertise a product but not in a catalogue or television commercial format. Advertising is specifically sought after for tearsheets in a model's portfolio.

❖ Age/Looking the Ages Of

This question was posed to agents worldwide in the form of "what age do models have to look on print?" This does not mean the models' real age, but what age category they fall into when viewed on print or film. For teenagers, see "junior/teens". For adults, we specifically requested agents to keep it ages 18 and up in regards to appearance. For example, a model can be 15-years-old but look the ages of 18-22 on film. Thus, the model would be an adult model even though the true age is that of a teenager. Most markets do take older than the maximum age in our adult age quotients, but we tried to keep it to the primary ages used for adults.

❖ Athletic

In the fashion world, this does not mean being as buff as a super weightlifter. Most markets use fashion models for athletic clients and sportswear. In a nutshell, to be "athletic" for this type of client means being able to do some sports, and having a body that is in great shape but not overly "buff".

❖ Board

A term used for the different divisions of a modeling agency. For example, the men's board, the women's board, the main board, the new faces' board, and the development board.

❖ Buy-out

A term used by clients to book a model for a job for a set price usually covering a wide variety of possible usages, and/or a longer set of time that can go from several months to infinity. Clients may opt for

MODEL MARKETS OF THE WORLD
GLOSSARY

a buy-out instead of renegotiating every time for renewal or additional usage.

❖ Campaign

Advertising that is booked by major designers, fashion/retail houses, and top product clients. Product campaigns are usually booked by fashion, health, beauty, or hair care clients. For example, a model can book a Gucci campaign or a Revlon campaign that involves a model doing a series of ads for the client, or the client is taking one or two images and using them for a specific timeframe. Campaigns can be local, regional, national or worldwide.

❖ Castings

Also referred to as "go-sees" and "appointments." Models go to meet the client for a specific job and date, or for any yet-to-be-scheduled future work. Castings are usually held at the decision maker's company or at a modeling agency. People who make decisions for castings can be anyone from the photographer, the art director, a specific casting service, the hair and make-up stylist, or the clothing stylist.

❖ Catalogue

Catalogues are books displaying fashion and/or products. Commonly known ones in the fashion business are JC Penney, Sears, and Spiegel. Models are referred to as "catalogue" models when they fit into this realm of the business.

❖ Cheap/Inexpensive

What one may think of as inexpensive, another may think of as very expensive. When we note "inexpensive" or "cheap" monetary figures, we are stating what is the least expensive in accommodations, transportation or food. For example, in one market a cheap hotel maybe $150 per night and in another market, the cheapest hotel maybe $450 per night.

❖ Clean

An essential term – "clean" can of course mean clean – in other words, to not be dirty or grimy. In our industry it also has other meanings. "Clean" can be minimal to none or keeping it natural and neat in the spectrum of make-up and hair, or "clean" can be clothing that is not cluttered and has simple lines and colors.

❖ Commercial Print

Basically, advertising that is not in video form. Agents and clients more often refer to advertising campaigns that are not fashion oriented as "commercial print".

❖ Composites

Essentially the models' business cards. Composites are usually 5x8 on heavy stock paper with a close-up shot on the front along with the model's name and agency. On the back will be a variety of smaller shots showing different images of the model along with the model's statistics including height, size, bust/waist/hip measurements, shoe, hair and eye color.

❖ Continental Size

This is also called "French" size. This

sizing system is different than that of North America for females. There was much debate on the difference in sizes in many of the international markets. Many markets stated Continental 36-38 for female models. Many international markets, especially Europeans, thought this transferred to an American 6-8. Without a doubt, it cannot be since most models coming from New York City that are successful in Europe or any other top international market are really fitting anywhere from a size 2-6. For the sake of moving onward, we chose to go with the most recent sizing chart, which puts Continental 36-38 as an American 4-6. Please be advised that in reality, this maybe an American 2-4. We recommend that female models check with the agency on the specific measurements required for their specific height. In regards to male models, we found the transfer from Continental to American sizes to be correct.

❖ Direct Booking

An agency books directly to their client's location and the model is traveling elsewhere. For example, the model is placed with an agency in New York City and lives in Vancouver, Canada. The New York City agency calls and books the model into New York City with one of their clients. That is a direct booking. It can also be a direct booking if the model is based in New York City and goes to a casting there, and then the client books the model to a location shoot in Hawaii.

❖ Editorial

Essentially has two meanings. A look that can be defined as a bit more high-end, edgier and unique than the typical fashion model, or pages in the middle of a fashion magazine that tell a story with clothing, jewelry, accessories, hair and make-up. These pages are sought after by models for their portfolios as the stamp of approval that they are a proven product. Basically, these pages are their resume to help them garner future jobs.

❖ Edgy

A word used in the business for having a bit more flare in the extreme sense. It's a stronger, more severe image than the average model, more of an editorial look.

❖ Established

A term used for models that have worked as models for at least 1.5-2 years. These models can only be referred to as "established" if they have a good resume of clients and tearsheets throughout their portfolio.

❖ Ethnicities

Agents were asked if they use Caucasian, Light Black, Black, Eurasian, Asian, Hispanic/Latin, Eastern, and/or Native American ethnicities in their markets.

❖ Exclusive/Exclusivity

Occurs when a client wants a model to work for their product exclusively and no others in the same product category, or sometimes, for no other products whatsoever. Clients pay a high price for this privilege.

❖ Fiscal Attestation

Documentation that helps Canadian models not have taxes deducted in international countries that Canada has agreements with. This letter states they will pay their taxes on monies earned abroad in Canada. Models must have this form with them or sent to the agency before leaving, or the agency will have to abide by their country's foreign model tax laws.

❖ Full-time

This means that models are completely focused 100% on modeling solely as their career. It does not have to mean they are making a full-time salary as of yet, although that is the desired outcome.

❖ High End/High Fashion

These are used for top of the line, fashion products. These products are usually very expensive and/or couture.

❖ Hip

This refers to the largest amount of hip size on a female model. Agents were wary to give the largest sizes as they feel the largest size is in accordance with a larger model. For example, if a market says "no larger than a 37" hip", this is not for a female who is 5'8" but for a female who is 5'11".

❖ Hourly / half day / full day / multiple days

"Hourly" is a job booked by the hour. "Half day" is usually a 4 hour booking. "Full day" is usually an 8 hour booking. "Multiple days" is usually a booking that is 2 or more days in a row.

❖ Infomercial

A term used for commercials that that market products and are usually 5-30 minutes in length. For example, Thighmaster or ProActiv skin care.

❖ Industrial

Images for in-house use for a client's company. In other words, the images are not to be used for advertising to consumers. They are usually in the form of an informative brochure or video presenting products to employees, sales reps and/or store buyers.

❖ IRS Tax Forms 8802 and 6166

These are forms to help USA models not have taxes deducted in international countries that the USA has agreements with. Models must submit IRS Tax Form 8802 to request IRS Tax Form 6166 be sent to them. This form states they will pay their taxes on monies earned abroad in the USA. Models must have this form with them or sent to the agency before leaving, or the agency will have to abide by their country's foreign model tax laws.

❖ Junior/Teens

Teens and juniors are a very specific

segment of the market. These are models that are appropriate for clients advertising towards this age group. Each market varies a bit on what age a model should look to fit into this category, but overall the models appear to look anywhere from ages 13-18. Some clients carry this into college age as well.

❖ Lifestyle/Relatable

A type of model that everyone can relate to as an average, good looking person. Usually, clients pick people that are fashion types, but aren't threatening in the sense of "this isn't a type that I can relate to from where I live and work." Most agents refer to lifestyle and relatable as "commercial". Not to confuse the reader with the terms "commercial print" and "TV commercial", we chose to use the terms "lifestyle" and "relatable".

❖ Medical Shots

Only one market we interviewed conveyed that medical shots or vaccinations against rare diseases might be necessary to enter the market. Istanbul felt a model should check with the agency before arrival.

❖ Metropolitan Area Population

We used this word to refer to populations for cities. This is not usually just the city borders itself, but the surrounding metropolitan, smaller cities and suburban areas as well. These metropolitan areas are usually the target areas for the local clients, and most agencies insist that these are their population demographics.

❖ Models' Apartments

Housing supplied by the agencies which are usually very cost effective by having several bunk beds in one bedroom so that the models can save instead of wasting money on living expenses. Think dormitory style.

❖ Model Bag

Usually smaller markets insist on models bringing this to all bookings. The bag is usually filled with basic necessities – black/brown shoes, black/brown belts, skin colored hosiery and lingerie/underwear, some jewelry, hair accessories and shaving utensils.

❖ Money Contract

A modeling agency or a specific client gives a model a contract for a set amount of money for a specific amount of time and/or bookings. Usually, as long as the contract is adhered to, models do not owe expenses back no matter what the outcome of the contract.

❖ Mother Agency

A very important term, especially to agencies, dealing with all management and development decisions with a model. Once an agency becomes mother agency to a model, they have the right to not only advise, consult and develop the model, but to place the model with other agencies in other markets as well. Since they have done the main base of work and usually discovered the model, they retain a mother

MODEL MARKETS OF THE WORLD
GLOSSARY

agency commission fee from other agencies for placement. This fee is usually anywhere from 5-10%.

❖ New Faces

A term used for brand new models or models still in a stage of development. Models are considered "new faces" for the first year or two of their careers, even if they have already accrued a resume of experience and tearsheets. Models can be considered "new faces" longer if their careers have not accelerated to an established level.

❖ Non-Union

These are jobs in TV, film and TV commercial that do not fall under the union rules and provisions (see Union or SAG/AFTRA). The rates for non-union jobs can be nebulous and are always negotiable. Usually, markets have an unspoken set of rules for rates and work provisions for non-union jobs even though they do not have to follow any set rules.

❖ On Stay

A term used by agencies for models that will base in a market temporarily while working there, instead of living there on a permanent basis. The term usually applies to stays of more than 1 week.

❖ Plus/Full-Size

Women's clothing on the larger end of the spectrum. Most markets look for women that fall into the range of sizes 10-22.

❖ Pocket Money/Weekly Salary

"Pocket Money" is used to describe the money advanced to a model that has arrived to a market penniless. This money must be reimbursed to the agency when the model is paid from future bookings. "Weekly salary" is paid when markets with guaranteed contracts advance weekly money to the model as part of the deal.

❖ Polaroids/Snapshots

These are Polaroid or snapshot images done by an agent or someone at home showing the model's face with no make-up at lots of different angles, including a smile shot, and then full-length in a bikini or underwear at different angles as well.

❖ Portfolio

Also called a "book". Typically, a 9x12 photo album housing 1 professional image per page for clients or agents to review.

❖ Print

Images shot on still film, photographs, and not on videotape.

❖ Repeat Bookings

When clients book models they have already used before.

❖ Residuals

Payment for a job based on percentages of markets and amount of time used. A term often related to TV commercials.

❖ Season

A timeframe in a market when it is busy.

❖ Short Ride in a Taxi

A term used to describe a taxi ride

of 7-10 blocks.

❖ Showroom

Models are booked at a designer's or retail company's place of business, which is called a showroom, and hired to wear the designer's line of clothing for prospective buyers. The model will change into many outfits in a short amount of time and walk out in as buyers discuss each outfit. The model may or may not have communication with the buyers depending on what the client has suggested. Some smaller markets also include "showroom" to mean when a model is booked for a clothing company's in-house staff meeting or customer meeting to premiere the new line.

❖ Sizes

See "Continental Size".

❖ Store Informal/Promotional Work

Somewhat separate terms, but we grouped them together because of the similarity. Store Informal is when models are hired to walk around in an outfit or spritz a perfume that the store wants promoted to its customers. Promotional work can be in a store promoting non-fashion products such as cigarettes or alcohol, or for example, at a car race registering people for a contest for Pepsi or Coca-Cola. Both of these types of work like to use good looking fashion types and the work can either be hourly ($10-30 per hour) or full day ($125-350 per day).

❖ Tearsheets

Pages from print advertising, campaigns, editorial magazine stories or catalogues that are used in a portfolio to exhibit the work of a model.

❖ Testing/Tests

An aspiring model pays a photographer to shoot different images for his or her portfolio. It is a necessary investment for a model to begin developing a career in the business as clients need to see a variety of looks to get a sense of what the model can achieve. Established models will test to refresh their portfolios if pictures are outdated.

❖ Trade Show Convention work

For example, automotive industry clients rent out a space of 30,000 square feet with many booths promoting different aspects of their industry. Auto clients call local modeling agencies and hire models to either work as booth representatives or demonstrators. Trade show promotions pay $150-500 per day.

❖ Trips

These are bookings that usually involve multiple days and are booked to a location outside of the market.

❖ Union or SAG/AFTRA

For example, SAG and AFTRA unions have been established in the USA to protect TV, film and TV commercial actors with provisions for appropriate work conditions, hours and pay scales. Jobs falling under the SAG and AFTRA unions are usually referred to as "union" jobs or "union pay scale" – meaning either of these union's rules and pay rates apply to the specified jobs.

❖ Usage

Applies to how a client uses images from a booking. For example, a client could book a model for a full day. Then, the client could use the images for a catalogue, a newspaper, in-store point-of-purchase, or a billboard. Each of these separate usages can have separate fees applied in addition to the day rate.

MARCIA ROTHSCHILD MOELLERS **NOTES** 223

MODEL MARKETS OF THE WORLD
NOTES